Why Associations Matter

Why Associations Matter

THE CASE FOR
FIRST AMENDMENT PLURALISM

Luke C. Sheahan

 University Press of Kansas

Published by the University Press of Kansas (Lawrence, Kansas 66045),
which was organized by the Kansas Board of Regents and is operated
and funded by Emporia State University, Fort Hays State University,
Kansas State University, Pittsburg State University, the University of
Kansas, and Wichita State University.

Library of Congress Cataloging-in-Publication Data
Names: Sheahan, Luke C., author.
Title: Why associations matter : the case for First amendment
    pluralism / Luke C. Sheahan.
Description: Lawrence : University Press of Kansas, 2020. | Includes
    bibliographical references and index.
Identifiers: LCCN 2019039081 (print) | LCCN 2019039082 (ebook)
    ISBN 9780700629251 (cloth)
    ISBN 9780700629268 (epub)
Subjects: LCSH: Freedom of association—United States. | Associations,
    institutions,etc.—Law and legislation—United States.
Classification: LCC KF4778 .S54 2020 (print) | LCC KF4778 (ebook) |
    DDC 342.7308/54—dc23
LC record available at https://lccn.loc.gov/2019039081
LC ebook record available at https://lccn.loc.gov/2019039082.

British Library Cataloguing-in-Publication Data is available.

Printed in the United States of America

10 9 8 7 6 5 4 3 2 1

The paper used in this publication is recycled and contains 30
percent postconsumer waste. It is acid free and meets the minimum
requirements of the American National Standard for Permanence of
Paper for Printed Library Materials Z39.48-1992.

To my forebears: Thomas, Patrick, and Daniel,
Whose rights these were.
And to my children: JJ and PE,
Whose rights these will be.

Multiply your associations and be free.
—*Pierre-Joseph Proudhon*

Contents

Acknowledgments

Divining precisely how an idea germinates, finds sustenance through a period of incubation, develops into chapters, and finally blossoms into a full-length manuscript is an impossible task. The elements of the intellectual and social milieu from which ideas come are not easily identifiable. But I will make an effort to thank those who I know contributed to that milieu in some way. The list is woefully nonexhaustive.

Thanks to Claes Ryn, David Walsh, Dennis Coyle, Phil Henderson, Mike Reardon, Gary Ferngren, John DiIulio, Daniel Cheely, Richard Avramenko, Tim Shiell, Brad Birzer, Adam Kissel, Don Downs, Nathanael Blake, Josh Bowman, Lucie Miryekna, Ben Clark, Jeff Nelson, Nigel Ashford, Bill Glod, Clyde Ray, Greg Collins, Sam Sprunk, John Mickey, Connie Field, Mike Tolhurst, and my colleagues at the Freedom Project: JP Messina, Nazan Bedirhanoglu, Shingirai Taodzera, and Caryn Sowa. Also, thanks to Greg Lukianoff, Robert Shibley, Sean Clark, Alisha Glennon, Azhar Majeed, Will Creeley, Samantha Harris, Peter Bonilla, and Peyton Cudaback. Thanks to my mom and dad for patiently teaching me to read and write and to Calvin and Tanner for learning along with me. Thanks to Michael Gillespie, who gave invaluable edits to a version of chapter 3 in a writing workshop at Duke University. I am grateful to Michael Munger, who provided time and space for me to work on the manuscript at Duke. He was (proudly, I am sure) a cattle prod to productivity. Likewise, I am grateful to Katherine Lynch and Tom Cushman for similar environs at Wellesley College. A little-known fact is the behind-the-scenes work of Emily Corwin to bring Nisbet's *Quest for Community* back into print. That was an important and hitherto unacknowledged contribution to the continued study of this important thinker. I situate my argument in the work of three First Amendment scholars: John Inazu, Paul Horwitz, and Steven Smith. As of this writing I have only met one of them in person, but it is difficult to exaggerate the intellectual debt I owe to all of them for their scholarly work and perspectives. I am grateful to David Congdon, my editor, who came on board at Kansas with my proposal sitting on his desk. He caught some problems with my argument throughout the manuscript and no doubt saved me much embarrassment after publication. The same should be said of the three anonymous readers who also offered important corrections to the manuscript. Remaining defects cannot be blamed on the four of them.

I need to thank the talented editors at the *Kansas Journal of Law and Public Policy*. My analysis of *CLS v. Martinez* in chapter 3 appeared in an earlier form there, and they were most helpful in whipping my argument and prose into shape. I have been studying and publishing on Robert Nisbet for a few years now. I first discussed the voluntary association in Nisbet's thought in *Perspectives on Political Science* (2019), available online (DOI: 10.1080/10457097.2019.1653064). My other articles on Nisbet have appeared in *The Political Science Reviewer* and *Studies in Burke and His Time*. While the writing in this book is not taken from those articles, I did explore Nisbet's ideas in these places and I am grateful to the editors and anonymous reviewers who helped me think through various aspects of his work.

I chose to dedicate this book to three young men who fled their homeland under duress in the middle of the nineteenth century and to two children born while the book was in progress. A picture of Thomas sits on the bookshelf in my office alongside my children. They are the poles of a filial continuum of which I am the link. After arriving in America, Thomas, Patrick, and Daniel taught themselves to read (education was forbidden in their homeland) and started families. They devoured newspapers (thus enjoying the fruits of a free press), exercised their religious freedom and free speech with fervor (naturally, while assembling with others), and bragged to their children about the liberties they had acquired in their new land. No doubt the stories told of these men to a child stirred the fires of that young imagination. As I became capable of contemplating constitutional questions as an adult, I suspect that the accounts of their experiences exerted an enormous influence on my own understanding of these issues and motivated me to pursue their study. As I wrote this book, I thought of them often, and I wondered if they would approve of what I had done with their freedoms and of what I am doing with them now. Five generations on, I hope that I have made them proud. *Quid enim est aetas hominis, nisi ea memoria rerum veterum cum superiorum aetate contexitur?*

1. Political Sociology and the Problem of the Vanishing Freedom of Association

In *Harry Potter and the Order of the Phoenix*, Hogwarts School of Witchcraft and Wizardry is annexed by the Ministry of Magic, the government agency that oversees the magical realm in J. K. Rowling's fantasy world. Of the many regulations that the Ministry places upon the school, one of the most egregious is a moratorium on student groups that stray from Ministry-approved viewpoints and activities.[1] This restriction is part of the Ministry's effort to centralize all authority in the magical realm within the Ministry and to shape each individual student to serve its purposes.

The impetus for this policy is an informal group formed by Harry Potter himself. Unhappy with the lack of instruction they are receiving in their class on the "Defense against the Dark Arts" from the Ministry's approved teacher and High Inquisitor of Hogwarts, Dolores Umbridge, Potter and his friends start a student group to educate their fellow students on the material excluded from the classroom. After all, no (living) student has more experience on fighting the dark arts than the book's young hero. Disliking the Ministry's meddling at Hogwarts and its interference with Albus Dumbledore's authority as headmaster, they call their secret organization "Dumbledore's Army," after their beloved headmaster, now shunted aside by his enemies within the Ministry.

Why is the Ministry of Magic so opposed to student groups? What is it about an alternative source of authority, even one as mild as an independent student group, that so rankles the Ministry? What is there to fear in students giving allegiance to something other than the Ministry itself?[2]

What the Hogwarts students are experiencing is a violation of their freedom of association. These questions regarding conflicts in authority and allegiance strike at the very heart of any discussion about this important freedom. Rowling's depiction of restrictions upon freedom of association as a key instrument in tyranny has a long line of predecessors going back at least to the Greek philosopher Aristotle, who writes that tyrants will prevent the formation of private clubs to keep their people from establishing and nurturing friendships, parallel allegiances that exist apart from—and outside of—a tyrant's authority.[3] While the Harry Potter fan may think that the world governed by the Ministry of Magic is far from the world they inhabit, there are some unfortunate parallels between the policies of the Ministry of Magic and recent Supreme Court jurisprudence on the freedom of association. This book is about that jurisprudence and what can be done about it.

THE PROBLEM OF THE VANISHING FREEDOM OF ASSOCIATION

Freedom of association as a substantive right within First Amendment case law has shrunk significantly in the last few decades, as the Supreme Court has subsumed it into freedom of speech before finally discarding it as an independent right in *Christian Legal Society v. Martinez* (2010).[4] In that case, the Court ruled that a public university could require a religious student group to allow anyone to join the group, regardless of whether the excluded person agreed with the stated religious beliefs and practices of the group. The student group was registered in the university's student organization forum, which the Court has insisted is a type of "public forum," a place where First Amendment rights are practiced. Rather than a robust freedom that suffuses and undergirds the panoply of First Amendment rights, the Court sidelined freedom of association on behalf of other rights and values, including freedom of speech. This development has been noted and discussed among scholars of constitutional law, but it has evaded adequate treatment from the perspective of jurisprudence and political theory.

Constitutional scholars John Inazu and Timothy Tracey have noted the vanishing freedom of association in recent Supreme Court jurisprudence and attributed its decline to the formulation it received as a product of both the right to free speech and the right of assembly in Court jurisprudence in the late 1950s and 1960s.[5] While most scholars have accepted the Court's formulation and only regard freedom of association as *expressive association*,[6] as a species of freedom of speech, rather than an independent First Amendment right, Inazu has argued that the right of association is a newer iteration of the textual right of Assembly that dates in its practical application to the 1790s, just shortly after the ratification of the First Amendment. But the Court's mid-century jurisprudence failed to anchor association in the right of assembly alone.[7] As more cases emerged, the Court increasingly relied on speech rights to undergird freedom of association, and the right to association eventually became a species of speech and lost its moorings in assembly entirely. I will argue later that the Assembly Clause is a better textual location for the right of association as it is a right that, by definition, can only be practiced in association with others.[8] The right to free speech is an individual right and one that does not necessitate association. By anchoring association in the right to free speech, the Court ignored its fundamentally communal nature.

The limitation on a general right to associate as the right to associate when expression is the goal of the association has broad ramifications for the liberty of institutions and associations throughout American society. Associations that serve important functions in the lives of individuals may continue to thrive but they may no longer enjoy constitutional protection. Consider the following examples: a gay social club (as distinguished from a gay rights club), a Catholic gay club, and a college sorority.[9] The gay social club exists to provide an "exclusively gay environment" where gay persons may "feel safe, build relationships, and develop political strategy."[10] It is not primarily expressive because it does not exist to advocate gay rights as a gay rights club might.[11] The Catholic gay club exists to encourage LGBTQ persons to live celibately in accordance with traditional Roman Catholic teaching. Perhaps it even encourages its members to seek religious vocation. It does not advocate *against* gay rights any more than the gay social club advocates *for* them, so it too is not expressive. The college sorority exists to bring together young women for social reasons. It does not have any particular viewpoint to advance, and it engages in explicit sex discrimination (as do fraternities) as it requires its members to be female.[12] Since the purposes of these groups are not expressive, they do not enjoy constitutional protection under the Court's current jurisprudence on freedom of association. It is possible that the Free Exercise Clause would provide the locus of protection for the Catholic gay club, but it is far from clear that the standards established by the Court in *Employment Division v. Smith*[13] would protect such a group without a strong judicial sense for the autonomy of religious associations beyond explicitly religious institutions like churches, synagogues, and mosques.[14]

While at least some scholars of constitutional law have approached the problem of the vanishing freedom of association in their scholarship, a more comprehensive and more theoretical treatment of the problem has not been attempted.[15] This book aims to fill that gap in the scholarship by providing an account of freedom of association that complements recent constitutional law scholarship. It revises the demotion of freedom of association in the constitutional constellation of rights by providing this right with a more complete theoretical basis, one that takes seriously the social basis of freedom of association.

Political Sociology and Freedom of Association

Since the freedom of association implicates social groups and institutions and the relation between these groups and the state, one perspective that may offer insight into the problem of the vanishing freedom of association is political sociology, the study of the relationship between the political state and social groups and institutions. One of the most prominent and influential political sociologists of the last century is the American sociologist Robert Nisbet.[16] In his 1953 book, *The Quest for Community*, a classic of political sociology, Nisbet describes the decline of community in western democracies.[17] According to his account, in the modern world the state has come to claim "the supreme allegiance of men" and offered psychological and material refuge from the insecurities of modern life. Where previously a number of western associations would perform many functions for individuals and, in turn, demand as many respective allegiances, the state increasingly restricts the role of the smaller associations and replaces their function and demand for allegiance with its own. These changes in the political structure of modern societies have rendered the functions of associations defunct, and groups now have a reduced capacity to hold a position of moral centrality in the lives of their members.

Nisbet locates the philosophical basis for his argument in the political philosophy of Plato, Thomas Hobbes, and Jean Jacques Rousseau. The salient characteristic of these thinkers' political theory is that the state and the individual are its two basic conceptual units. Associations of all types are, at best, distractions from the good found in the unity of the state and the freedom of the individual. At worst, these groups form a rival locus of individual allegiance and authority to that of the state. Their political philosophy is primarily designed to denigrate social institutions and to bolster the supremacy of political power to the purported benefit of individuals, which Nisbet styles "rigorous social nihilism and political affirmation."[18]

Plato is the first to describe the political state as essential to the quest for the good life. Membership in the political order is superior to all other types of membership, including membership in the kinship group, religious organization, or local community. Plato attributes a redemptive quality to political citizenship. The state saves the individual from the social disorder generated by the conflict between social groups. Nisbet writes, "The vision of the political community, like that of the religious community, is born in perceptions of anticommunity, of a world overwhelmingly characterized by strife, dissention, and uncertainty."[19] This leads Plato in *The Republic* to abolish kinship, at least for the elite ruling class of guardians, and to insist on unity over plurality. Plato would abolish or diminish the importance of social groups, but affirm the absolute value of the political state and the individual's membership in it. The political state both liberates individuals from the uncertainty and predations of social life and provides them with psychological certainty, liberating each person from the conflict of allegiances inherent in social life and centralizing those allegiances in the state. As Nisbet writes, both "rigorous social nihilism and political affirmation are on full display in Plato."[20]

For Nisbet, these two values, social nihilism and political affirmation, form the essential foundation of later political thought. Thomas Hobbes provides the first modern account of the Platonic political state, demonstrating in his work "relentless hostility to all groups or allegiances intermediate between sovereign and citizen."[21] Like Plato, Hobbes finds the conflict of civil society intolerable and he articulates an order that has as its primary conceptual units the individual and the state. Hobbes's state of nature begins with the reasoning individual in a state of war who realizes through rational calculation that his condition is better under a sovereign state that protects him from his fellow man than in the state of nature. This individual, though rational, is asocial, abstracted from the web of social relationships in which we actually encounter human beings.

The state that emerges in Hobbes from the contract between these individuals is, like Plato's, redemptive and absolute. It redeems individuals from social conflict through the exercise of absolute power. Nisbet writes, "Apart from [the state's] absoluteness there could be no protective society and man would sink once again into the dismal condition of fear and brutishness that had characterized his beginnings."[22] No association is immune from state power. The family exists for procreation and the authority of parents only persists through the consent of their children.[23] Associations in general cause dissension and disunity in the state. Like the family, they make claims of authority over individuals and demand allegiance in return. Nisbet writes, "The state became for Hobbes the legal-political community that is Leviathan: a community which

does not permit within itself any lesser form of community that could con-
ceivably challenge its unity, its indivisibility, and its absolute authority."[24]

Like Hobbes and Plato, Rousseau's state is redemptive and his political theory is characterized by "social nihilism and political affirmation." But where
Hobbes was primarily focused on order and redemption from *social* disorder, Rousseau is concerned with virtue and redemption from *moral* disorder.[25]
Nisbet argues that Rousseau's vision of the moral nature of political order has
made the political state "the single most attractive vision for modern man."[26]
Not only does the state redeem the individual from social disorder, it redeems
him from the moral disorder caused by conflicting social allegiances. Individual virtue is found in the individual's liberation from the authority of a
plethora of associations and in its subsequent unity with other individuals in
the state. Nisbet writes, "It is Rousseau, more than any other modern, who has
given the political state the guise of community who has made it the image of
a fortress and a refuge against the tyrannies and injustices that seem always to
be a part of traditional society."[27]

Individual freedom is an essential component of Rousseau's political philosophy, but his idea of freedom requires liberation from social authority,
not immunity from state power.[28] Nisbet writes, "[The state's] mission is to
effectuate the independence of the individual from society by securing the
individual's dependence upon itself."[29] Through this liberation from social institutions and unity with the state, the individual achieves true freedom by
release from the "partial will" of associations—which is Rousseau's term for
the independent goals and authorities of nonstate social entities—and sub-
mergence in the "general will" of the state. An individual who objects to the
general will must be compelled to obey, but according to Rousseau, this is not
a violation of individual freedom but "merely means that [the individual] is
being compelled to be free."[30] For Nisbet, this identification of the exercise
of political power over the individual with social freedom is Rousseau's most
significant contribution to political philosophy.

The essential goal of each of these thinkers is "social nihilism and political
affirmation," the destruction of associational authorities and the transference
of that authority to the political state. The result is a dichotomous dynamic in
political thought where the concept of intermediate associations is subsumed
into concepts of state and individual which become the exclusive modes of
philosophical, political, and social analysis, precluding from consideration any
type of social group as an independent point of analysis. When transcribed

from political philosophy into concrete social change, these concepts take the form of social processes that Nisbet calls *individualization* and *politicization*. These processes reduce the value of associations, dichotomizing their functions into either the political state on the one hand or the individual on the other.

Individualization is "the release of the individual from the ties and constraints of community." It is "the process or processes whereby human beings come to feel conscious of themselves *as individuals* rather than primarily as members of a group."[31] Individualization produces individual self-awareness and a sense of personal initiative, personal responsibility, and recognition of individuality.[32] These motives and responsibilities would have previously been attributed to the groups of which the individual was a part. This process of individualization has taken place many times in the course of human history, largely as the result of the intrusion of political power.[33] This is Nisbet's "social nihilism."

Politicization is "the process whereby power, or the assertion of power, or the struggle for power, or the extension of power becomes a dominant consideration in a social order, with strongly modifying effects."[34] The process of politicization has three elements: the territorialization of authority, the individualization of preexisting social aggregates, and the centralization of authority.[35] These elements reinforce each other. The territorialization of authority is the monopolization of power in a specific geographical area. Various preexisting sources of authority must submit to this central power, even if their authority is not territorial in nature. The sublimation of these preexisting authorities individualizes members of social groups, transferring members' primary loyalty to the central territorial power, what we call the political state. This is Nisbet's "political affirmation."

Individualization and politicization are parallel processes, politicization often begetting individualization and individualization contributing to the centralization of authority in the political state. Nisbet writes, "Paradoxical as it may seem, the political state has been the means, at many junctures in history, of creating individualism—through its distinctive concept of citizenship and through the powerful ideas of rights and freedoms directly granted by the state."[36] Rights and freedoms often first appear as immunities from social authorities fixed and enforced by the state in order to bend those groups' purposes to serve the state's prerogatives. In Nisbet's words, "social nihilism and political affirmation."[37]

This brief account of Nisbet's thought cannot do justice to the concepts he works out over the course of hundreds of articles and nearly twenty books nor can it provide the historical background and philosophical caveats necessary to fully flush out his ideas. Nonetheless, Nisbet's understanding of a political philosophy that reduces social thought to the individual and the state and his concepts of individualization and politicization as processes of social change are useful for the analysis pursued in this book because Nisbet studied the way in which political powers invade and hem in, if not eliminate, the functional significance and authority of social groups. While Nisbet's analysis applies to all sorts of social groups, I am particularly concerned with the fate of voluntary associations, the type of association at issue in *CLS v. Martinez* and common more broadly in modern liberal democracies. Nisbet was impressed with the potential of voluntary associations to fulfill the social role once held by static groups such as clans and tribes or even more historically recent institutions such as guilds and churches. His argument regarding the state's inclination to undermine traditional social groups, such as guilds and churches, applies just as readily to the state's failure to respect the autonomy of new social groups, such as the voluntary association.

The First Amendment Dichotomy

Nisbet's ideas of state and individual can illuminate the processes of politicization and individualization in Supreme Court jurisprudence on freedom of association to produce what I call the First Amendment Dichotomy, the theoretical construct that guides the Supreme Court's reasoning in its freedom of association cases. The First Amendment Dichotomy consists of two concepts, the individual and the state. These terms are conceptually abstract and analytically exclusive. The Court's incorporation of these concepts into its jurisprudence on freedom of association triggers the processes of politicization and individualization such that authorities, initiatives, and rights that may have resided in free associations are transformed into either a facet of the sovereignty residing in the centralized political state or an aspect of rights and responsibilities of the individual citizen. When associations do otherwise, Court jurisprudence finds them suspect.

The Court conceives of the individual as separated from its social context according to what William Galston calls "liberal autonomy" defined as "individual self-direction."[38] In Nisbet's terms, the individual is "discrete . . .

autonomous, self-sufficing, and stable."[39] He is more or less interchangeable with other individuals. The term is abstract and exclusive, by which I mean that the Court will understand the individual as abstracted from his social context in associations and institutions, the communities of belief and action in which he is actually found, and consider his exercise of rights in isolation from their real-world context. When the Court considers constitutional rights, it will limit them to the rights of individuals considered in their solitary state. Rights that emerge from interactions between individuals, such as the rights to association and assembly, are circumscribed by an overriding concern for their origin in the individual.

The state in the Court's conception is the political authority defined in the tradition of Plato, Hobbes, and Rousseau: monolithic in power and reach, absolute in sovereignty. This does not mean that the state is undemocratic. In the Court's conception, the state is democratic and, as such, democratic citizenship is the primary mode of membership for individuals, overriding their memberships in other groups. Galston describes this theory of the democratic state as "civic totalism."[40] The important point for Nisbet is that the state takes on the role of the ultimate community.[41] The political power is supreme in authority and importance over lesser social authorities that are contained within it. This is related to the Roman law concept of concession: an association only exists when the state *concedes* its existence, a concession it may revoke at any time for any reason. Rights that the individual has against state power apply just as readily to immunities from the authority of associations and the state will limit an association's claim to associational authority over individuals to accord with the state's own power, purposes, and limits. This is what Nancy Rosenblum calls "congruence," the conceptual approach that "thinks it imperative that the internal life and organization of associations mirror liberal democratic principles and practices."[42] Associations must be the larger political community "writ small." In constitutional law, this concept of the state is applied by the Court when it subsumes the idea of the association into its understanding of the state and treats associational activity as essentially state activity, protected only insofar as it supports state objectives. This happened in *Martinez* when the Court allowed the state (in the form of the state university) to exclude from campus associations that would restrict their own membership in a manner impermissible to the state.[43] Under the conceptual framework of the First Amendment Dichotomy, the Court will only protect freedom of association when it either furthers the rights of individuals or when it is considered beneficial to the functioning of the democratic state.

Why We Should Care about Freedom of Association

Associations are important for a variety of reasons, but their discussion in political theory largely hinges on their instrumental benefits to democracies. In First Amendment jurisprudence, associations are valued for their ability to facilitate expression because where the people rule they must be free to discuss and come to agreement about how to govern.[44] Associations are important to democracy because they provide a context where diverse viewpoints may take shape and find adequate expression and promotion. A collection of individuals with no ability to bind themselves together around a viewpoint remains weak in their ability to advance, or even meaningfully preserve, their viewpoint. This utilitarian argument for the importance of associations fits with the consensus pluralism of David Truman and Robert Dahl.[45]

However, the importance of associations in a democracy runs deeper than its relation to democratic governance. Alexis de Tocqueville, a nineteenth-century thinker Nisbet considered of central importance to understanding the modern world, argued that associations are necessary in a democracy because there are few powerful citizens that command a large enterprise on their own by virtue of their aristocratic status.[46] In democratic societies all citizens are equal. While there are many benefits to democratic equality, one drawback is that such equality is an equality in weakness. Tocqueville writes, "[Democratic citizens] can hardly do anything by themselves, and no one among them can compel his fellows to lend him their help. So they fall into impotence if they do not learn to help each other freely."[47] Associations in a democracy are not a means to self-government; they are self-government. They are not one option for the ordering of human life; they are the order of human life.

This strikes at the heart of Nisbet's contention that persons are fundamentally communal beings. Their search for order and moral meaning is primarily a "quest for community." The history of social thought and history itself is primarily driven by the search for an adequate source of community for individuals.[48] Associations provide the context in which persons relate to others as social beings. The associational context revolves around some function the association performs, which includes anything from bearing and raising children to playing chess. This functional value in associations performs two services for the individual. The first is the protection of individuals *from* political power offered by social authority resident in various associations. These groups are *intermediate* associations, mediating between political power and the individual, shielding the individual from the abstract, rationalized power that resides in large-scale territorial aggregates such as the modern political state. In other words, associations protect individuals from the ravages of individualization and politicization.

The second is the communal value the individual garners from shared allegiance with others. These two functions are related, Nisbet writes on the connection, "Major groups which fall in between the individual and the sovereign state become intermediating influence between citizen and sovereign. They are at once buffers against too arbitrary a political power and reinforcements to the individual's conception of himself and his own powers."[49]

Nisbet's scholarly focus on social groups stems from their ability to provide individuals with communal value. From this comes the psychological and emotional support necessary to humane existence. It is in various social groups that one's very personality is shaped and within which one finds identity and purpose. When a particular social group ceases to offer this functional value, it rightfully disappears and is replaced by other social groups that do offer such value. But this should not be taken as a statement that associations are merely instrumental to individuals, as if individuals could just as well do without them. They are intrinsically necessary to humane life, and they are necessary for what they enable individuals to do with others.

Nisbet's concern with the social group and the notion of community is inseparable from his concern for the well-being of the person. On the first page of his dissertation he notes that the nineteenth century's obsession with the individual was odd given that the individual never existed outside of a social group. At the same time, groups come and go, but they are always composed of individuals and derive their very existence from the value they offer to individuals.[50] The political role of such groups, both as intermediary institutions between state and individual and as facilitators of the democratic system, is secondary to and derivative from their importance to the person.

I begin from the premise that Nisbet's contention that associations are necessary to the flourishing of individuals is correct and that it is within associations acting as communities that personality is formed in all its complexity and individuality. I do not attempt to substantiate those claims in the social science research. The purpose of this book is to show that freedom of association is the constitutional doctrine that reflects the theoretical principle of the importance of social groups to the flourishing of individuals and that current judicial doctrine fails to recognize this fundamental aspect of freedom of association. Freedom of association is first the freedom of an aggregate of individuals to be a community. It is a right that is predicated on an acknowledgment of the socially situated nature of persons in concrete historical reality rather than on the fiction of discrete individuals. The Supreme Court's decision in *Martinez* reflects the state's disdain for the role of associations as a threat to the unity of distinct and socially liberated individuals in the democratic state.

We are pursuing the question of *why* we should care about associations. But a more fundamental question in the context of First Amendment law is whether we can ask this question at all. We must consider whether associations as such have rights under the First Amendment or if First Amendment rights only attach to individuals. The substance of this question becomes more clear if we acknowledge individuals as bearers of First Amendment rights who may practice those rights in conjunction with others, and then ask whether the associational structures within which they act have rights of agency to practice First Amendment rights which attach to the association as distinct from any individual member as such. Put another way, is an association a mere aggregate of individual rights-bearers, or is it an entity that itself is a rights-bearer? If it is, it would mean that each First Amendment right contains an associational component as well as an individual component. The rights of religion, speech, press, assembly, and petition may be practiced by an individual acting alone and they may be practiced by associations of individuals acting in unison.

Recent scholarship on religious institutionalism increasingly advocated by scholars such as Richard Garnett and Steven Smith makes the point that the Religion Clauses of the First Amendment are intended primarily to protect the rights of religious institutions. To put it in Smith's terms, the First Amendment renders religious institutions beyond the jurisdiction of the government. This is not meant to diminish the rights of individual would-be worshippers. The right of conscience, the right of the "inner church" to be free from coercion is derived from the right of institutional churches to be free of coercion. The religion clauses defend the individual right to worship within any of a vast array of religious communities, or in solitude, whichever the individual prefers. Stephen Monsma writes, "Attempts to protect the religious freedom of individuals without protecting the religious freedom of the faith communities and religious associations within which faith is given birth, nurtured, practiced, and passed on from one generation to the next make no sense."[51] The right of religious liberty attaches to both the individual conscience and the institutional place of worship. But the institution must be free to operate distinct from whether any given individual chooses to worship there, and it must have the authority to determine who among individuals is allowed to worship as part of its communion. The religious liberty of the religious organization must be independent of the claims of any given individual's right to religious liberty.

Likewise, freedom of speech applies to expressive associations, as well as institutions such as corporations when they engage in free speech,[52] and to individuals acting within expressive associations or speaking on their own. Freedom of the press attaches both to the institutions that publish as well as the individual journalists and writers who publish through those institutions. The right of assembly means the right of the individual to assemble with others of like mind and like intention, and the right of the particular people assembled to act in unison. The right to petition the government for a redress of grievances includes both the right to petition the government as an individual and the right to join with others in the act of petitioning.

Essentially, the First Amendment presupposes associations. In order for the free exercise of religion to be meaningful, religious institutions must exist within which individuals may freely exercise their religion. Most speech acts take place through the activity of expressive associations, and journalists are made effective as journalists through their role in the institutional press. As for the right to assemble, "the verb 'assemble' presupposes a noun—an assembly."[53] The right of assembly means the right of the assembly, or association, to organize itself and to gather in whatever and by whatever means it determines are best.

Some renderings of First Amendment freedoms describe them as essentially individual in origin and the rights of association as derivative of the rights of individuals.[54] Other accounts reverse this priority, seeing first a freedom of institutions and only second a freedom of individuals, derived from the freedom of the associations. Essentially both of these views amount to a First Amendment Dichotomy, either of state and individual or of state and social group, both of which I am trying to avoid.

What I wish to emphasize in this discussion is the importance of associational freedoms, both the individual freedom to associate, by which I mean the freedom of an individual to engage in association with others, and the freedom of association, the freedom for an association to exert authority over its members to ensure that they act as a unit in accordance with the end for which the group exists. Recognizing these two aspects of association, of the individual and of the group, is essential to the full practice of First Amendment rights for individuals. Here is the catch: one cannot adequately defend the right of individuals to associate without recognizing, without treating as conceptually distinct, the right of associations to a fundamental autonomy that does not reside in the individual as such. Rather, it resides in the association itself, in the social bonds between individuals. This social space is what I believe is protected by freedom of association.

This discussion of the dual nature of freedom of association is complicated in that while the rights of individuals to associate and the rights of associations to act as a unity are conceptually distinct, they are in social fact but two aspects of the same phenomenon, two parts of the same freedom. In order for individuals to have a right of association, a right to associate with others to worship or to speak, the association must have a right to organize worship and to shape the message it seeks to express. There must be a structure within which individuals can act but which exists apart from any particular individual's acting. The right of the association to act independent of the state is the right to act in a way that has a restraining effect on the individual in a moral sense. Associations that are free under the First Amendment are entities that have authority distinct from state power in the realm of religion, speech, press, and assembly to shape and censure their individual members. The authority they exercise over their members is one that the state is explicitly forbidden from exercising.

The threat to freedom of association is a threat to the freedom of individuals to act within associations. Along with the decline of associational rights, as one scholar notes, "has come the loss of important rights traditionally attaching to individuals acting within mediating groups."[55] To focus only on the right of individuals is to ignore perhaps the most effective right of individuals: *the right to act corporately.* The individual right to act corporately in any First Amendment sense is the right to act in an association which may restrain, discipline, and even expel that individual. But it is precisely this right of associations to act autonomously that allows for the concrete right of individuals to act corporately. And to understand the right to act corporately as emerging only from the individual is to diminish the concrete ability of associations to act—which in turn is a diminishment of the ability of individuals to act in associations. To properly preserve the right of individuals to act corporately, we must take seriously the corporate structures, the associations, within which individuals are acting. These structures must be treated as intrinsically valuable, as existing in their own right, because they do.

My thesis is agnostic as to whether the individual or the association is the original source of rights in a final philosophical sense. I posit for the sake of my argument that the rights of individuals and the rights of associations exist side by side in the First Amendment, neither taking precedence over the other, and each deserving independent protection from state restrictions. The reason for my agnostic position on the origin of the right of association is that I think my analysis of the nature of associations is helpful to partisans of both sides of this debate in describing the associations that both believe are essential to the proper scope of First Amendment rights. Both agree that there are structures of authority within which individuals act. One side sees these structures as an extension of the individual right in question and the other sees them as residing in the institution. Both would benefit from a better understanding of what these social structures are and the realm of autonomy they require to thrive.

In light of the above discussion of the dual nature of First Amendment rights it is clear that First Amendment rights are severely diminished if associations do not have a wide degree of autonomy. Associations are not merely a way of organizing life. Associations are human life. Any given association may be optional, but associations as such are not. This is what I call the *reality of the social*. Law must recognize the reality it governs. Associations are the primary reality of the First Amendment landscape, and First Amendment law must take account of their existence. In order for associations to appropriately reflect constitutional rights, they must be regarded as intrinsically valuable, a social reality that First Amendment jurisprudence ought to recognize. In other words, the Supreme Court must put the "social" into freedom of association.

Against the First Amendment Dichotomy, the tendency to attribute the concerns of social groups to the individual or the state, I am arguing for the necessity of a recognition of a plurality of rights bearers in the First Amendment, individuals to be sure, but also the plethora of associational structures within which they reside, by which they are shaped, and through which they make themselves manifest to the world and to each other. While these associational rights bearers may practice their rights to the benefit of the democratic state, that is not the essential purpose of these rights. I call this plural view of the First Amendment, appropriately, First Amendment Pluralism. First Amendment Pluralism relies for its orientation and its name on Robert Nisbet's four principles of pluralism (discussed in the next chapter) to provide a grounding for freedom of association which secures the functional autonomy of associations, preserving freedom necessary for associations to function according to their diverse purposes. The courts must broaden their understanding of what First Amendment rights are in order to properly account for the social reality of the First Amendment landscape, including the full practice of individual rights. This means that at the heart of the First Amendment is the right of association, the right of both individuals to associate and of associations to autonomy.

We have addressed the importance of freedom of association and its presence in the First Amendment. Another issue with my thesis is whether it matters if associations are granted rights. While the Court has focused on individual rights, the right of association has nonetheless prevailed in a number of cases. In *NAACP v. Alabama,* the Court ruled unanimously to protect the rights of the NAACP against the state of Alabama. Likewise, in *Wisconsin v. Yoder*[56] and *NAACP v. Claiborne*[57] the Court sided with the association, forbidding state interference with the internal practices of the group. The same could be said of *Boy Scouts of America v. Dale*[58] and of *Hurley v. Irish American Gay, Lesbian, and Bisexual Group of Boston.*[59]

I grant that the current jurisprudential basis for association works. At least, it works . . . until it doesn't. As I mentioned in the opening of the chapter, freedom of association failed to protect the membership requirements of the CLS chapter at a public law school. It also failed to protect the Jaycees in *Roberts v. United States Jaycees,*[60] to protect a variety of communist groups during the 1950s and 1960s, the same period it protected the NAACP.[61] It fails to protect fraternities,[62] sororities, gay social groups, prayer or meditation groups,[63] and some foreign charities.[64] What I am pointing out is that individual rights as the Court has conceived them are inadequate as a theoretical point to fully account for the breadth of constitutional rights, which means that they are inadequate from a jurisprudential perspective because they fail to protect the full scope of rights guaranteed by the First Amendment.

WHY ROBERT NISBET?

Various thinkers have discussed the importance of community and contributed to political sociology.[65] Why draw from Robert Nisbet for a discussion of Supreme Court jurisprudence? Nisbet was an important figure in American twentieth-century sociology and political thought. His scholarship was wide-ranging and his books were favorably reviewed in scholarly and popular publications.[66] Nisbet's training as a sociologist gave him a unique perspective in discussions of politics, making him sensitive to the effects of political power upon social groups. Freedom of association is a constitutional principle that, along with other freedoms like the free exercise of religion, negotiates the relationship between social groups and the state. While Nisbet had little to say about freedom of association as a constitutional principle,[67] he had much to say about the relationship between the state and the social group and the importance of the freedom of nonstate associations and social institutions, issues which bear directly upon the subject of this book. Other writers have discussed these themes, but few, if any, have drawn as broadly from political philosophy, history, and sociology or published as widely in scholarly and popular outlets. Nisbet demonstrated a deep understanding of the subject matter as well as an ability to make his ideas resonate with a variety of audiences. He studied the processes through which the political state infringed upon the authority and autonomy of the social group, the core issue in the decline of freedom of association, and he offered a tentative solution to the problem of the conflict between these entities. While Nisbet's scholarship is largely descriptive, he defined and advocated a philosophy of pluralism that would allow for a plethora of social groups and associations in society.

Central to Nisbet's contention is that human beings are primarily social beings, persons in search of community. Nisbet's concern for associations was not mere nostalgia, bemoaning the relics of a bygone era that have long since lost their function and significance in human life.[68] Rather, he sought the context in which new associations may be created in response to the human need for community. The problem is that in the absence of meaningful community the individual will continue to search for that connection with others. If he does not find it in healthy forms, such as in voluntary associations, he will search for it in destructive forms, such as the totalitarian state, or live in withdrawal and alienation, with all of the problems that entails including the self-destruction of suicide.[69] Nisbet writes, "The quest for community will not be denied, for it springs from some of the powerful needs of human nature— needs for a clear sense of cultural purpose, membership, status, and continuity."[70] The solution to individual alienation will not be through the revival of traditional groups per se, but through the creation of new ones.[71] It is this possibility in Nisbet's idea of a "laissez-faire of groups" discussed in the next chapter that provides a powerful argument for, as well as a description of, the constitutional right to freedom of association. Nisbet's diagnosis and recommendations offer a theoretical framework for thinking about the relationship between the state and the social group in the realm of freedom of association jurisprudence. The judicial test and legislative proposal presented in chapter 4 to address the problem of the vanishing freedom of association in Supreme Court case law are based on Nisbet's philosophy of pluralism and his idea of a laissez-faire of groups.

FIRST AMENDMENT SCHOLARSHIP AND THE FREEDOM OF ASSOCIATIONS

Nisbet's description of the historical and philosophical condition of the social group is especially relevant to the study of First Amendment law. The dichotomous relationship between state and individual that Nisbet argues is central to the political theory of Plato, Hobbes, and Rousseau governs First Amendment jurisprudence as well, often casting First Amendment rights in terms of the lone soapbox speaker against the state and ignoring the social context in which the speaker actually exists and is empowered to speak and to do everything else he does in life.[72]

I will explain and correct this problem in First Amendment law by utilizing Nisbet's diagnosis of the problem of the missing social group in modern political theory and his philosophy of pluralism to provide a means whereby the Court can recognize social groups as a third concept in First Amendment analysis, in addition to the concepts of the individual and the state. Instead of a *dichotomous* theory in First Amendment law, one that bifurcates First Amendment concerns into the categories of individual or state, this book will argue for a *plural* theory consisting of three basic units—state, individual, and association. This theory recognizes the inherent plurality of associations and of the individuals who compose their memberships and therefore recognizes a wide swath of freedom for a variety of associational forms. It will propose a judicial test and a legislative solution to resuscitate freedom of association by providing a framework for courts to recognize the existence of the social group, especially the voluntary association, in First Amendment law. The goal is to provide a practical means for federal courts to conceive of a third entity in political and social reality, the association, as an independent subject of judicial analysis—to put the "social" into freedom of association.

Some recent First Amendment scholarship has recognized the problem of the dichotomous relationship between state and individual in First Amendment law. Below are three prominent examples. John Inazu argues in *Liberty's Refuge: The Forgotten Freedom of Assembly* (2012) that the right to associate was originally preserved in the Assembly Clause of the First Amendment, which contained a right to form nonreligious groups. Steven D. Smith's book *The Rise and Decline of American Religious Freedom* (2014) makes the point that the religious liberty preserved in the First Amendment was understood as the freedom of religious institutions for most of American history.[73] Paul Horwitz argues in *First Amendment Institutions* (2013) that the judiciary should take account of the context in which First Amendment rights are exercised, namely, in what he calls "First Amendment institutions," such as churches, newspapers, and voluntary associations. As I describe the arguments of these scholars I will explain how my proposal is different from, although often complementary to, their solutions to the problem of the vanishing freedom of association. An additional point is precisely that this perspective is emerging in First Amendment scholarship. The lack of associational protection in constitutional law is receiving increased scholarly attention, which means that First Amendment scholarship is ripe to consider my perspective.

John Inazu and Freedom of Assembly

Freedom of association as a constitutional term was coined by the Court in the 1950s, but as John Inazu argues in *Liberty's Refuge*, its pedigree as a practice, and a constitutionally protected practice, is much older. The Court did not have an operative doctrine of "freedom of association" when Tocqueville described such associations. Nonetheless, they formed an essential part of the lives of many Americans. Their constitutional protection was anchored in the Assembly Clause of the First Amendment, not in the doctrine of freedom of association. The right to assemble was not limited to "petitioning the government" or to exercising the freedom of speech and thus participating in democratic governance. Rather, Inazu writes, "the text of the First Amendment and the corresponding debates over the Bill of Rights suggest that the framers understood assembly to encompass more than petition"[74] and much more than simply holding public meetings. It was written with the intent of protecting dissenting groups. The Assembly Clause lacks a formulation of "for the common good," and thus is not bound by what the majority in society wants or even what a democracy needs.[75]

At the drafting of the First Amendment, a right to assembly was included in every state constitution.[76] Case law supports the right of dissenting groups to assemble around their message regardless of what the government would otherwise want. Inazu writes, "The understanding of assembly as a presumptive right to form and participate in peaceable, noncommercial groups has long been ingrained in our constitutionalism."[77] The political assemblies protected under the Assembly Clause are separate from the state and free from state interference in both their beliefs and internal structure, *who* they assemble. The point is not that the Court can fit an association neatly within its dichotomous doctrine, but that the group can exercise its liberty apart from government interference. The Assembly Clause begins with an assumption of liberty regarding associations.

Inazu's analysis forms the basis of much of the first part of chapter 3 and I return to his thesis in chapter 4. Here it will suffice to note that while his textual proposal is intriguing, the Court simply lacks the theoretical apparatus to be able to recognize the very associations that Inazu argues the Assembly Clause protects. The dichotomous conception of state and individual that controls the Court's analysis precludes, from a theoretical point of view, the ability of the Court to recognize groups. To put it another way, the Court has ignored the Assembly Clause because its theoretical lens only permits recognition of individuals as speakers and expressive associations as groups of individuals speaking in unison. The right of assembly is inherently social and relational in a way that speech is not. As Inazu writes elsewhere, "One can speak alone; one cannot assemble alone."[78] The theoretical lack of a concept of an association limits the Court's ability to conceive space for the social group in any constitutional sense, regardless of the force of textual and historical arguments. The Court lacks the theoretical tools necessary to give to the Assembly Clause Inazu's reading, or any reading at all, no matter how historically and constitutionally plausible it may be. It has not ruled on an Assembly case in over thirty-five years. Without the proper lens that First Amendment Pluralism offers, the Court will remain unable to conceptualize the social contours of an assembly and Inazu's proposal will lack full force. The proposal in this book is complementary to Inazu's approach, providing a theoretical framework that will bolster the case for his textual proposal in constitutional law.

Steven D. Smith and the Freedom of Religious Institutions

Smith argues in *The Rise and Decline of American Religious Freedom* that the emphasis on the conception of freedom *from* religion or even the government's religious neutrality is a departure from what he calls the "American settlement" on religious liberty in the First Amendment. The American settlement was anything but a settling of the disagreements over the meaning of religious liberty. Everyone believed in religious liberty, but there was no agreement over what religious liberty entailed. Did it mean secular government? Did it mean neutrality between Christian denominations? Did it mean simply freedom of individual conscience? He refers to this state of affairs as "open contestation."[79] There was an open contest as to the meaning of religious liberty. Contrary to popular and scholarly opinion, none of the above principles were elevated in the First Amendment. There were advocates of neutrality as well as advocates of state churches who supported the First Amendment. This settlement, or lack thereof, was *preserved* in the First Amendment.[80] To little fanfare the federal government was forbidden from interfering in state or private establishments of religion, a power it never had to begin with. "[The religion clauses] were simply a reaffirmation of jurisdictional arrangement under which religion was within the jurisdiction of the states, not the national government."[81]

Implicit in this understanding of religious liberty as a matter of jurisdiction was the idea of *libertas eclessiae*, freedom of the church. Smith argues that this understanding of the American settlement entailed a freedom for the church as a *social* institution. Freedom of the church from secular control had been a theme in western political thought since at least the investiture controversy of the eleventh century.[82] After the Reformation and the splintering of Christendom, national churches largely became departments of their respective national states. But, Smith writes, "The ideal of a church free of state control did not so much die as go underground."[83] It showed up in the ideas and practices of dissenter immigrants to the American colonies, including the Puritans. The principle of the freedom of the church meant the separation of church and state but not the separation of religion and state.[84] All sorts of religious pronouncements were regularly made at the federal level. The separation of church and state aimed not to subdue the church to the state, but to preserve the freedom of the church as an institution beyond the reach of state jurisdiction. It is historically ambiguous how precisely the principle embodied in the phrase "separation of church and state" is related to the idea of freedom of the church. What is clear is that both communicated the long-standing Christian distinction between the jurisdiction of the church and the jurisdiction of the state. In effect, it divided sovereignty between church and state. From this perspective, the principle of the separation of church and state protects the freedom and sovereignty of the church from state interference.[85]

Freedom of conscience was also an important principle in American religious liberty. But rather than being in tension with freedom of the church, freedom of conscience was *libertas ecclesiae* applied to the individual mind, which was conceived as a sort of "inner church." In this view, freedom of conscience is derivative of freedom of the church. Just as the institutional church is beyond government jurisdiction, by analogy the conscience, the "inner church," is also beyond government jurisdiction. Smith's thesis is that the American settlement viewed government intrusion into church or conscience as jurisdictionally impossible. He writes, "To say that the government ought not to do something is not strictly equivalent to—is in a crucial sense weaker than—saying that government has no jurisdiction to do something."[86]

Smith's thesis, and the contention of freedom of the church made by other scholars, has been criticized on a number of grounds.[87] First, the historical case for freedom of the church draws from a historical period where there was only one church, and its clergy and institutional actions were thoroughly entwined with activities that today are generally considered to be under the province of the government.[88] The political and social context of the time does not parallel the context for debate over religious liberty today and therefore makes the concept inapplicable. Second, the idea of sovereignty does not accurately apply to the authority attributed to religious institutions. Churches do not have full coercive power over a given territory, the very definition of sovereignty, therefore it is inaccurate to describe their authority in matters of religion as exercise of sovereign powers. Third, relatedly, the concept of church sovereignty does not translate easily into the theoretical and jurisprudential concepts applicable in the modern context, let alone, American context.[89] Simply put, the sovereignty of the church as an institution comparable to the sovereignty of the state does not apply to a political and social context where there is a variety of churches and religious institutions operating in a plural society.[90] Fourth, the term "sovereignty" suggests there are no bounds to the authority that ought to attach to religious institutions. The purpose of churches is to "save the world," and that purpose would admit no inherent limit that would circumscribe the church's autonomy.[91] Fifth, Smith describes the freedom of conscience as derivative of the freedom of the church. He essentially argues for a First Amendment Dichotomy (at least regarding the Religion Clauses) that attributes First Amendment concepts to the state and the church and only by implication to individuals.[92]

As I have noted already, contra both Smith and his critics, my theory suggests that the individual's freedom of conscience (among other individual rights) and the corporate freedom of the church (and the freedom of other associations) are rights conceptions that exist side-by-side with neither taking precedence over the other. Rights attaching to both individuals and associations are protected in each clause of the First Amendment, and the rights of the individual are bolstered in a meaningful way by the autonomy and freedom of institutions, which is not the same as saying that the autonomy of associations is necessarily derivative of individual rights or that individual rights are derivative of the autonomy of associations.

These potential objections aside, Smith's thesis supports my argument by pointing to an institutional freedom that undergirds the First Amendment. He focuses specifically on *libertas ecclesiae*, the freedom of the church, and how this idea informs the concept of religious liberty. While there may be historical and jurisprudential problems with how this idea is articulated, especially as it is described in terms of sovereignty and jurisdiction, the fundamental movement toward recognition of a realm of authority where associations and institutions act and interact with individuals and with each other is valuable in focusing discourse over First Amendment rights on the proper issue, namely, what the First Amendment may require in terms of securing the autonomy of associations.

My contention is that freedom of association is analogous to, while not being identical with, freedom of the church. When I talk about freedom of association, I am discussing a similar realm of autonomy to that surrounding Smith's idea of freedom of the church, while not describing it in terms of jurisdiction or sovereignty. But when the text of the First Amendment protects religion, speech, press, and assembly, it is protecting associations that engage in each of these rights. To list a variety of textual rights suggests that there are differences in the nature of autonomy attaching to institutions practicing each of them. The text and history of religious freedom indicates that the autonomy of religious institutions is or ought to be profound. The category of institutions that may form under the other clauses of the First Amendment may also have their own realm of autonomy appropriate to the practice of those rights.

The right to protect confidential sources may attach to the freedom of the press, but not freedom of speech, and so on.[93] I am especially interested in how this realm of autonomy applies to voluntary associations.

Fundamentally, Smith's book lends credence to the idea that the First Amendment was not simply for the protection of the individual from the state, although it does do that through protection of the right of conscience. Rather, the First Amendment protects social groups and institutions, as well as individuals, from the state. Certainly, Smith's inquiry demonstrates the importance of this book for understanding the breadth of constitutional rights beyond freedom of association, including religious liberty.[94]

Paul Horwitz and First Amendment Institutions

Horwitz explicitly recognizes the problem of the First Amendment Dichotomy identified above in his book *First Amendment Institutions*. He writes, "[First Amendment experts] habitually ignore real-world context and focus instead on one central distinction: that between the speaker and the state. On one side is the speaker, often thought of as an individual soapbox orator. . . . On the other side is the state—powerful, coercive, censorious, an imposing and undifferentiated mass."[95] Courts often engage in "institutional agnosticism," ignoring the fact that it is rarely a single speaker who speaks or engages in other rights protected by the First Amendment. Rather, it is almost always in the context of institutions that such rights are practiced. Horwitz emphasizes that the First Amendment was designed to protect broad engagement in public discourse. He defines a First Amendment institution as "one 'whose contributions to public discourse play a fundamental role in our system of free speech.'"[96] He wants the courts to pay attention to the "infrastructure of free expression"[97] in First Amendment law. This requires developing judicial doctrines regarding the institutions that make public discourse possible.

By "public discourse," Horwitz means, quoting First Amendment scholar Robert Post, "those speech acts and media of communication that are socially regarded as necessary and proper means of participating in the formation of public opinion."[98] Public discourse is important for legitimate self-government. Citizens must be able to take part in shaping public opinion. Horwitz, contra Post, emphasizes the breadth of this definition. Public discourse shapes culture in a broad sense not limited to the formation of political ideas and practices. Under Horwitz's understanding, democratic political processes are only part of public discourse and by no means the main part. His conception of public discourse would provide more protection for speech that does not engage in the democratic process than would Post's.[99]

Two problems emerge in Horwitz's approach. The first problem is similar to the problem with Inazu's proposal, namely, that the Court cannot theoretically conceive of a nonstate, nonindividual entity, as Horwitz acknowledges.[100] The point of his book is to explain the presence and importance of such institutions. But in order for such institutions to come into focus, the Court must begin with a triangular conceptual framework that accounts at the outset for the presence of associations. Otherwise the Court will treat such institutions as mere aggregates of individuals or as reliant upon the state. In other words, Horwitz does not provide a way for the Court to emerge from the theoretical dichotomy of state and individual that currently shackles First Amendment jurisprudence and produces this jurisprudential blindspot regarding institutions.

The second problem in Horwitz's approach is that the basis for the protection of institutions is their role in public discourse. As I will discuss throughout this book, such a conception ignores that the First Amendment protects the existence of institutions and associations that do not engage in "public discourse" even in Horwitz's broad sense.[101] An institution that is not outwardly focused or message-based would be denied the broad protections of the First Amendment, which is the very problem addressed by Inazu. While Horwitz distances himself from Post by not limiting First Amendment protection to what affects democratic processes, he still subscribes to a sort of consensus pluralism that sees the diversity of institutions as necessary for democratic dialogue. He understands the discussion protected by the First Amendment to be taking place at a general cultural level, but his pluralism is attached to public discourse. It still limits First Amendment rights to speech in a broad sense.

Horwitz would extend protection to institutions for their instrumental contribution to the broader social dialogue, but not for being communities that are functionally relevant to the persons that compose their memberships. In many ways the protection of institutions for their instrumental value to speech compounds the first problem. Valuing institutions and associations only for their ultimate role in facilitating the function of democratic society reinforces a conception of the group as existing only insofar as it contributes to the health of the democratic state, which is the theoretical reason why the Court ignores institutions in the first place. I will reserve a full critique of consensus pluralism for chapter 3. Suffice it to say here that First Amendment institutionalism lacks Nisbet's understanding of a pluralism of groups that do not exist chiefly for the sake of public discourse, no matter how broadly conceived, but in recognition of the profound and ineradicable diversity of personal views and personal needs. Horwitz does acknowledge the types of associations that emerge from diverse personal views. He argues that a prime characteristic of First Amendment institutions is that "they are places in which public discourse is *formed* and *disseminated*, in social ways and for social purposes. Their social nature is just as important as the experience of individuals within them."[102]

Horwitz further acknowledges the need for "constitutional institutionalism," recognizing that First Amendment institutionalism does not protect institutions like the family, at least not in a sense adequate to the fundamental importance of the institution for persons.[103] However, he does not focus his analysis on the importance and preservation of institutions *as such*. He emphasizes institutional rights as related to their institutional role in public discourse that makes their protection dependent on their effect on the democratic state, broadly understood. This error is reflected in Supreme Court doctrine regarding freedom of association that will be examined in chapter 3.

The proposal made in this book is both more general and more specific than Horwitz's. It is more general in that it intends to provide a theoretical framework for the Court to recognize groups and institutions as social entities both categorically distinct from the state and irreducible to the speech of their individual members. Social groups and institutions often function as pre-expressive institutions in that they prepare individuals for social engagement while accomplishing activities related to group goals, thus preparing individuals for engagement in public discourse. But the preparation of individuals for democratic dialogue is not the primary purpose of these associations' existence. It is merely incidental to their main purpose, and the autonomy granted them through the freedom of association should not depend on such an effect. Some institutions may actually claim that they are withdrawing from public discourse, providing an alternative means of living and believing in contrast to and apart from the broader culture.[104] There will necessarily be implicit dialogue between such institutions and the broader culture, but framing the issue of constitutional protection in terms of "public discourse" seems to miss the real importance of these institutions, which is not their role in public discourse but their associational existence as nonstate associations.[105] My proposal is more specific than Horwitz's in that it provides a concrete judicial test for the Court when examining the status of voluntary associations. Horwitz offers a way for the courts broadly to recognize various First Amendment institutions, but his proposals for analysis are broad and multifaceted and, as he admits, would come with transition costs.[106] While it demonstrates the value and high quality of his scholarship, this book has a more straightforward proposal that could be implemented when next a federal Court hears a freedom of association case or members of Congress or state legislatures draft legislation to protect freedom of association.

Two other aspects of Horwitz's position are worth noting in the context of this book. The first is his critique of the public/private distinction.[107] Because he wants to focus on institutions as categorically significant, it is less important for Horwitz's analysis that an institution be public than that it be a particular type of institution. For example, a public university would be treated simply as a university in a manner similar to private universities because a public university is in the same institutional category. The fact that it is public would be largely insignificant for judicial reasoning. The principles of academic freedom that govern universities as institutions are more similar between private and public universities than between public universities and public libraries, even though the latter are both public. Problems with the public/private distinction are fairly obvious, as Horwitz writes, "It is what leads courts—at least in theory—to conclude that Harvard University is more like Wal-Mart than it is like the University of Michigan and that the University of Michigan is more like Michigan Department of Motor Vehicles than it is like Princeton University."[108] For Horwitz, institutional categorization is the governing principle. This distinction is important because it leads Horwitz to a different conclusion regarding *CLS v. Martinez* from the one articulated here.

My approach does not require anything so drastic as a change in the understanding of public and private. It simply requires that the private realm protected by the First Amendment be recognized as consisting of individuals and the groups in which they associate. It allows the courts to continue to rely on the public/private distinctions which are still meaningful and relevant in current jurisprudence. For example, no public university would be allowed to use the sort of religious tests that private universities are able to use under the same circumstances and in the same institutional context. They also must treat public forums as realms where First Amendment rights are protected. The same forum at a private university would not be governed by the First Amendment but by the institution's own goals and norms.[109]

The second aspect of note in Horwitz's approach is his critique of acontextuality in First Amendment law. He argues that First Amendment scholars and jurists tend to think in terms of acontextual legal categories, such as state and individual. [110] The problem with such an approach is that it ignores the real-world contexts in which the law actually operates. Horwitz writes, "One snare of acontextuality is that carving up the world into legal categories may not help us to see the world as it really is and to make relevant distinctions between different kinds of conduct. . . . [L]aw does not operate in a vacuum. It must have something to do with what I value *in the world*."[111] The public/private distinction discussed above is Horwitz's primary example of an acontextual distinction.[112] On the ground, as the theory of First Amendment institutionalism demonstrates, the public/private distinction is much messier than the acontextual theory would indicate. That said, the public/private distinction is itself an attempt to contextualize institutions, to see them in light of their purpose. Our society is ordered according to public and private spheres so an analysis that ignores whether an institution is public or private may be guilty of ignoring relevant context, however messy it may be in practice.[113]

This book's argument for a conceptual pluralism consisting of triangular relations between state, individual, and association in First Amendment law could be accused of precisely the acontextualism that concerns Horwitz by simply positing a third abstract category alongside the individual and the state. However, the goal of this project is precisely to articulate a contextualism that recognizes the *reality of the social*. "Law does not operate in a vacuum," Horwitz writes. As we have said, law must recognize the reality it governs. First Amendment law regarding freedom of association must recognize the social reality, the associations, that it governs. Current jurisprudence is inadequate in this regard. A proper context does not mean the abolition of the categories of state and individual, but the reintroduction of a social category. This book corrects the Court's flawed theoretical vision so that the social context of the real world can be perceived properly. Language of the social, of a plurality of social groups and associations, is "unavoidably locally specific."[114] As chapters 2 and 4 indicate, the very practice of focusing on the social sphere places emphasis on the contextual and the concrete.

The scholarship produced in recent years by Inazu, Smith, and Horwitz demonstrates another point, First Amendment scholarship is currently recognizing the problem of the First Amendment Dichotomy identified in this book, while not properly diagnosing it, and is searching for solutions to the

Court's conundrum of how to treat associations and institutions, while not adequately reorienting its theoretical perspective. Each of these scholars is concerned that the Court's current First Amendment jurisprudence has inappropriately limited the autonomy of associations. They differ greatly in how they pursue their respective inquiries, but they are animated by the same fundamental concern that animates this book.

Anxieties over the autonomy of associations demonstrate the relevance of my thesis to broader public policy concerns that implicate the relationship between non-state institutions and the state. For example, my argument regarding the necessity of institutional autonomy for the integrity of associations is relevant to current debates over the independence of faith-based organizations and their relation to state funding.[115] My thesis would indicate that to the extent organizations receive state funding, the state must be careful to avoid co-opting private associations for its own purposes and allow them to remain free to pursue their own goals. We should avoid a situation where contact with government funding or programs automatically deputizes the receiving association and it immediately becomes merely an arm of the state.[116]

Horwitz writes at the end of the introduction to *First Amendment Institutions,*

> I do not presume that First Amendment institutionalism will dissolve all the problems of current First Amendment theory and practice. Rather, I hope to start a productive conversation—not only about the First Amendment, but about constitutional law and theory more broadly. First Amendment institutionalism is just one of a number of emerging legal theories that embrace a shared role for legal and social institutions in our constitutional and political culture.[117]

This book engages in and expands that conversation with the goal of contributing toward an increased judicial and legislative recognition of the role of the *social*, which means a revived freedom of association.

STRUCTURE OF THIS BOOK

This book will explain the problem of the vanishing freedom of association in the Supreme Court case law by using Robert Nisbet's understanding of the conflicted relationship between the state and the social group to provide a theoretical account of the ethos behind the Supreme Court's jurisprudence. The Court, as a representation of the political state, has come to exhibit disdain for the social groups that operate under the aegis of freedom of association. A theoretical basis for freedom of association founded upon Nisbet's understanding of the function of social groups justifies freedom of association in a truly plural society. What follows is a brief outline of the structure of the rest of this book.

In the next chapter I explain what I call the "theory of the social" drawing from Nisbet's four principles of pluralism (functional autonomy, decentralization, hierarchy, and tradition) to explain the theoretical perspective that would allow the Court to perceive groups in addition to the individual and the state in its analysis. This examination results in the necessity of what Nisbet called a "laissez-faire of groups." Then I turn to political sociology and explore Nisbet's description of the identity and characteristics of the social aggregate. The goal of the rest of the chapter is to describe in detail all sorts of social institutions and groupings that are left out of a judicial analysis that focuses only on state and individual. I identify the seven components of a *functional community* including dogma, function, authority, hierarchy, solidarity, status, and sense of superiority. These elements render an association or institution able to function in the lives of its members as a source of meaning and locus of allegiance, providing individuals with a sense of membership and belonging as well as functional value and purpose.

After describing the nature of social groups across a variety of Nisbet's categories including size, open or closed, personal or territorial, *Gemeinschaft* or *Gesellschaft*, and reference group I define the character of the voluntary association across the same sociological categories and I explore its potential to serve as a functional community, to be a source of identity and meaning for its individual members. My goal is to demonstrate the importance of the type of association at issue in freedom of association case law. Furthermore, I demonstrate that the elements of Nisbet's functional community are essential to the ability of any social group, including a voluntary association, to function meaningfully in the lives of its members. What I am getting at here is the particularly "social" nature of the social groups protected by freedom of association.

In the next chapter I present a detailed analysis of the problem of the First Amendment Dichotomy in freedom of association case law, beginning with its inception in *NAACP v. Alabama* (1958)[118] and culminating in *Christian Legal Society v. Martinez* (2010). I spend most of the chapter describing and dissecting the Court's analysis in *Martinez* according to the logic of the First Amendment Dichotomy, categorizing the Court's arguments as resulting from its conception of either the individual or the state. This analysis is intended to demonstrate that the First Amendment Dichotomy is the organizing principle of the Court's freedom of association analysis; it is the theoretical framework through which the Court *sees* freedom of association. Such a conception reduces protections for voluntary associations, the type of association at issue in the *Martinez* case. The membership requirements of the voluntary association were described by the Court as a potential threat to the autonomy of individuals and the unity of a state institution.

The argument of this book hinges on the link between the ability of the voluntary association to serve as a functional community for its members and the Court's reasoning that denies the voluntary association the constitutional protection necessary to instantiate the qualities of community, such as enforcement of dogma and function through the exercise of authority. These elements of community are the aspects of association that allow it to function as a source of meaning and belonging for its members. By failing to recognize membership requirements as an essential element of freedom of association, the *Martinez* Court deprived voluntary associations of the constitutional protections that would allow them to function in their members' lives as meaningful communities. Of course, voluntary associations may continue to function as this sort of community throughout American society in spite of the *Martinez* ruling. Any fair observation of the contemporary social scene would identify such associations as operative today. However, the important point is that *they now lack the constitutional right to do so*. The Court's decision in *Martinez* denied the constitutional protections that would secure the role of functional community for voluntary associations as a matter of First Amendment jurisprudence. State policy that intervenes in the inner workings of associations in a manner that deprives them of their functional autonomy and ability to effectively integrate members through the exercise of authority around shared dogma will not encounter resistance from the realm of First Amendment law. This book argues that it would be appropriate for the Court to grant constitutional protection to voluntary associations through a freedom of association that properly recognizes the nature of associations as functionally autonomous communities.

This last point implicates the dual nature of constitutionalism. On the one hand is the written document that prescribes certain rights, on the other are the constituent social institutions to which the written rights apply. This book points to the relationship between a First Amendment freedom of association, long located in the Assembly Clause and presumed for a proper functioning of most First Amendment freedoms, and the social group, such as a voluntary association, to which those rights are attached. For those rights to be meaningful, to operate as concrete constitutional protections, they must recognize the nature of the institutions and associations they are protecting: functional communities with the qualities of dogma, function, authority, hierarchy, solidarity, status, and sense of superiority. Freedom of association is only worthy of the name if it protects the qualities of functional community that allow an association to operate according to its proper function.

The question that follows is: what would judicial reasoning look like if it took into account the qualities of Nisbet's functional community in its freedom of association analysis? To explore this question, I turn in chapter 4 to Nisbet's philosophy of pluralism to explore relations among state, individual, and social group. Where a dichotomous framework inappropriately confines a vision of political and social structures to the state and the individual, a plural framework opens political and social thought to a plethora of social groups, including voluntary associations. I explain how a theory of pluralism provides a means of conceptualizing social groups as functional communities. By recognizing the necessity of functional autonomy, functional integrity, limited authority, and conditional allegiance in the inner workings of associations I demonstrate the way in which the framework of Nisbet's philosophy of pluralism allows voluntary associations to function as meaningful communities. In this chapter I apply Nisbet's principles of pluralism to voluntary associations to determine how the principles of a functional community would concretely operate in the sort of association at issue in *CLS v. Martinez*. The example of a chess club shows in a banal way how important membership requirements are to a group's ability to maintain its functional integrity by operating according to purposes articulated in a group's central tenets and expressed through its prescribed practices. A chess club has a central tenet regarding the importance of playing chess at club events and a function that is to provide a forum for chess. The club can only serve its function if it has the authority to enforce its central tenet, that playing chess is important, and certain prescribed practices, such as playing chess at club events. Then I turn to the example of a hypothetical religious student group, the Shakers, to serve as an illustration of the application of Nisbet's philosophy to ideological or religious organizations that are likely to assert a strong and possibly controversial link between their central tenets and prescribed practices.

Then I turn to the relation between the broad claims of Nisbet's principles of pluralism and judicial analysis to develop a specific method by which the Court can instantiate First Amendment Pluralism by recognizing associations in its First Amendment jurisprudence. I formulate a four-part "functional judicial test" based on the four principles of pluralism outlined by Nisbet. This test is designed to provide the judiciary with a concrete means of identifying and protecting voluntary associations within the bounds of its First Amendment case law. I also present a legislative proposal I call the Freedom of Association Protection Act (FAPA) based on the Religious Freedom Restoration Act (RFRA). This proposal provides a legislative solution to the judiciary's diminution of freedom of association. These exercises aspire to concretize a *theory* of associational rights, to help the Court conceptualize associations for the purpose of constitutional analysis. Through the functional test, the Court can instantiate First Amendment Pluralism as a theoretical framework for recognizing the role of state, individual, *and associations* in First Amendment jurisprudence. In other words, it can put the "social" into freedom of association.

In offering this challenge to the hitherto dominant dichotomy of individual and state, I am calling into question an assumption basic to modern political thought, and I am offering an alternative way of perceiving political society more broadly. The theoretical pluralism at the heart of First Amendment Pluralism offers a conceptual paradigm to understand the associational dynamics of political society that include groups and institutions in addition to the state and the individual.

2. Pluralism and the "Social" Nature of the Social Group

Associations exist, and they are plural. The potential for groups to manifest a multitude of characteristics across a variety of criteria produces a vast array of concrete social entities. Nonetheless, there are certain characteristics that associations have in common, at the heart of which is "function" and "dogma." These qualities make associations functional communities, meaningful associations that provide a psychological and social anchor for their members. Principles derived from Nisbet's philosophy of pluralism would secure the functioning of a diversity of associations in a particular state of freedom that Nisbet dubbed a "laissez-faire of groups." In terms of constitutional rights, a laissez-faire of groups provides an accurate depiction of the social setting protected by the freedom of association.

In this chapter I will describe a "theory of the social" that provides an account of what I called in the last chapter the *reality of the social* as well as the doctrinal goal of a properly conceptualized freedom of association. I will begin by describing the four tenets of Nisbet's philosophy of pluralism that undergird his understanding of a plural social reality, a laissez-faire of groups. Then I will describe in detail what social groups are, especially the voluntary association, the type of group at the center of the *Martinez* case. My definition will utilize a variety of sociological criteria found in Nisbet's work. The important point is identifying the particularly *social* elements of associations.

A *THEORY* OF THE SOCIAL

Let's begin with a theory of the social. The use of the term "theory" would seem to indicate inherently abstract and acontextual reasoning, but it need not be so. The term "theory" comes from the Greek word *theoria*, which can mean "beholding a spectacle" or "a way of seeing something." Originally *theoria* could be applied to observers at Olympic Games and other sacred festivals in a kind of "sacrilized spectating." In theology, *theoria* can be applied to the highest knowledge or experience of something. To have a theory of something means to know that thing more than superficially, to perceive the fundamental issues of whatever is under analysis. To have a theory of the social means to have a way of perceiving the social that acknowledges it, that actually *sees* it, now for purposes of analysis. I am critiquing a particular theory of politics and law as flawed, as *seeing* only the individual and the state, and I am arguing for a pluralist theory of politics and law that *sees* the individual, the state, *and* the social realm, that perceives human beings as creatures of their memberships. The term "social" includes the plethora of groups and institutions that matter to the person and that shape the person but are not the state. They are composed of individuals, but, by virtue of their communal component, are more than the sum of their parts. The social structures of authority and allegiance they compose cannot be reduced to any constituent. They are inherently social, communal. There are qualities that emerge from the interaction between individuals that are captured in social groups and that cannot be explained in purely individualist terms.[1]

I have defined this theory by reference to triangularly related concepts of state, individual, and social group interacting in complex ways. The state interacts with individual and social group, the social group interacts with—and intermediates between—state and individual, and the individual is a member of both the state and various social groups, each of which makes distinct claims upon him and provides him with consonant benefits. While the triangular language is helpful to conceive of actual relationships, the geometrical metaphor should not be taken too literally lest it become acontextual. This account is nonperfectionist. I am not arguing for an abstract, geometric relationship between these categories that can be ideally defined. Rather, I am attempting to help the Court to *see* the social group, to have a theory that accounts for the actual context of human political and social order, which is made up in large measure of nonstate social institutions, associations, and relationships.

The First Amendment Dichotomy is an acontextual construct that blinds the Court to the reality of the social group. First Amendment *Pluralism* articulated in this book is intended to remove blinders from the Court's analysis at a theoretical level, allowing the Court to *see*, to have a *theory* of, the social group, especially the voluntary association. But I do not claim to articulate a definitive, ideal relationship among state, individual, and association. The goal of my theory is to offer a practical means whereby the Court can acknowledge associations and the large role that they should play under the Constitution, while recognizing the need in future case law for doctrinal balancing and contextual definitions. It is in this context that Nisbet's scholarly work and theoretical perspective are essential. At the center of his political sociology is a philosophy of pluralism that recognizes the importance of a plurality of social groups. Nisbet's philosophy offers a way to secure the context for the preservation of meaningful groups as well as the creation of new groups through a robust conception of freedom of association under what Nisbet dubbed a laissez-faire of groups.

The Reintegration of the Individual into Community

According to Nisbet's description, the state has effectively dismantled the status-based associations of the past.[2] To the extent that associations can exist in modern society beyond such necessary biological associations like the family, they are largely voluntary. Nisbet does not lament this development. Rather, he expresses concern that as traditional groups declined in modern society, new groups did not arise to replace them in terms of moral and psychological significance in the lives of individuals. Nisbet writes in *The Quest for Community*,

> The common assumption that, as the older associations of kinship and neighborhood have become weakened, they are replaced by new voluntary associations filling the same role is not above sharp question. That traditional groups have weakened in significance is apparently true enough but, on the evidence, their place has not been taken to any appreciable extent by new forms of association.[3]

One reason that new forms of association, such as labor unions, industrial corporations, and government bureaucracies, do not, according to Nisbet, adequately integrate individuals into their structures is that they are too impersonal.[4] These groups have the qualities of *Gesellschaft*, not *Gemeinschaft* (terms I will define later) and cannot be integrating communities for individuals by offering the psychological function of membership that Nisbet believes to be central to personhood.[5] Nisbet writes, "New associations have arisen and continue to arise, but their functional value is still but dimly manifest for the greater number of people, and their moral and psychological appeal is correspondingly weak."[6]

In the last chapter of *Twilight of Authority* Nisbet offers several observations on possible sources of social renewal including a "renascence of kinship" as well as recommendations for broad social change. His recommendations are not specific or policy-based. His goal is to provide a theoretical framework to help to create a plural society, one that recognizes a plethora of social groups including many voluntary associations, built on what he sees as the ruins of the political community. He spends a good part of the book describing the decline of the modern state. It will suffice to point out that he titled the first chapter "The Political Community at Bay" and the second chapter "The Crumbling Walls of Politics." In sum, his argument is that the political community is not capable of providing the sense of community, of operating as what Nisbet called a Gemeinschaft association, that it promises by transferring functional authority and individual allegiance from social groups to itself. As a result, the political community is having an increasingly difficult time maintaining order.[7] The most relevant of Nisbet's proposals for our purposes is his promotion of a philosophy of pluralism and a resuscitation of voluntary associations.

Nisbet expresses doubt in *The Quest for Community* about the prospect of voluntary associations replacing traditional associations in providing functional value to individuals, but he believed that this form of associating held great potential for a large role in the healthy development of individuals. He does not question the form of functional community that the voluntary association represents.[8] Rather, he questions the present ability of voluntary associations to operate as functional communities given the present conditions created by the modern state. I believe that Supreme Court jurisprudence on freedom of association is an example of the state-created conditions that make voluntary associations difficult to form in a meaningful sense.

In *Twilight*, Nisbet revisits the topic of voluntary associations with more optimism regarding their prospects than he expressed in *Quest*. He writes, "Crucial are the *voluntary* groups and associations" because they provide the context in which "individual energies become stimulated, strengthened, and, finally, focused."[9] For Nisbet, individual accomplishment is never the result of the individual acting alone, but always the result of the individual acting under the inspiration and with the support of others with whom the individual associates. "Despite the American creed of individualism, which locates motivation and achievement in the recesses of the individual mind and character, human accomplishment in almost any form is the product of association, usually in small and informal structures whose essence is a high degree of autonomy."[10] However, voluntary associations, like status-based associations of the past, require authority, the ability to garner allegiance, in order to function meaningfully in the lives of individuals. This calls for the development of a new pluralist philosophy that will account for voluntary associations that perform *functions*, exercise *authority*, and command *allegiance*. "Function," "authority," and "allegiance" are technical terms of association that I will explain in detail throughout the rest of the book. Nisbet writes, "What would be immensely beneficial is the development of a clear philosophy of voluntary association that could take its place alongside philosophies . . . of the local community and of decentralization."[11] The purpose of the rest of the chapter is to explain Nisbet's philosophy of pluralism and a concept of the voluntary association using Nisbet's political sociology. The goal is to understand the essential elements that would allow voluntary associations to flourish so that I can transfer those elements into constitutional law to articulate a judicial philosophy that appropriately grants voluntary associations the freedom and autonomy necessary to their success.

Robert Nisbet's Philosophy of Pluralism

Nisbet outlines four elements of a pluralist philosophy that he argues would provide an account of how to effectively protect the presence of voluntary associations and to allow for the reintegration of the individual into meaningful communities. The four elements are functional autonomy, decentralization, hierarchy, and tradition. His explanation in *Twilight* is intended to provide direction for reform, although he does not provide specific policy proposals. Later I will translate these principles into proposals for judicial and legislative reforms of free association jurisprudence.

The first element of a philosophy of pluralism is functional autonomy.[12] A function is the end for which the association came into existence. It is the reason its founders created the group and its members joined it. Each group must be autonomous as to its function, it must be able to perform its major functions with the most freedom possible within its sphere of competency. The concept of function is essential to the concept of association and I will discuss it in detail later in this chapter and in chapters 4 and 5.

The second principle, decentralization, is related to the first. The centralization of function that occurred as the state accrued power in the vindication of individual rights must be reversed and each association must be granted independent authority. Functions must be decentralized in order to be autonomous.

The third element of pluralism is hierarchy. Every community has "some form of stratification of function and role" that emerges necessarily from the function it performs in the lives of the individuals that compose the group.[13] Every group exists for a purpose and every group has leaders that determine its purpose, establish the means to accomplish its purpose, and apply an enforcement mechanism to ensure that members accomplish that purpose. Nisbet points out that this aspect of authority is frequently ignored because of the present obsession with "a vain and vapid equality [that] takes what is in effect leveling as the desired norm of justice."[14] But every group requires authority in order to perform its function. An understanding of the need for hierarchy, of difference in role, is necessary for integrating the individual into meaningful community, including voluntary community.

The final element is tradition. By tradition, Nisbet means, "The reliance upon, in largest possible measure, not formal law, ordinance, or administrative regulation, but use and wont, the uncalculated but effective mechanisms of the social order, custom, folkway, and all the uncountable means of adaptation by which human beings have proved so often to be masters of their destinies in ways governments cannot even comprehend."[15] The roadmap to accomplishing an association's function cannot be deciphered ahead of time, but accrues over time through the practical application of "what works" within the concrete social context of each group. The notion of tradition for Nisbet's idea of plurality means that the internal structure of the group must be determined by the collective experience of that particular group. It cannot be determined by a central authority or by an outside source at all. The concept of *interaction* discussed later in this chapter is relevant in an analysis of group tradition. The interaction of group members with each other over time produces the particular character of the group that is embodied in its tradition. This involves a give and take between the hierarchy and the membership and between past group members and present group members. While tradition has the connotation of being formed over a long period of time, when applied in the context of voluntary associations it simply means that the ways and means of a specific group are the result of the accumulated experience of that particular group, even if it is not multigenerational. The lessons of that experience and the legitimacy of its authority as tradition for a particular group can only be utilized as well as challenged from *within* the group, not from an outside authority.

The Laissez-Faire of Groups

What would such a society look like if it implemented the principles of Nisbet's philosophy of pluralism, even the society limited to the college campus?

Nisbet calls his solution to the dichotomy of state and individual in political theory and public policy the laissez-faire of groups. He writes of it briefly in two of his most popular books, *The Quest for Community* and *Twilight of Authority*.[16] Nisbet chose the term "laissez-faire of groups" because he believes that the old laissez-faire of individuals has produced a populace of alienated individuals and a monolithic state that claims to be the supreme authority, asserting its central role in community, while simultaneously failing to adequately integrate individuals in the most basic psychological sense. He writes, "To create the conditions within which autonomous *individuals* could prosper, could be emancipated from the binding ties of kinship, class, and community, was the objective of the older laissez-faire. To create conditions within which *autonomous groups* may prosper must be, I believe, the prime objective of the new laissez-faire."[17] Nisbet advocates freedom for a plethora of groups to form around every conceivable interest and function so that the need of human beings for community, to do things together, is met in a variety of ways.

The term "laissez-faire" requires some further explanation. While it is an appropriate term for Nisbet's meaning, it can create confusion. Laissez-faire means "letting go." It emerged from the philosophy of release, of freeing the individual from social bonds. The use of the term is appropriate for Nisbet because what he means by "letting go" is the release of groups from the bonds of the state so that they may retain functional autonomy, exert authority, and claim the allegiance of individuals. However, the use of this term is misleading because the new laissez-faire of groups allows the exercise of authority over individuals, which, Nisbet contends, can often be to their benefit. Such a restraint upon the individual was anathema to the old laissez-faire.

In addition to freedom of groups to pursue their own function must be the freedom for new groups to form and to fulfill needs not adequately met by groups currently existing. Nisbet uses his discussion of the new laissez-faire in *Twilight* to introduce the concept of *social inventions*. He writes, "The overriding objective of the new policy of laissez-faire would be that of stimulating *social inventions*."[18] By "social invention" Nisbet means "creations of structures which become elements of the social bond; some minute, others very large and widely diffused."[19] Nisbet believes that in times of change social structures are created to adapt to those changes. Kinship structures, the origins of which are lost to history, are a prime example. He points to local community as another instance of the human race adapting to changed circumstances, in that case, to a static lifestyle following the agricultural revolution.[20] The scientific institutes and academies of the eighteenth century are yet another of Nisbet's illustrations of society "uniting the creative impulses of individuals" in ways made possible by the historical context. Even the political state, which is criticized by Nisbet and throughout this book for the disruption it may cause in the social sphere, was a social invention that served and continues to serve a variety of beneficial social purposes.[21]

I believe that a primary condition for a laissez-faire of groups and the presence of social inventions in a constitutional democracy is the constitutional right to freedom of association. To put this contention another way, the constitutional right of association ought to be understood primarily as securing a laissez-faire of groups and through this arrangement the capacity for social inventions. The goal of First Amendment Pluralism is to secure a laissez-faire of groups as a matter of constitutional rights.

Nisbet's goal with his new laissez-faire is to keep the "liberal purposes of individualism" but to change the means whereby those purposes are attained.[22] The benefit of a laissez-faire of groups and First Amendment Pluralism is that they maintain both the autonomy of the individual *and* the autonomy of the association. Nisbet writes, "We need a laissez-faire that will hold fast to the ends of autonomy and freedom of choice; one that will begin not with the imaginary, abstract individual but with the personalities of human beings as they are actually given to us in association."[23] Privacy and personal choice are essential to individualism. But they require the very context of small groups that are functionally autonomous in order to secure for the individual the privacy and personal choice that individualism holds to be so important. Nisbet writes, "It is the intimacy and security of each of these groups that provide the psychological context of individuality and the reinforcement of personal integrity. And it is the diversity of such groups that creates the possibility of the numerous cultural alternatives in a society."[24]

Nothing in Nisbet's solution should be understood to challenge the autonomy of the individual preserved in the right of exit. To the contrary, Nisbet believed that individualism as a philosophical point had produced incredible insight into the importance of the person. However, it had faulty premises which devalued the psychological importance of associations to individual personality. Nisbet writes,

> No fault is to be found with the declared purposes of individualism. As a philosophy it has correctly emphasized the fact that the ultimate criteria of freedom lie in the greater or lesser degrees of autonomy possessed by *persons*. A conception of freedom that does not center upon the ethical primacy of the person is either naive or malevolent. . . . Any freedom worthy of the name is indubitably freedom of persons.[25]

The laissez-faire of groups and consequently the theory of pluralism and freedom of association advocated in this book are intended to preserve the freedom of persons as they exist concretely, historically, and socially. The triangular language I used to describe First Amendment Pluralism underscores this point. The introduction of the social group into First Amendment analysis does not extinguish the rights of the individual. If the common conception of the First Amendment Dichotomy is the lone individual soapbox speaker vs. the state, First Amendment Pluralism proposed in this book depicts state, individual, and a plethora of social groups interacting with each other in complex ways. This triadic conception diversifies the Court's analytical tools, but the individual remains an important part of the theoretical paradigm. I am not arguing for the replacement of the First Amendment Dichotomy of *state and individual* with the First Amendment Dichotomy of *state and social group*. I am instead arguing for a First Amendment *Pluralism* in constitutional doctrine that adequately takes account of a third component, the social group, in all of its plurality. Nothing argued here would diminish the concrete rights of individuals. An express purpose of my theory is to extend and secure the individual right to act *corporately*. This right is only meaningful if the corporate social structures within which and through which individuals act are themselves constitutionally secured.

It is to the sociology of these social structures that I now turn.

THE VOLUNTARY ASSOCIATION AS SOCIAL GROUP

The first part of this chapter may have been frustrating to read because so many terms were left undefined. What *is* the elusive "social group" that can neither be reduced to its individual members nor subsumed into the state? What are authority and allegiance? Why are they important? For that matter, what is Christian Legal Society at Hastings Law School? What is the "association" that I argue is excluded from the conglomeration of doctrines that I call the First Amendment Dichotomy? What are the "social" qualities of the associations that are ostensibly excluded from the Court's analysis of freedom of association? The rest of this chapter aims to answer these questions by turning to Nisbet's political sociology to identify the key elements of a certain type of social group, the voluntary association, the type of group at issue in *CLS v. Martinez* and freedom of association jurisprudence more broadly. Later in the book I will use this analysis to develop the means whereby the Court can protect the voluntary association. The presence of the social group in the Supreme Court's theory of the First Amendment would abolish the First Amendment Dichotomy described in the previous chapter and establish First Amendment Pluralism as the governing conceptual paradigm.

In the course of our investigation of the social group I will not ignore the state or the individual. In the process of investigating the dynamics of the social group, I will describe the state across the same sociological categories that I use to describe the voluntary association. But this chapter is concerned primarily with "the major elements of the social bond, the mechanisms and processes through which human beings become members of the social order and by which they remain members."[26] The term "social group" infers this social context and these social processes. Nisbet writes, "Just as modern chemistry concerns itself with what it calls the chemical bond, seeking the forces that make atoms stick together as molecules, so does sociology investigate the forces that enable biologically derived human beings to stick together in the 'social molecules' in which we actually find them from the moment, quite literally, of their conception."[27] This chapter is also about what is lost when constitutional law ignores the social context in which human beings necessarily, "from the moment of their conception," are to be found. Nisbet writes, "I do not really see 'individuals' in the sense of discrete, elemental human particles in the world around us. I no more see 'individuals' in this sense than I see the smallest elements of matter with which physicists work. I do indeed see human beings. In fact, that is all I see."[28] But they are found only in the social context of community, only in their memberships in various social groups.

I will begin by discussing the nature of a "functional community," an association that provides the essential social elements that bind individuals to others, according to seven qualities that Nisbet believes characterize a community. Important to this discussion is *dogma*, the element of community that forms the center of every social group. Then I will describe the various elements of social aggregates, which together define every possible type of social arrangement. I will discuss social aggregates in terms of size, whether they are closed or open, personal or territorial, Gemeinschaft or Gesellschaft, and whether they are a reference group. The term "social aggregate" refers to any type of social arrangement defined along any combination of the aforementioned qualities. The term "social group" refers more narrowly to the especially "social" as opposed to "political" social aggregates. The political state and the voluntary association are only two types of social aggregates. There are others, but they are beyond the scope of our discussion, and I will touch on them only in passing.

Various typologies of social aggregates demonstrate an inherent pluralism in the concept of the social group. When we speak of "the social group," we inevitably must speak in the plural; we must speak of "social group*s*." There are so many possible combinations of characteristics of social aggregates to produce a dizzying array of potential types that any discussion of this third prong inevitably implies plurality.[29] After the discussion of the types of social aggregates, I will explain how social groups interact with individuals using the concepts of social roles, statuses, and norms, creating even more complexity and plurality among social groups in terms of how individuals interact with them. I will turn to the concept of authority, which binds a social group together, and explain how authority is related to function, the purpose for which every group is created. After setting the stage by explaining in detail all the possible categories of the social aggregate and how individuals interact with them, I will turn to the voluntary association, the particular type of social group at issue in *CLS v. Martinez*. I will explain voluntary associations in terms of Nisbet's typology of social aggregates: the components of community, the elements of social aggregates, the exercise of authority, and how they enable individuals to embody roles, statuses, and norms. The point of this section is to demonstrate the importance of voluntary associations to individuals as social persons through their ability to exert authority and offer functional significance in the lives of their members. I will also demonstrate how the CLS chapter at Hastings Law School possesses the qualities of a voluntary association.

SOCIAL AGGREGATES

Nisbet discusses the nature of the "social aggregate" in *The Social Bond*. The terms social group, association, and political state denote certain general types of social aggregates. The social aggregate is the essential context for any type of social interaction. Its essential characteristic is that it exists where persons "*do something* together."[30] Social aggregates are "those specific clusters, assemblages, gatherings, and groups within which social behavior is to be found in the human species."[31] They are not statistical clusters or imaginative constructs. Social aggregates require interaction and "may be as large as nations, as small as intimate dyads."[32] The Jewish people, the Roman Catholic Church, Sunni Islam, England, The Humanist Association of America, the city of Chicago, fans at a hockey game, are all social aggregates. The association may be loose or suffocatingly cohesive. "But," Nisbet writes, "What is essential to the social aggregate is the sense of *mutual awareness*, either directly in a face-to-face manner, as in the small primary group, or through common possession of symbols, as in a vast nation or world-wide church." Members "are aware of each other and are influenced by each other."[33] The term "social" implies mutual awareness and a sense of membership. Each member has a sense of belonging to the aggregate.[34]

Why Do Social Aggregates Exist?

Social aggregates exist to accomplish some purpose, for individuals to do something together. Social groups come into existence around various ends, performance of a function of some sort, such as raising and socializing children, educating a populace, cheering for a sports team, or organizing suitable religious ceremonies. Aggregates exist to provide community around some goal which the community hopes to accomplish. The characteristics of social aggregates cohere with the particular function that any given aggregate performs. In *The Degradation of the Academic Dogma* Nisbet describes a community as having seven characteristics: *function, dogma, authority, hierarchy, solidarity, status*, and *sense of superiority*. These elements strike at the very heart of Nisbet's concern with the demise of the social group.[35] These elements are what make groups psychologically and materially significant in the lives of their individual members. I will explore each of these characteristics briefly below and tie them into the elements of the social bond.

Function can be anything "from crime or conspiracy to worship, scholarship, or child rearing." The function is the end for which the aggregate came into existence. A mosque comes into existence to worship Allah and an orchestra comes into existence to play music. *Dogma* is the "sense of some transcending purpose" that infuses the group's function. Whatever function orients the group must be articulated as a dogma, a transcendent ideal that is a "deeply felt, profoundly held value."[36] Dogma is composed of the beliefs that form the *central tenets*, the essential orienting beliefs or purposes that ground a particular group. For example, a Christian group has a dogma in the deity of Christ, and a Muslim group has a dogma in the truth of the teachings of Mohammed. We tend to think of dogma in terms of fundamental religious teachings, but the dogma of a group need not be religious. A chess club also has a dogma regarding the value of playing chess, a soccer club has a dogma in the value of playing soccer, a choir has a dogma in the value of singing, and so on. I will often use the term "central tenets" as a synonym for dogma because it does not have the negative connotation nor the strong association with religious doctrine as does the term "dogma," but I mean precisely the same thing.

Authority is the means through which a community's function and dogma are made effective for its members. Authority is not power. It may use force, but authority does not rely on force for its legitimacy as does power. The legitimacy of authority arises from group consensus and tradition. By tradition, Nisbet means acceptance of group authority by the group members through time. This implicates the development of consensus derived from interaction both between members of the group and between the membership and the authority structure of the group.

Hierarchy is the ranking of social roles into varying degrees of status. Various roles in a community cohere more or less to the norms of the community, "and it is impossible to array all of these roles on the same line of equality."[37] Depending upon the nature of the community, its dogma and function, there is necessarily a hierarchy of values and social roles. Even the simple distinction between leader and general member present in every group in some form is a reflection of hierarchy of role and function.

Solidarity means that there is a sense of "we" in the group. The group is more than a mere statistical aggregate but a unified community. Nisbet writes that solidarity in a group means that "corporatism is at premium; individualism at near nullity."[38] Members of the group see each other as fellow members, as part of the same enterprise.

Nisbet describes status or honor (he uses the terms interchangeably for this particular characteristic) as subordination of merely material or utilitarian interest to group goals. The status of membership in the community is valuable in itself apart from anything that might be gained materially by membership. Members have an overriding fidelity to the group that attaches to personal identity, a sense of honor that imbues their loyalty to the group such that their membership and participation cannot be reduced to merely utilitarian terms.

Last is the quality of superiority, "measured in terms of what one's own community does and is and what the rest of the world does not do and isn't." The community not only sees itself as separated from the rest of the world in some way, but actually better than the rest of the world. This is true of all communities in all societies. As Nisbet points out, "We are told that in the Middle Ages even beggars, pickpockets, and prostitutes—all communally organized, of course—possessed this sense; able . . . to look down upon nobles and kings."[39] The qualities of *honor* and *superiority* relate directly to the concept of a "reference group" discussed below.

These qualities provide the individual with both a functional end that orients her life and a dogma, an overriding purpose. Through authority the social group enforces the dogma and accomplishes the function. Hierarchy, solidarity, honor, and superiority give the individual a sense of value for her role in the group and a sense of belonging to something beyond herself. This in turn invites the individual to give her allegiance to the group. It is impossible to separate an individual member's allegiance to a group from the qualities outlined above.

Types of Social Aggregates

An aggregate may be categorized based on size, whether it is open or closed, personal or territorial, Gemeinschaft or Gesellschaft, and whether it is a reference group. Recall that any given social aggregate will possess one quality in each of the above categories, and there is no necessary correlation between types of aggregates across categories. Discussing the small size of a group does not necessarily determine that it is necessarily closed rather than open or "communal" rather than "social." Having certain qualities, such as small size, will contribute to having certain other qualities, such as possessing Gemeinschaft rather than Gesellschaft, but it is not determinative. Any given social aggregate, including the state and the voluntary association will be characterized by one type in each of the categorical descriptions discussed below. I should further note at the outset that social behavior has an underlying unity. It is impossible to separate the various elements of social entities including the categories of social aggregates from social roles, social statuses, and social norms. Each is a different aspect of social groups that can be conceptually distinguished to better understand social behavior and the nature of social groups, but they are intertwined in concrete human society.[40]

Size

The size of a social aggregate may affect its nature. Smaller groups may have intimacy impossible in groups that are too large for face-to-face interaction. The dyad, consisting of only two persons, is the smallest possible aggregate. A monogamous marriage is the prime example of this type. By its nature it invites intimacy and is associated with the most private thoughts, hopes, and feelings.[41] The triad is the next larger aggregate in size. When a child is born, a marriage becomes a triad. Social dynamics between two persons can be altered when a third is added, but the potential for intimacy is hardly less than in a dyad. Dyads and triads need not be like a family or even sexual. A friendship between two people constitutes a dyad. A group of three friends or coworkers is a triad. These basic forms of the social aggregate are important because they are universal. Nisbet writes, "No matter how vast the scale of organization of a society, how formalized or bureaucratic, how deeply rooted in law or tradition, all human associations are composed of dyads and triads."[42] Throughout international corporations and nation-states there are innumerable dyads and triads, groups of two or three people who live, work, or commune together in some way. They may serve the purposes of the larger group. or they may have their own goals apart from if not contrary to any larger group.

Small groups are the next smallest form of association, larger only than the dyad and the triad. This group is small enough that members know each other and are in frequent association such that there are relationships between members that are substantive and involve sentiments, relational stimuli, and responses in an interactional intensity that makes the small group a substantial influence on its members. Small groups can include the family, military squad, academic department, or jury, to use some of Nisbet's examples.[43] It could also be a group of friends or, of special relevance to our discussion, a student group at a university. The small group is of primary importance "to the formation of human personality and to the diversities of personality and conduct that we see from one culture to another."[44]

Nisbet's description of the small group draws from Charles H. Cooley's concept of "the primary group." Such a group involves face-to-face contact that persists over time such that the small group can exert influence over each member. In this group persons develop "the successive awareness of membership in the social order; of relation to the fundamental values of the larger society and internalization, through interaction of these values, thus forming the sense of self, of character, and identity."[45] The family and small neighborhood are "primary" in this sense, but other small groups fit this description as well. The important point is that small groups are the context of shaping fundamental personality characteristics and values to an extent impossible in larger aggregates.

Dyads, triads, and small groups are all characterized by smallness, and they are the context for the expression of values associated with what the Court has called "intimate associations," such as love and understanding.[46] But, Nisbet writes, "there is no magic in smallness. Dullness multiplied by two or three or ten is still dullness."[47] And while these various forms of small associations are the unique settings of love and intimacy, they also can be characterized by hate and cruelty with an intensity often unknown in larger organizations. The smallness intensifies the passions of the members according to the nature of the group, for better or for worse.

Large-scale aggregates are characterized by "greater impersonality, diminished intensity of personal interaction, greater formality of character, and a minimum of face-to-face association in which the participants are 'whole personalities.'"[48] Size is not related to the moral worth of a group, but it does affect the quality of the interaction between members. The type of interaction that takes place between individuals in a dyad presents different possibilities than what exists between individuals who are members of a large-scale aggregate like a nation-state.

Nisbet discusses two types of large-scale aggregates, organizations and masses. An organization is formal and has relatively clearly defined roles for its members. It is rational in makeup, and there is division of labor between roles. Unlike small groups, dyads, and triads, large-scale aggregates are impersonal. Members are recognized for their role within the organization, not for their worth as whole personalities, which is often true in smaller aggregates that involve face-to-face interaction. Masses are not organized but are still unified. A mass is not simply a statistical aggregate, but has "a certain unity, a certain sense of mutual awareness, and an occasional capacity for acting in unison."[49] Nisbet points to the phenomena of the television public, the crowd at a football game, and political parties as examples of masses in this sense. The people are unified but not organized. Individuals who are part of a mass do not have a particular role per se in the aggregate. But all members of the mass are unified around something nonetheless. That unifying thing could be a television show, a sports team, or a political party platform. The mass is generally united by a single aim or a set of simple ideas. A mass of individuals may be joined in little else than cheering for the same sports team or voting for the same candidate. Masses may be largely passive, but they can be incredibly influential. Nisbet writes, "The mass may be quiescent, it may limit itself to the spectator role, or it may become, as it does frequently in history, extraordinarily active, its members given the sudden sense of almost intoxicating unity and purpose."[50]

Any particular size of aggregate does not automatically carry a connotation of "good" or "bad." While size relates to function in that a mass cannot provide the same personal qualities one may find in a small group such as a family, any aggregate of a given size may be destructive or constructive to its individual members and to society at large depending upon the historical circumstances, the qualities of its members, and the value of their interactions. Furthermore, while there is a limit to the effect of a large social aggregate on its members, it may be effective in a concrete way through myriad smaller aggregates. While the Roman Catholic Church is a massive organization, it is composed of parish churches, small groups that have the potential to operate effectively in their members' lives and engage their members in a more comprehensive way. Often large organizations follow this model, intentionally making themselves effective to their members through the use of small groups.

Closed and Open

In addition to size, the character of social aggregates is "affected by the degree to which their membership is closed or open."[51] An aggregate is "open" when membership is not denied to anyone who wishes to participate in whatever function or norm or idea that serves as the impetus for the aggregate's existence. An aggregate is "closed" when, "irrespective of an outsider's desire to join, membership is denied on the basis of some rule or consideration or sharply limited by special conditions."[52] Most aggregates fall in between these extremes. Aggregates are open or closed for a variety of reasons including tradition, rationality, values, and expediency.

Reasons for limiting membership in an aggregate are legion. Nisbet writes, "There is literally no type of consideration that is not somewhere at some time operative as a condition of membership."[53] Tribes and clans are limited by kinship and marriage, religion by ritual affirmation and acceptance of beliefs and laws, and universities by academic merit, to cite a few of Nisbet's examples. These groups may be very severe in their requirements. For example, a religious group may have strenuous doctrinal "tests" and strict conduct regulations to make sure that adherents are true believers. Alternatively, they may have lax guidelines, content with vague spiritual affirmations and laissez-faire regarding personal conduct. Likewise, universities may have strict standards regarding academic merit, or they may be willing to accommodate students with weak academic records but proof of work ethic or some other quality or skill transferable into academic achievement in the university context.

The difference between open and closed aggregates is relative. An organization that has strenuous requirements that cross several categories, such as race and religion, for example, will be much more closed than an organization that is closed in one category but theoretically open to all. For example, the Ku Klux Klan is much more closed than Phi Beta Kappa, even though it is still quite difficult to be accepted into the latter. The Klan has strict racial, religious, and ideological requirements while Phi Beta Kappa has only a merit requirement, however high it may be. An organization with a single standard may still make that standard quite high and their group quite exclusive, but it would still be considered relatively open if it allows anyone to join who meets even a high level of achievement.

There are numerous combinations of aggregates that mix the qualities of open and closed. Prisons and insane asylums are closed in the sense that individuals are forced to be in those institutions based upon particular qualities, such as insanity and the social deviance of criminality. Other individuals, those who are sane and law abiding, are excluded from these institutions. Some associations are closed as to exit, but not entrance. Monasteries, military schools, and hospitals are often open to all, or nearly all, but often require permission to exit. Other groups, such as Ivy League universities, may be very selective in terms of who may join, but allow any member to exit if they so choose.[54]

Personal and Territorial
Personal and territorial aggregates are distinguished by whether the binding quality is personal or merely geographical. Kinship, religion, and ethnicity are

the major forms of personal aggregates as they are formed by qualities that adhere to the person, such as family ties, personal beliefs, and blood. Tribes, clans, and war bands are also personal.[55]

Territorial aggregates generally follow personal aggregates chronologically. Tribes and clans give way to a political state attached to a particular geographical area. One of the earliest incidents of this happening is the Cleisthenean reforms of the late sixth century that created the polis of Athens as a distinctly political unit in place of the clan structure of ancient Athenian society. When this happens the locus of authority shifts from personal sources in kinship and religion to a political source based upon geographical location. Under personal aggregates one is bound by the authority of the tribe or clan based upon blood or marriage. That authority has nothing to do with location. But under territorial aggregates one is bound by the authority of the territorial power. Geographical location is everything. With this shift in the locus of authority, there is a shift in the notion of self-identity. With the rise of the territorial political unit citizenship emerges as a distinct form of membership. What is important for individual identity is the source of citizenship in the territorial aggregate. Rights and duties arise from the territory in which one resides, and not from the bonds of religion or kinship. When loyalty moves from personal aggregate to territorial, emphasis on the personal ties of kinship and clan declines and the rights and duties of citizenship, such as economic and geographic mobility, political individualism, and greater intellectual and cultural freedom, become more central.[56]

The struggles between personal and territorial aggregates continue after the formation of the political state. Even in the postmedieval period where the modern political state has achieved the greatest degree of unchallenged authority in its history, there is still struggle between the state and personal aggregates. Nisbet points to the examples of ethnic loyalties in the African American and Mexican American communities clashing with claims of the federal government and to similar conflicts between state and family and state and religion. He also points to the flag-salute cases and the refusal by individuals to submit to the military draft as other examples of personal loyalties clashing with the authority of the territorial aggregate.[57] Recent examples of this conflict include the refusal of portions of the Catholic Church to submit to the contraceptive mandate in the Patient Protection and Affordable Care Act[58] and clashes between members of African American communities and police forces over the shooting of young black men.[59]

Totalitarian societies are the most extreme example of this conflict in the modern period. Political leaders of totalitarian nations sought "to dissolve or thoroughly subordinate traditional personal unities in the population and to make the territorial state itself serve as the single, total manifestation of society."[60] But it need not go that far. Every territorial unit is in some conflict with the personal loyalties of those who reside within it. Nisbet writes,

> In a whole variety of matters—education, and administration of welfare funds, among others—we are witnessing conflict between powerful, deeply evocative personal social aggregates (in this case racial or ethnic) and those aggregates, such as municipalities or states, which are territorial and which are the official units of government in these matters. Again let us emphasize that, first, this type of underlying conflict is not new in history—it is one of the oldest we know anything about. Second, here as elsewhere, the conflict is based upon allegiances, loyalties, and authorities that are the very stuff of human society.[61]

The struggle for freedom of association is another example of the clash between the modern territorial state and personal aggregates. Voluntary associations form on the basis of personal loyalties and beliefs, not territory, and they can be perceived as a challenge to the authority of the territorial state because they make claims on the person that may conflict with the claims of citizenship. This conflict is at the heart of *CLS v. Martinez*, and it underlies much of the discussion in the coming chapters.

Gemeinschaft and Gesellschaft

Nisbet draws from Ferdinand Tonnies the concepts of Gemeinschaft and Gesellschaft, notions that describe the communal quality of the social group. Gemeinschaft could be translated as "community" and Gesellschaft as "society," but I will use the German terms, as Nisbet did, because he believes that the English equivalents do not do the concepts justice. What Nisbet means by these terms is that when an aggregate has the characteristics of Gemeinschaft, it is a "community" in the sense that the relationships contained in the aggregate deal with human beings in their "full personalities rather than the single aspects or roles of human beings." Gemeinschaft aggregates are highly cohesive, have a strong sense of community between members, and endure throughout

time. Historical examples are kinship groups, village communities, castes, religious organizations, ethnic groups, and guilds.[62] There is a strong sense of
unity in each of these aggregates, and they lay claim to the whole personality
of each member.

The quality of the *community* is what matters for Gemeinschaft and Gesellschaft, not its correspondence to previous designations of social aggregates.
That said, the kinship group is the archetype for Gemeinschaft, involving as
it does the whole person. Other forms of Gemeinschaft follow its pattern
and even borrow its terms. Religious groups use filial terms such as "father,"
"brother," and "sister," labor unions use the term "brotherhood," and fraternities and sororities are a familiar academic example of an aggregate that bor-
rows filial language. The use of filial language indicates that these identities
involve, or attempt to involve, the whole person in the privileges and responsibilities of the aggregate just as the family does.[63]

Gesellschaft is generally translated as "society." It too can be any combination of the previous designations of a social aggregate. However, the difference
between Gemeinschaft and Gesellschaft is that aggregates characterized by
Gesellschaft engage the individual in only one or a few aspects of his personality. Gesellschaft aggregates are less cohesive, demanding less loyalty and less
commitment from the individual. These groups can be based upon common
religious, economic, or cultural interests, but Gesellschaft aggregates do not
make as great a claim upon the whole individual as do Gemeinschaft.[64]

Historically, there are periods where social aggregates in general are best
described as *Gemeinschaft* and others best characterized as Gesellschaft. Reasons behind such a historical shift are complex. They have to do with the rise
of motivations and incentives that alter the fundamental character of the aggregate in such a way that the aggregate either involves less of the total personality of its members or it involves more. While this shift from Gesellschaft to
Gemeinschaft may happen to a variety of aggregates, a salient example from
recent history is the nation-state. The modern state arose as a matter of military defense. But over time it took on the character of Gemeinschaft, making a
greater and greater claim to the loyalty of its citizens. At its founding, the state
required little of its subjects and seldom involved itself in their ordinary lives.
It was little more than a king demanding tribute of his subjects in return for
protection. However, through the rise of nationalism and the doctrine of sovereignty, the nation-state adopted a position of supreme personal allegiance

and membership. The intense allegiance given by citizens to the modern state arises from its Gemeinschaft nature that would have previously been conferred on church or family.[65] The use of filial designations for territorial units, such as the use of "motherland" and "fatherland" by Russia and Germany in the twentieth century, indicate the nature of this shift.

The attempted Gemeinschaft nature of the modern state contributes to the conflict between the state and traditionally Gemeinschaft aggregates such as the family, the local community, religious organizations, and the small group. The conflict between state and social groups is not a conflict between a Gemeinschaft and a Gesellschaft aggregate but a conflict between two aggregates that both seek the qualities of Gemeinschaft. *CLS v. Martinez* is an example of this conflict. The public university, as an extension of the state, jealously guards its access and claims upon its members, the students, even against voluntary organizations such as student groups.

The nature of the state as an exclusive concept discussed in the last chapter emerges from its territorial quality combined with its Gemeinschaft quality. As a territorial entity, the state applies membership (i.e., citizenship) to every (or nearly every) individual in its territory. That does not present an inherent conflict with Gemeinschaft groups such as filial and religious aggregates. However, when the state combines its insistence on applying membership to every individual in its territory and makes that membership a Gemeinschaft relationship between citizen and state, then it makes a claim on the total person of every individual in its territory. The definition of the citizen becomes the definition of the whole person. This puts the state in sharp conflict with other Gemeinschaft groups making similar claims on the identity of the person. I will explore the extent of the state's claims in this context in the next chapter.

Reference Groups

Reference groups are any type of aggregate described above organized around any possible interest. What makes a social aggregate a *reference* group is that it is the "social aggregate to which an individual 'refers,' consciously or unconsciously, in the shaping of his attitudes on a given subject or in the formation of his conduct. It is the social aggregate toward which he orients his aspirations, judgments, tastes, and even his profoundest moral or social values."[66]

This concept is vitally important because, while individuals are members of various combinations of the above social aggregates, they may not take their primary identity from those aggregates, even ones that are Gemeinschaft in character. However entrenched in a number of aggregates an individual may be, he probably primarily identifies with only one of those groups, and it may not be a primary aggregate, such as his family or local community. A particularly religious person may refer primarily to his religious association, even while coming from a nonreligious family or working and living with nonreligious individuals. Deviant behavior is often the result of an individual drawing identity and social norms from a group outside of the primary aggregates of which he is a part, such as neighborhood, family, and religious community.[67] Consider the trope of the rebellious teenager who defies his parents and breaks the law at the instigation of his friends. He violates the norms of the local community and his family by taking his primary identity and cues for action, i.e., his reference, from an outside aggregate, his friends. The reference group may be a means of encouraging the individual to leave his present circumstances and beliefs, or a means of reinforcing his current belief systems and conduct.[68] The reference group "serves as both a standard for *comparison* of one's self with a set of norms, that is, for self-appraisal, and also as the *source* of the varied norms and values that operate in a given individual's life."[69]

The concept of reference group is the most penetrating of the qualities of social aggregates in terms of demonstrating the group source of individual self-satisfaction. It encapsulates the fundamental reason social groups are so important to individual development. The individual finds his primary identity by reference to the group. Its values, ideas, and constraints shape individual identity and personality. By being a reference group, groups speak to their members, shaping them in ways they may not understand. While a reference group can operate in this unconscious way, this concept illuminates the manner in which groups can be *consciously* influential on an individual. An individual may *choose* to identify with the reference group and adopt its values. Take, for example, a person raised in a conservative evangelical home who leaves her childhood religion behind during college. While her primary aggregates of family and church community still surround her, at least relationally, she is consciously referring to a different group for her primary values and identity. This point is especially important for the discussion of voluntary associations later in this chapter. An individual may consciously and voluntarily join an association to represent her values thereby consciously choosing to have them shaped by a particular group representing a specific set of values.

The political state as well as most social groups can serve as reference groups. An individual can find his primary identity in his political citizenship and therefore find expression for his identity in patriotism. He can "refer" primarily to his religious institution and find expression for his identity in piety. An individual can identify with the values and standards of his occupation and find expression for his identity in his work. Like the Gemeinschaft/Gesellschaft distinction, the concept of a reference group identifies a source of conflict between the state and the social group as well as the conceptual origin of the state as an exclusionary concept. Out of all the groups of which an individual may be a member, only one or a few will serve as conscious or unconscious reference groups, sources of identity formation. The state's claim to sovereignty is, among other things, a claim to be the primary reference group for individuals within its territory. This conflicts with the claim of social groups of all sorts that provide individuals with values, dogmas, and functions that render each of them a potential reference point for individual identity.

The Person and the Social Aggregate:
Roles, Statuses, and Norms

In the above sections I discussed the properties of social aggregates, touching upon their functional value to individuals. In this section I turn to the place of the person in social aggregates by considering the individual's interaction with social groups in terms of the individual's role, status, and capacity to absorb and reflect the norms of the group.

Social Roles

"Persons as Roles" is the title Nisbet gives the first section of his chapter "Social Roles" in *The Social Bond*. He argues that we do not know *individuals* but *persons*. Person, as derived from "persona," is a theatrical term for mask. A "person" is the role played. Human beings interact with each other in their various roles, and the person cannot be separated from the role or roles that he plays in society. Roles are "parts that have already been written by time and circumstance before we are born."[70] New roles come into existence over time and old roles are modified and occasionally discarded. This is the process of *inter*action, "with the individual modifying, shaping, and adjusting the successive roles he encounters in life."[71] A person cannot be other than a role, however diverse and varied these roles may be in actual social life.

Nisbet attributes five characteristics to roles. First, "roles are *ways of behavior*, distinctive, more or less prescribed, and handed down from generation to generation." Human beings have taken action in various ways throughout history, but only some ways of behaving have become embodied in roles. Nisbet describes this process as "some kind of natural selection in social history" to explain how some ways of behavior become fixed in society and some disappear. Second, every social role embodies social norms, the ideal types of a particular kind of participation in society. Behavior defined by role is determined by social norms. Third, "a social role is invariably a part of some structure or system of interactive relationships." This denotes reciprocity and complementarity in the social order. The role exists in terms of other roles to which it reacts and interacts and with which it complements and coheres. "For the social role to exist . . . there must be other, complementary or reciprocal roles that alone can give the particular social role meaning as well as function."[72] Fourth, social roles connote legitimate action. Human beings accept particular behavior as long as it corresponds to what is expected from that particular social role. "Arresting" someone is considered legitimate when an officer of the law carries it out, but the same action is considered "kidnapping," an act of social deviance, when one who does not have a social role in law enforcement takes the same action. The same is true of a physician's actions, some of which would be considered invasive and even abusive if carried out by someone who is not in a physician's social role. A role is legitimate if the person carrying it out is in the social role of the person who has social sanction to carry it out. Fifth, a social role is characterized by duty. The person in the role has a strong sense of duty to engage in whatever behavior is required by the role. Nisbet writes, "The idea of duty is a manifestation of the larger system of authority that exists in any social aggregate."[73]

Social roles fall into two general categories, ascribed and achieved. Ascribed roles are those associated with age, sex, race, occupation, religion, and social class that denote a role by virtue of a person having the characteristic. There is no necessary reason the role is ascribed in this fashion. Racial minorities do not biologically have to be ascribed certain roles, but in some societies racial minorities are given an ascribed role based solely on race. In other societies, occupations are ascribed by caste. Achieved roles are, in theory, open to everyone based on an understood definition of merit appropriate to the position. The level of merit may be general or it may be very particular and specialized.[74] Many occupational roles are achieved in this way.

Social Status

The first section of the chapter on "Social Status" is titled "Persons as Statuses."[75] Status refers to the hierarchical ranking of social roles. The concept of status depends upon "*a vertical perspective that permits considerations of 'higher' and 'lower' to become relevant.* Hierarchy, stratification, and rank are the very essence of status."[76] Nisbet describes status in the same five categories that he ascribes to role: it is a way of behavior, part of a social circle, bounded by norms, implicates legitimacy, and is accompanied by a sense of duty. Nisbet points to the example of the aristocrat in medieval Europe. Status accorded to an aristocrat is vertically described as "higher" than other social roles within the social order; it requires manners, a certain way of behavior; it embodies certain norms; certain behaviors of aristocrats are considered legitimate and socially acceptable if carried out by an aristocrat; and it requires certain duties, such as those inferred by the maxim *noblesse oblige.*[77]

While role and status are related, role does not contain an inherent implication of higher or lower. Status denotes vertical ranking and is inherently bound up with the hierarchy embodied generally in the social order or in a particular social group. Just as social roles are essential in a society due to the variety of functions, so status, defined as social esteem for a particular function, will immediately arise from the same diversity of functions.[78] As soon as a society has determined that there is a necessary role for hunter and gatherer, parent and child, laborer and leader, it will rank these roles based upon perceived social importance. Status can be based on sex, age, wealth, political authority, ethnicity, education, job, and kinship.

Status is not the same concept as class. Democratic society, which does not have classes in the static sense of medieval Europe, is still rife with statuses, even if all statuses are achievable by persons of high ability. The concept of status is important because it "best enables us to deal with all the myriad, shifting, and complex patterns of social mobility in contemporary society"[79] in a way that the concept of social class does not. Nisbet pointedly explains that denial of the existence of static social classes is not a denial of inequality, as some social scientists assume.[80] Social status is more fluid than social class, but nonetheless it is a real social ranking even in a democratic society that does not have distinguishable social classes. Personal identity is derived from various social aggregates besides class. Social authority and social allegiance emerging from social aggregates[81] play a large role in socializing and shaping human beings, providing them with a worldview, a reference point, and a sense of the relative importance of affiliations to various social aggregates.

Social Norms

"Human nature is human *normative* nature. All efforts to derive human nature and its modes of behavior directly from man's biological heritage are fallacious."[82] Nisbet focuses his chapter in *The Social Bond* on "Social Norms" on the reality of norms as the guiding force for human conduct within a given social aggregate. Human life cannot exist without social norms to orient its moral direction. But Nisbet emphasizes the *social*, not the biological, nature of norms. Nisbet writes, "Much behavior that appears at first sight to proceed unmediatedly from man's biological nature—expressions of joy, pleasure, pain, hate, violence, love, and others—in fact proceeds from culture and its ways of defining the ends which produce these ways of behavior, although of course man's *capacity* for them is biological, as is his *capacity* for thought and speech."[83]

Nisbet writes, "Norms are the vital core of *culture*."[84] Every social aggregate contains norms or values that provide the aggregate with its distinctive character. They emerge from the dogma of the group and they help to uphold its function. Norms are the *prescribed practices* that mark one as a member of a particular social aggregate. They are learned by persons and transferred to subsequent generations during the process of socialization. The locus of the perception of norms is the individual conscience where the person perceives norms and adjusts his behavior accordingly. Perception of norms takes the form of a series of "oughts." Norms make right by legitimizing behavior in the social context of any given aggregate.[85] This concept of norms as prescribed practices, moral imperatives of the group, is an important part of the *Martinez* case and freedom of association more generally. Each association has norms of behavior that are essential to that particular group, that make it unique. This is why freedom of association must protect not only association around dogma, but norms as well.

Social aggregates, statuses, roles, and norms are all inseparable aspects of human behavior. The concept of norms clarifies how these facets of social order can be discussed as conceptual distinct, but phenomenally inseparable. Nisbet writes, "*Which* norms will be dominant in an individual's way of life is a function of what social aggregates he has been influenced by, of the status level he belongs to, of the social roles he occupies, and of the types of *social authority* that are strong in his life."[86] Aggregate, status, role, and norm are integrally related facets of human social behavior and cannot be discussed but in the context of each other and, for Nisbet, all are necessary to understand the concept of the person.

From the idea of social norm arises necessarily the concept of sanction. "Sanctions . . . *are forms of retributive action* for violations of norms in a social group or order."[87] When norms or values are violated, there is an ensuing sanction. The nature and quality of the sanction varies. It may be weak and diffuse, or it may be strict and onerous in its effect on the violator. Even when norms are violated with seeming impunity, there is often a sanction or the relic of a sanction residing under the social surface. The sanction may be social in terms of how the violator will be treated by the group. It may be legal. The sanction may be constrained to a loss of esteem and good opinion among other members of the group. Nisbet explains, "Retributive action may be as mild as a mother's disapproving glance or as harsh as the sentence by a court of law upon a felon."[88]

Sanctions are essential to the social bond of each particular social aggregate. They are what give the social bond meaning because sanctions make the purpose of the social aggregate functionally significant in the lives of its members. Essential to this functional significance is the ability of the social aggregate to enforce its terms, the binding agreement and the social norms, the code of honor and conduct that makes the social aggregate a social unity in some way. Aggregates that serve as reference groups for individuals are especially prone to providing sanction through means that are nonforceful. Given the inherent importance of a reference group to the individual member, forceful coercion is seldom necessary to enforce the norms of the aggregate. The individual takes his primary identity from the group. He follows its norms out of an internal motivation that requires very little in terms of sanctions other than the disapproval of other members of the group or the understanding in his own mind that he has trespassed the boundaries of its norms. The threat of expulsion or even chastising is sanction enough to persuade such an individual to follow the norms of the social aggregate.

Authority

Authority is the enforcement mechanism for social norms and the glue of the social bond. Every community necessarily has constraints and discipline as part of its essential social bond. Without them, there would be no community. Authority is one of the essential components of a functional community discussed earlier in this chapter. It is the component that enforces sanctions and thus ensures unity and continuity in the group. I will spend more time on this element because it is central to the discussion of exclusion and exit, issues essential to freedom of association.

Society only exists when there is "authority over individual mind and behavior."[89] In an important way, authority constitutes society. Drawing from the sociologist Emile Durkheim, Nisbet explains that the presence of authority directs individuals through discipline and social constraint, providing unity for a social aggregate. This authority is expressed through traditions, codes, and roles, which socialize individuals through limits unique to the particular social bond.[90] For Nisbet, "Authority, in its relation to man, not only buttresses moral life; it *is* moral life." The moral center of a group is related directly to its ability to constrain individuals according to the moral vision of the group. The limits are not necessarily the result of the application of force, but often arise from within the individual herself, who feels herself to be part of the group, attached to its moral center, and under the direction of its ultimate moral purpose. Only in this manner can an individual's character and personality be shaped by the group.[91] Authority is this ability to constrain and to direct individuals.

Nisbet is careful to point out that authority as Durkheim understands it cannot be understood as "synonymous with unitary nationalism or centralized economic collectivism."[92] Authority is not a strictly *political* term. Durkheim argues for a plurality of *social* authorities. Person interacting with person across different spheres leads to a plethora of these moral centers, a multitude of authorities producing a variety of intermediary associations. Nisbet writes, "Authority is the bedrock of society. But for Durkheim authority is plural, manifest in the diverse spheres of kinship, local community, profession, church, school, and labor union as well as in political government."[93] Authority functionally exists to bind individuals to the group. It is the substance that gives structure and direction to the group and its mission. Nisbet writes, "The function of authority is integrative, the indispensable cement of association, the constituent tie of human loyalties. Loyalties and obligations to the group would waver, would be constantly threatened with atrophy, were it not for the hard, unyielding structure of authority that serves not only the mission of the group and its values but also the vital tie between individual and group."[94] Without authority, the individual is adrift, unmoored from the group and detached from its moral purpose.

Above I have emphasized the pervasiveness of authority in social structures and pointed out how all members are subject to the authority of the group. However, while every member is subject to group authority, that authority is *conditional* upon the consent of the members. Unless membership is absolutely compelled (Nisbet points to prisons or asylums as examples of compelled associations), then there is an element of consent. A group's authority can only be exercised over members insofar as they consent to it and agree with it. Authority is conditional in that it "is binding solely upon those who are members of the association that contains the system of authority. Authority is therefore conditional upon membership."[95] Rather than a source of intrinsic oppression, authority is consensual, interactive, and grounded in a variety of associational locations.

Consent is essential to the exercise of authority. Leaders may tell members what to do, but those members may vote with their feet and leave the organization and defy its authority structure. A person consents to all sorts of filial, occupational, and social associations throughout his life. He also defies those social structures at different times. A person may find himself in a position where the organization takes a course of action with which he disagrees but to which he is still bound. Nonetheless, he may refuse to take part in the organization's decision and even leave the organization. This may result in personal hardship, such as being fired from a job or shunned by his family or religious institution, but it reflects the element of consent that is present in any authority structure.

Authority is *interactive*. Nisbet writes, "Domination, far from being one-sided, as it might at first sight appear to be, is in fact determined by expectation of the nature of the *obedience* it will receive."[96] The authority of the group over members is better conceived as the structure of *interaction*, of reciprocity, between the group member and the group authority structure. The very nature of interaction denotes a limitation upon each interacting party. Sure, the hierarchy of a group may be able to make a claim upon its members, but that claim is directly linked to its ability to garner voluntary obedience. The smaller the group, the less domineering this interaction will be, but the larger the group, the less reciprocity between individual member and group and the more dominance of the group over the individual member. Nisbet writes, "The group—and by no means the political group alone—conceives of its members, not as confronting it, but as being included by it as its own links. This often results in a peculiar inconsiderateness toward its members, which is very different from a ruler's personal cruelty."[97] Smaller groups are less likely to be oppressive from this perspective precisely because they are so dependent upon the interaction and cooperation of their members in a way that a large organization, including the nation-state, is not.

The third element of the conditionality of authority is the diversity of its sources, not only among different groups but within them. Group authority may lie in a formal hierarchical structure, reside in an executive board, find embodiment in a single individual, be spread throughout the group, or be located in a set of principles to which each member adheres.[98] It may be formal or informal. Informal authority resides in the individuals who do not have official authority, but who exert undue influence within the organization and have considerable authority despite their lack of formal position.[99] The authority exercised by informal authorities within a group relies on consent, upon other members of the group allowing the informal authority to influence their position. Formal authority exists in the official channels within the organization, such as the executive board of a nonprofit or the CEO of a corporation. The nature of formal authority gives a sense of oppressiveness because of its top-down mode of enforcement, but it abides by the same rules of consent as informal authority. In some cases, it may actually be weaker than the informal authority in the sense that members will be more likely to follow informal authorities within the organization than the formal authorities, or be dedicated to the goals and purposes of the group because of the endorsement of the informal authorities rather than the actual decisions of those formally in authority.

Types of Authority

Nisbet distinguishes between several types of authority. He organizes the categories in terms of opposing binaries: traditional and rational, personal and territorial, limited and total.

Traditional and Rational

Authority may be traditional or rational. Nisbet refers here to Max Weber's important distinction between the two types of authority. Whether authority is traditional or rational depends on where the authority finds its sanction and source of legitimacy. Traditional authority "derives its efficacy from being handed down from the past."[100] This type of authority is legitimate because it is old and it has worked for generations. Traditional authority may operate in any sphere, economic, religious, political, or filial, and it may be written or unwritten. The important point is that this authority derives its legitimacy from what has been. Past practice functions as an imperative, determining for the present how things ought to be.

Rational authority derives its legitimacy "from conscious and calculated effort to make the authority correspond to the express needs of the situation and to the norms of reason and logic."[101] Weber used the concept of "legality" as an example of rational authority. A statute is legal insofar as it is derived from rationally created rules. What makes the law legitimate, what gives it authority, is how well it can be defended upon rational grounds. There is not a necessary opposition between traditional and rational authority. Traditional authority could be defended on rational grounds, but traditional authority's rationality is not the primary reason traditional authority is obeyed. Traditional authority is obeyed because it derives from tradition. Rational authority is obeyed because it is perceived as rational, even if it is also derived from tradition.

Personal and Territorial

Nisbet distinguishes between personal and territorial authority. This distinction corresponds to the distinction between personal and territorial aggregates discussed above. Personal authority is the oldest form of authority in history. It governed human relations in kinship, religion, and ethnic groups for thousands of years and still governs many of them today. Personal authority derives its legitimacy from the identity of the authoritative person and the position that person holds within the organization. For example, the position of a father or a mother in the family is derived from that person's position as parent. Territorial authority attaches to a particular geographical area. One's obedience is conditioned not by personal relation of some sort, no matter the distance, but by location within particular geographic boundaries. As territorial aggregates chronologically follow personal aggregates, so territorial authority tends to follow personal authority. Political states are territorial authorities and tend to build their own authority at the expense of personal authorities flowing from tribe, family, and caste.

Nisbet identifies three effects of the movement from personal to territorial authority. [102] The first effect is individualization, a concept I explained in the introductory chapter. Territorial authority grows at the expense of personal authorities that exist within the territory. The effect of this development is to weaken the memberships of various groups by weakening the authority of groups over their members. Persons come to identify primarily as individuals, not members of groups. They prize the rights, privileges, and responsibilities of individual members of the territorial unit and the identity of citizen over the duties and identity of the personal group. The second effect is centralization of authority, a key aspect of politicization discussed in the introduction. Territorialization centralizes all authority within a territory into a single entity that exercises jurisdiction over the entire territory regardless of diverse personal authorities previously existent. In contrast, organizations built upon personal authority are concentric, with gradations of authority based on a variety of traditional criteria, including age. This authority is diffuse and plural because the sources of personal authority are diverse. For example, if age is a source of authority, there will be a number of elderly persons and therefore multiple sources of authority at any given time within a single structure. Third, territorialization creates the mass, "an aggregate of individuals, of whatever size, that is devoid of kinship, religious, ethnic, or other types of social and traditional relationships." [103] Territorial authority exerts its sovereignty over all individuals as a mass despite their membership in various groups and regardless of diversity of culture, religion, kinship, caste, or other designations. The creation of the mass by territorialization is directly related to the process of individualization. Members of various groups are treated as discrete individuals, separated from their primary identities drawn from those groups and all lumped together under one territorial authority.

Personal authority can continue to exercise great influence even in the presence of a territorial authority. In the modern territorial state, where sovereignty resides explicitly in the government of the nation-state, personal authorities still abound. Some persons, such as the Mayors Daley of Chicago, exert personal as well as territorial authority. Their authority is derived not only from their position in the territorial government but also from their personal status as members of the Daley family. The same could be said of members of the Adams, Kennedy, and Roosevelt families as well as the Bush and Clinton families and other lesser-known persons who run local or state political party machines. [104]

Limited and Total

Authority can be limited or total. I explained above the conditional nature of authority. Conditionality means that authority is always limited by certain factors inherent within the authority itself. Authority "is restricted to some given form of association, to a single relationship, or to a single function. By its nature it does not encompass all aspects of the individual's life."[105] It is limited primarily by membership. The authority of the Roman Catholic Church extends to Roman Catholics, not to members of other churches and religions. The authority of a business extends to its employees and perhaps contractors, but not to those employed at other businesses. The exercise of authority over members varies in degree between groups. The authority of churches in the United States is generally weak, and individual parishioners may withdraw at will with little or no institutional repercussions. At most, the cost may be shunning, but that is rare and even in those circumstances restricted to other members of the religious community and not to members of the territorial community at large.

Total authority, however, affects an individual's whole existence. The territorial authority of the modern nation-state is total in that it claims sole sovereignty over all individuals within its territorial boundaries, "at least in theory and in potentiality."[106] Even a democracy's claim to be the sole legitimate practitioner of sovereignty within its geographical territory is a claim of total authority. Constitutional guarantees can be set aside through legitimate political channels. Limitation in practice, which is common in democracies, is not the same thing as limitation in theory. For Nisbet, the totalitarian state is simply the total theory of sovereignty that governs democracies taken to an extreme in practice.[107]

Legitimacy and Function

Authority is legitimate insofar as it is "*spontaneously* and *willingly*" obeyed.[108] The reason that authority is spontaneously and willingly obeyed depends on the type of authority it is. Traditional authority is *legitimate* because it accords with the customs of the social milieu that surround it. Rational authority is *legitimate* as it accords to rationality. An important part of legitimacy is the now familiar notion of *function*. Nisbet writes, "[We] regard authority as legitimate if it arises necessarily from discharge of a given function in society. The authority of the teacher is legitimate as long as it is confined to the function of teaching."[109] The same could be said of the parent, the priest, and the policeman. Each is a legitimate authority insofar as it is carrying out its function. This is related to our discussion of social roles above. A person carrying out a function acts legitimately when she is in the role of one who carries out the function as part of her role. A person exercising authority exercises authority with legitimacy when she is in the role of someone who ought to exercise that authority.

The concept of legitimacy demonstrates the difference between authority and power. Authority is bound to the norms of the social aggregate, but power is not. Power exerts control and influence, but not within the social channels of roles, statuses, and norms native to the particular social aggregate. Nisbet writes,

> [Power is] the effort to exact obedience or compliance of others to the will of one or more persons in a way that, however moral or right it may be in some ultimate ethical sense, is *not* derived from the recognized norms of the social aggregate concerned, that is *not* perceived as legitimate by those who come under the brunt of the power, and that does *not* flow directly from the established patterns of role behavior or form the common and normal patterns of role and status interaction.[110]

VOLUNTARY ASSOCIATIONS

The typology outlined above is designed to describe every type of social aggregate, from nation-states to kinship groups to sports teams to student groups. The concepts of social roles, statuses, and norms are tools to help us understand the intricacies of social interaction that takes place between group and member. I will use these typologies and tools to discuss the voluntary association, the type of social aggregate at the center of *CLS v. Martinez*, and the right of association more broadly.[111] Understanding the social dynamics of the type of social group implicated in that case will make clear the ramifications of the Court's decision. Our discussion will follow the same structure I used above. I will begin by explaining how a voluntary association reflects the seven elements of what I called the "functional community." Then I will identify its features as a social aggregate before exploring how persons acquire social roles, social statuses, and social norms within voluntary associations. Last I will discuss the role of authority in the voluntary association. By understanding the properties of the voluntary association, we can better determine how courts ignored the essential social nature of the voluntary association in its case law and how they might better protect these social entities in the future, a task I will take on in chapter 4.

Why Do Voluntary Associations Exist?

Voluntary associations exist for the same reason that every social aggregate exists, to accomplish some purpose, for individuals to *do something together*. I can describe voluntary associations according to Nisbet's seven attributes of a functional community that he enumerates in *The Degradation of the Academic Dogma*: *function, dogma, authority, hierarchy, solidarity, status* or *honor*, and *sense of superiority*.

Voluntary associations perform a *function*, which could include activities as diverse as proper worship (as with CLS), building houses for the homeless, or playing chess. Closely related to function is *dogma*, the "sense of some transcending purpose" that formed the impetus for the founding of the group in the first place. To be a community, voluntary associations must have *authority* to enforce their function and dogma. A voluntary association has a *hierarchy* of roles between leaders and group members. The voluntary association has a sense of *solidarity*, a sense of "we" in the group. Solidarity around the dogma and function of the voluntary association is the reason members founded the group in the first place. A sense of *status* or *honor* accompanies a voluntary association because members only join when they support the group's function and dogma. Last, voluntary associations are imbued with a sense of *superiority*. Members join the group because they think it is a better use of their time than something else. They consider the mission and activities of the group they join superior to the functions of other groups, which is the reason they join that particular association instead of another.

Voluntary Associations as a Type of Social Aggregate

In terms of size, a voluntary association is generally a *small group*. While the small group may be part of a larger organization, the larger voluntary association is organized as small groups of persons that work closely together around some shared purpose. A person may be a member of the Sierra Club, but if he is an *active* member it is almost certainly in the context of a small group where he works in concert with other active members. Likewise, a member of the Catholic Church is active in the church through his local parish or even a smaller group within the parish. It is through these smaller associations that his allegiance to the Catholic Church at large is made concrete. Nisbet writes, "No matter how large, impersonal, and bureaucratic an organization may appear to be from the outside, careful examination usually reveals the existence of whole networks of small, informal, social groups within the larger structure. Often these can prove decisive to the success of the large organization."[112] Even in large organizations composed of thousands or even millions of members, the crux of the group's effectiveness is the small group. This may apply informally to groups of individuals who accomplish work on behalf of the larger organization. Or it may apply formally to an organized chapter, a small group that gathers to advance the goals of the overarching organization.

This concept applies to student groups. While there might be a large national organization, such as Christian Legal Society, in terms of many members across the country, the organization is made effective through individual chapters on each campus. The crux of the importance of student groups is not whether they are part of a large organization or unique to their particular campus, but that, whatever its larger affiliation or lack thereof, the small group actually exists on a *particular* campus. That particular chapter is then able to function as a small group.

A voluntary association has aspects of being both *open* and *closed*. Generally, it is open to all who would join as long as they agree with the founding dogma of the association. The College Democrats are open to all persons, as long as they agree with the platform of the Democratic Party or at least with a certain prescribed number of Democratic tenets. But it is not closed based on kinship, race, or religion. A campus religious group, such as the Muslim Student Association, may be closed on the basis of religion, requiring dedication to the founding dogma of the group, but open based on race, national identity, and political affiliation. The Sierra Club might be closed as to dedication to the cause of environmentalism and conservation, but open on all other criteria.

Aside from being closed as to dogma, voluntary associations are open as to entrance and exit. Individuals may join, as long as they agree to the dogma of the group, and they may leave if, for whatever reason, they abandon the dogma or choose to prioritize other dogmas or other associations over those of a particular voluntary association. The important point is that voluntary associations are voluntary. The right of exit is absolute. Nonetheless, the right of entry, and the continued right of participation, depends upon dedication to the dogma of the group. I will explore the nature of entry, exit, and exclusion in more detail later in the book. There may be further nuance regarding whether a group is open or closed. A group may allow anyone to attend meetings but limit leadership to those who uphold the dogma of the group. CLS limited voting membership and leadership to those who affirmed the "statement of faith," the dogma of the group, but they were willing to allow nonmembers to attend meetings and participate in the group to a limited extent even if they did not adhere to the dogma of the group.

Voluntary associations are personal rather than territorial. While voluntary associations may generally exist in a certain area, they are not organized primarily around the geographic area but around the quality of belief that attaches to the person. A person's belief about the dogma of the voluntary association, not geographic area, dictates membership. A student group, such as CLS, may be organized around a particular dogma but also require a particular status for prospective members, such as a student designation at a particular university. A student must actively attend a particular university in addition to holding to the dogmas of the group. However, the primary affiliation of the group is personal in that the priority of group affiliation is based on the characteristics of belief and action that attaches to the person and not primarily to the territory. CLS at Hastings did require its members to be students at Hastings Law School, but the primary identification with the group was around its founding dogma encapsulated in the "statement of faith."[113]

Voluntary associations have great potential to be Gemeinschaft organizations, to have the cohesive qualities of community that involves the whole person. But voluntary associations also may have the rationalized structure of Gesellschaft. It simply depends upon the nature of the association itself. The potential to have a tight-knit community certainly exists in the small group, but the small group may be loosely organized and thus not involve the total personality of its members in group activities. The potential for both Gemeinschaft and Gesellschaft in the voluntary association is what makes the voluntary association valuable for a variety of reasons. Individuals may pursue Gesellschaft associations to accomplish in unison certain tasks or work for certain causes that they cannot accomplish alone. Tocqueville points to this utilitarian aspect of Gesellschaft voluntary associations in *Democracy in America* when he writes,

Americans of all ages, of all conditions, of all minds, constantly unite. Not only do they have commercial and industrial associations in which they all take part, but also they have a thousand other kinds: religious, moral, [intellectual,] serious ones, useless ones, very general and very particular ones, immense and very small ones; Americans associate to celebrate holidays, establish seminaries, build inns, erect churches, distribute books, send missionaries to the Antipodes; in this way they create hospitals, prisons, schools. If, finally, it is a matter of bringing a truth to light or of developing a sentiment with the support of a good example, they associate.[114]

None of these activities necessitate a Gemeinschaft nature. Associations that are primarily utilitarian and accomplish some good and useful purposes for various individuals may not provide the communal function of Gemeinschaft. Nonetheless, these associations are valuable to their individual members and to society at large.

That said, while Gesellschaft associations are valuable in their own way, the primary benefit of voluntary associations to individual persons is their ability to cultivate a *Gemeinschaft* character that brings more psychological and emotional fulfillment to members by cultivating a tight-knit community that involves the whole personality of its members. Some examples that Tocqueville gives in the passage quoted above would also fit this category. Even some of the utilitarian examples, such as associations for building inns or distributing books, may involve a dedication by individuals and the context for cultivation of friendship and comradery that would indicate an underlying Gemeinschaft nature to the group, even if the official purposes of the association are only instrumental. The point is that while the voluntary association can be either Gemeinschaft or Gesellschaft, this type of social group, unlike a large territorial state, provides a profound opportunity for Gemeinschaft, for the personal communion that, according to Nisbet, all human beings crave. A student group such as CLS provides an important opportunity for Gemeinschaft, for a small group of individuals dedicated to the group to come together around the values of the group. Such a group may involve its members as whole persons, caring for them intellectually, emotionally, spiritually, and even physically. As anyone who has been involved with a student group knows, these are the contexts for profound friendships around deeply held beliefs that invite a dedication and loyalty to shared values that goes far beyond mere assent to ideological tenets.

The last quality of the social aggregate discussed above is the *reference group*. Nisbet describes a reference group as the "social aggregate to which an individual 'refers,' consciously or unconsciously, in the shaping of his attitudes on a given subject or in the formation of his conduct."[115] Voluntary associations can operate as reference groups for individuals. Individuals may choose which groups they join and therefore which groups serve as a reference for them, both a source and a reflection of the values they hold. Some groups with which an individual is affiliated will not be a reference group for that individual. The groups may simply be affiliations for an individual's social or networking purposes or even simply a means to accomplish some utilitarian purpose, as discussed above. However, the notion of reference group as applied to voluntary associations allows individuals to associate themselves with a group of their own choosing that both reflects and reinforces their personal identity and values.

The opportunities voluntary associations afford for the presence of Gemeinschaft, combined with the potential to function as a reference group demonstrates the profound importance of voluntary associations for human fulfilment. CLS as a small group provides students with the potential to be closely connected to other persons who share their fundamental beliefs and have the same life goals. This is the aspect of Gemeinschaft that can only be truly cultivated in a small group. Students who consider themselves devout evangelical Christians and aspiring lawyers can use CLS as a reference group, the group to which they connect their primary identity religiously and occupationally, both as evangelical Christians and as future lawyers.

Not only can voluntary associations perform this function, but *they are versatile enough to perform this function for virtually anyone*. This statement is not true of any particular voluntary association, of course, but of voluntary associations as a category of social aggregates. The same voluntary association will not be able to function meaningfully in the lives of everyone, but various voluntary associations may perform that function for a variety of individuals. While CLS performed the function of a Gemeinschaft reference group for a handful of evangelical Christian law students at Hastings, OUTLAW had the potential to perform the same function for LGBTQ law students at Hastings. The danger of the *Martinez* decision is that the reasoning of the Court relies only upon the exclusive notions of state and individual and thus denies the existence of social groups as essential, inherent constructs in society. Even a voluntary association cannot perform a Gemeinschaft function or serve as a reference group if it is denied the functional requisites of those types of aggregates. The concept of a voluntary association as a reference group is one of the most important aspects of voluntary associations in terms of their value to individuals.

Roles, Statuses, and Norms

Following the structure of the sections above, I now turn to the concepts of social roles, social status, and social norms in voluntary associations. Each concept revolves around the place of the person in this particular social aggregate and demonstrates how these concepts implicate the value of associations in the lives of individuals, revealing in sociological terms how voluntary associations function in the lives of their individual members.

Roles

Let's begin with Nisbet's description of "persons as roles." Every individual that we encounter is playing a role, and often the role played in modern society is in a voluntary association. Recall that roles have the following characteristics: they are ways of behavior, they embody social norms, they are part of a structure of relationships, they define legitimate action, and they connote a sense of duty.

A member of a voluntary association behaves in a particular way. He contributes to the group through voting habits, volunteer activities, meeting attendance, and so forth, depending upon the activities appropriate for the purpose of the group. Ways of behavior for voluntary associations exist, but they may not be as long-standing as social roles more broadly, which are "handed down from generation to generation."[116] They are not likely prescribed in the same way as traditional social roles. Nonetheless, the roles in voluntary associations are "ways of behavior."

The way of behavior for a member of a voluntary association embodies the social norms of the group. An environmental group may require members to pick up trash along the highway on a given day or write letters to members of Congress advocating for environmental legislation. A religious group may require participation in worship and adherence to certain religious practices, such as daily readings or prayers, as well as prohibition of certain activities, such as consuming alcohol.

The social role of voluntary associations is also part of a structure of relationships. There is a leadership hierarchy in a voluntary association that may organize particular group activities and determine group purposes. Members participate in their roles based upon direction from those in leadership roles and participation by other members. This *interaction* is essential to the associational aspect of voluntary associations just as it is to other types of social aggregates. Behind this interaction, there is a structure of relationships that makes the interaction possible. All persons in the group embody a role somewhere in the organization and only through that role do they participate in and become part of the group.

The concept of the structure of relationships relates to the notion of legitimacy. Legitimate action arises when it is carried out by individuals in the appropriate role. Above I discussed this in relationship to parents, law enforcement officers, and physicians. In the context of the voluntary association, legitimate action happens when action is carried out under the direction of the leadership of the voluntary association according to the norms and values of the group. What makes an action or an authoritative direction legitimate relates to the idea of role. Was the source of direction a leader in the organization? Was the given direction in line with the norms and values of the association? Is the person doing the action or receiving the direction in the appropriate role to follow direction? An affirmative answer to these questions indicates legitimacy in a voluntary association.

Members of the group, including leaders, act according to duty. They are personally devoted to the voluntary association, but beyond that their membership carries with it an expectation of action or participation. The level of participation and action depends upon the nature of the group, whether it is large or small, and whether it is Gemeinschaft or Gesellschaft. The important point is that the social role of membership in a voluntary association still carries with it obligation, a sense that there is something someone should do as a member of the group in whatever role they have, whether as a rank-and-file member or as a leader.

The social role involved in a voluntary association may be ascribed or achieved. Most roles in voluntary associations are not ascribed in the traditional sense by virtue of the fact that the groups are voluntary. However, the nature of the voluntary association as open or closed will relate to whether the association has ascribed or achieved roles in some limited sense. Fraternities and sororities have ascribed roles in that one must at least be male or female to be a respective member of a fraternity or a sorority. Similarly, one may have to subscribe to a particular religion in order to join a particular religious group.

The Knights of Columbus require members to be male and Roman Catholic. The ascribed characteristics of sex and religion are prerequisites to membership in the Knights of Columbus and to participating in a social role in that particular voluntary association.

Besides some ascribed aspects to voluntary associations, roles in this type of social aggregate are generally achieved. There are certain requirements of membership such as participation, payment of dues, and the like that anyone can do who meets the ascribed standards. Anyone can meet the volunteer requirements for an environmental group or worship requirements for a religious group if they choose to act in the required manner and affirm the group's particular beliefs. Additionally, anyone can attain a leadership position in the group as long as they meet the ascribed standards for admittance in the first place and achieve the appropriate merit. A Roman Catholic male may achieve leadership in the Knights of Columbus as long as he can prove to the membership his leadership potential and his devotion to the central tenets of the group.

Status
Status denotes a vertical ranking of roles. I have alluded to the concept of status in voluntary associations already. There is a difference in *role* between a mere member and a leader. Furthermore, there is a difference in *status* between the role of a leader and that of a member. The leader can exercise authority over the group and on behalf of the group. Different roles are necessary for a voluntary association because there are differences of function within the group. However, some roles are more important to the group or at least carry more social esteem among members of the group. The simple dichotomy of leader and member demonstrates this point. The leader generally has higher social status within the group for his ability to exercise authority. Furthermore, there may be distinction of status within the leadership hierarchy if there are offices such as president, vice president, secretary, director, and so on. Social status in a voluntary association is especially fluid. Leadership in a group usually changes, often frequently. The character and competence of various leaders will indicate in an informal way their prestige as perceived by the rest of the group. But status, especially that in a voluntary association, is always the result of *interaction*. It depends not only on roles, which are often achieved, but also on competence within the role and on the perceived status of the role within the group.

Norms

Nisbet's discussion of norms refers to broad social norms as well as the type of norms that exist within various social aggregates. Some large social aggregates, such as the modern state, may have general norms that more or less apply to all members of the state. Smaller aggregates have norms that may be peculiar to that *type* of aggregate, such as the family or a religious group, or more specifically to only that *particular* social aggregate, such as a *particular* family or a *particular* religious group.

Voluntary associations also have norms, "oughts" that are attached to membership in a particular group. There are certain expectations regarding belief and behavior in every voluntary association. Belief-based norms constitute the dogma of the group, its *central tenets*. Generally, a group's dogma also has *prescribed practices*, certain behaviors that are understood to appropriately attach to the group's dogma and constitute behavioral *norms* for group members. These practices are considered by the group to be prescribed by the dogma itself. For example, the dogma of an environmental group includes the central tenets of environmental preservation and conservation of wildlife. From the central tenets follow prescribed practices such as recycling, engaging in regular volunteer work cleaning up trash in state parks, writing to legislators, and so on. These practices constitute the norms of an environmental organization. Similarly, the dogma of a religious group, such as an Islamic organization, may be the worship of Allah. The prescribed practices will include praying five times a day, fasting during Ramadan, and celibacy outside of marriage. These are the norms of an Islamic organization.

When the norms of the voluntary association are violated, there are *sanctions*. Sanctions give meaning to norms. They provide a reinforcement mechanism to the prescribed practices of the group that are considered essential to the group's dogma, which is the orienting force of the association. In the context of a voluntary association, sanctions generally do not extend to legal action, unless the violator of norms also violated the law. When a member violates the norms of the group, sanctions can include removal from office (if the member is a leader), a loss of esteem among the other members, or suspension of membership or even expulsion from the group. Expulsion is the most punitive sanction for a voluntary association. The ability to exclude gives force to the authority of the group to be able to maintain the association's anchor in the founding dogma of the group by maintaining a membership that continues to hold fast to the central tenets of the group as well as the prescribed practices. The right of exclusion is the association's analogue to the individual's right of exit. Just as individuals may leave a voluntary association if it ceases to function for the good of the individual, so associations may exclude individuals who do not contribute to the functioning of the group. This latter point is necessary for the continued relevance of the group to the rest of the membership. I will return to this point in chapter 4 when I discuss how to uphold the functional value of associations.

Roles, Status, and Norms in CLS

I have established how roles, status, and norms function in voluntary associations in general. Now I will discuss how they function in CLS in particular. Laying the groundwork for how CLS operates as a voluntary association will clarify how disruptive the First Amendment Dichotomy is to the possibility of community.

Membership in CLS implicates the concept of social roles. Members engage in a way of behavior. They worship according to evangelical Christian practices, attend group meetings, and live by the standards outlined in the statement of faith.[117] This behavior embodies certain norms residing in evangelical Christian social values, including celibacy. There is an internal structure of relationships, a leadership that enforces the statement of faith and a membership that engages in various activities and also helps determine, through voting, the direction and values of the group. Legitimate action emerges when CLS members act in accordance with the values of the organization, as determined by the leadership. The notion of duty accompanies the actions of individuals within the organization. When members attend meetings, hold events, and abide by the statement of faith, they are acting in accordance with a sense of obligation attached to their membership in the group. Likewise, CLS's leaders are acting in accordance with a sense of obligation attached to their leadership in the group when they plan events that advance the group's dogma.

Along with the notion of role is the idea of status. The roles within CLS are ranked just as they are in every other social group. The facts of *CLS v. Martinez* related in the next chapter will highlight this point. The role of leader and even voting member carry more status within the group than does the role of someone who merely attends regular meetings. The fact that there is a restriction on voting membership and leadership to those who adhere to CLS's statement of faith was the subject of the Supreme Court's analysis. Exclusion was a dirty word for the Court at least in part because it denied equal status to persons within the group, even though such persons fundamentally disagreed with the central tenets of CLS.

Implied in the paragraphs above is the idea of social *norms* that attach to CLS. The group has requirements attached to internal social roles, which include both belief and behavior-based requirements that correspond to the central tenets and prescribed practices of the group. In the case of CLS, this means believing in the statement of faith and abiding by its prescriptions and proscriptions. The sanction that accompanies either a lack of belief in central tenets or defiance of the prescribed practices is exclusion from leadership and voting membership.

Authority

Finally I get to the concept of authority in the voluntary association. Authority is exercised within voluntary associations just as it is within all other social aggregates, and it provides the same function for the voluntary association as it does for other social aggregates: *it is the cement of the social bond between members of the group.*[118] The group associates around a dogma and from that arise certain social norms and social roles necessary to the proper functioning of the association. Authority is exercised pursuant to the purposes of the group to support group dogma and to uphold group norms. The conditionality of authority that exists in all groups is especially evident in voluntary associations. By their nature, they are voluntary, so any exercise of authority that is not legitimate, which means that it is not consented to by a given member, can be easily rejected by that member through the right of exit. The right of exit is an absolute check on any illegitimate exercise of authority by anyone in the group hierarchy.

Authority exercised in voluntary associations will tend to be rational, personal, and limited. It will be rational in that it will tend to take its legitimacy from its rational nature. When the leadership enforces the dogma and norms of the group, it will have to draw a rational connection between the two, a connection that must be accepted as legitimate by the membership. Authority will be personal in that the persons in charge of the organization will exert authority in a personal manner. Members will voluntarily constrain themselves to follow the association's authority based upon their personal choice to perpetually submit to the group. Unlike most instances of personal authority, the authority exercised by the voluntary association does not derive merely from who the authoritative person is, as is the case with the role of a parent in a family. However, there is still the same emphasis on group solidarity and a clear distinction between the type of authority exercised in a voluntary association and the type of authority exercised in a territorial aggregate. The authority of a voluntary association is limited. Unlike total authority, it does not touch the entirety of an individual's existence. Authority is necessarily limited to the dogma and norms of the group. It is only exercised pursuant to the very purposes of the association's existence. The right of exit is an inherent and absolute limitation on the authority of the voluntary association over its members.

Applied to CLS, the authority of the group to uphold its dogma and its prescribed practices is essential to the social bond between members of the group. The dogma, the statement of faith, is the reason members associate in CLS to begin with. The authority of the group, the actual ability of the group to enforce adherence to the statement of faith, is the sealant of that particular social bond. The social expectations that attach to membership in voluntary associations in terms of roles, status, and norms provide value to individuals as they implicate the dogma and function of groups. It is precisely this *social* function of associations that has been undermined by the First Amendment Dichotomy in Supreme Court case law in general and *CLS v. Martinez* in particular. It is to the jurisprudential origins and specific details of this problem that I now turn.

3. The First Amendment Dichotomy and Freedom of Association: State and Individual from *NAACP v. Alabama* to *Christian Legal Society v. Martinez*

What happens when the Court lacks a "theory of the social" in its consideration of the freedom of association? What happens when the Supreme Court ignores the "reality of the social" in its First Amendment analysis and pays attention only to the individual and the state?

In this chapter I argue for the presence of what I call the First Amendment Dichotomy, the Supreme Court's tendency in First Amendment jurisprudence to perceive only the individual speaker and the democratic state for purposes of constitutional analysis, subsuming characteristics of associations into these poles. The First Amendment Dichotomy is the primary theoretical paradigm in the doctrine and history of freedom of association that culminated in the 2010 Supreme Court case *Christian Legal Society v. Martinez*, effectively excising freedom of association from American constitutional jurisprudence in the name of the individual and the democratic state. The concepts of individual and state are analytically exclusive, meaning that by their nature they exclude from analytical consideration the existence of the third component of the conceptual trifecta of First Amendment Pluralism, associations.

To make my case, I begin this chapter with a discussion of consensus pluralism and egalitarian liberalism drawing from John Inazu's work on freedom of assembly to explore the theoretical background to the Court's articulation of freedom of association beginning in the 1950s. Still relying heavily on Inazu's insights, I then turn to a history of the Court's jurisprudential development of freedom of association and demonstrate how it bifurcated freedom of association into intimate associations and expressive associations. I explain how this development reflects the Court's conceptual paradigm of the First Amendment Dichotomy, rendering associations as nothing more than an amalgamation of speaking individuals or entities instrumentally valuable to the democratic state. At the heart of my argument is that the Court's continued reliance upon the Speech Clause relates directly to speech as an individual right that is uniquely valuable to governance of the democratic state.

In my discussion of the processes of individualization and politicization in the first chapter, I pointed out that these processes work in tandem. In the freedom of association jurisprudence, we see the Court increasingly ignoring protections for associational rights even while emphasizing the individual dimension of freedom of speech and its value to democratic government. In effect, the Court's reliance upon the right to free speech has an individualizing effect upon its concept of association. Simultaneously, the Court's appeal to the democratic value of associations because of their facilitation of speech politicizes the concept of association, making it jurisprudentially relevant only insofar as it bolsters state prerogatives.

We situate *CLS v. Martinez* as the culmination, or *reductio ad absurdum*, of the Court's doctrinal developments since the freedom of association's modern inception. The *Martinez* decision is analyzed in terms of the Court's bifurcated conceptualization of the individual and the state. Following the fundamental political theory of Plato, Hobbes, and Rousseau, the Court understands the individual to be discrete, self-sufficing, and more or less interchangeable with all other individuals. The state is the political power, as distinct from the variety of social authorities we discussed in the previous chapter. As represented in the state university, the Court considers the state the primary mode of membership for individuals such that the concept of association is subsumed into the state in a process of politicization and the activity of associations is considered by the Court to be state activity. Under this conceptual framework, the First Amendment Dichotomy, the Court will only protect freedom of association when it furthers the speech rights of individuals or when it is valuable to the democratic state. Freedom to associate as such is not part of the Court's doctrines governing freedom of association.

Six features of the *Martinez* decision reveal the presence of the First Amendment Dichotomy. The concept of the individual underlies the Court's decision to collapse freedom of association into freedom of speech, the abolition of the status/belief distinction, and the Court's use of "reasonable" and "viewpoint neutral." The concept of the state animates the Court's treatment of speech and the democratic state, the Court's notion of government property (manifested in its novel use of forum analysis, subsidy analysis, and application of the Fourteenth Amendment), and the Court's treatment of group regulation of conduct. The first three demonstrate the Court's concern with the individual as a discrete and self-sufficing unit, rather than a person with social context, as well as the process of individualization, the separation of individuals from their communal contexts. The latter three reflect the Court's concern with the state as the primary locus of membership as well as the process of politicization, the transfer of authority from the social units to the political state. All six result in a denigration of associations.

Throughout this discussion we are critiquing the Court's reasoning and not necessarily its holding. While I disagree with the Court's holding in *Martinez* for reasons I will explain later, it is the reasoning of the *Martinez* Court that I find devastating to freedom of association. One may disagree with my take on the Court's holding and yet be gravely concerned with the Court's dismissive treatment of freedom of association. As I will explain later, there are ways the Court could have reached the same ruling while respecting freedom of association as a substantive First Amendment right.

THE LEGAL THEORY BACKGROUND

Consensus Pluralism: Association on Behalf of the Political Order

In *Liberty's Refuge*, Inazu traces the theoretical underpinnings of the Supreme Court's freedom of association jurisprudence to two successive theoretical movements, consensus pluralism and egalitarian liberalism.[1] The first was dominant in political science circles in the 1950s and 1960s and the second in the 1970s. Both contributed to the theoretical background of the Court's decision-making regarding freedom of association. We will give an overview of his argument and point out that these two movements demonstrate a theoretical tendency toward privileging the state and the individual, respectively.

American pluralism defended the rise and existence of unpopular associations, specifically civil rights groups. However, this theory of pluralism was a justification for groups in a way that contextualized them within a democratic political order. Inazu explains, "American pluralism advanced its own insistent claim that politics relocated among groups achieved a harmonious *balance* within a broad *consensus* that supported American democracy."[2] Dissenting groups were defended on the grounds that there was an underlying agreement on notions of liberalism and democracy and that freedom of association would facilitate democratic debate. Inazu writes, "[Pluralism] established an implicit expectation that groups were valuable to democracy only to the extent that they reinforced and guaranteed democratic premises and, conversely, that groups antithetical to these premises were neither valuable to democracy nor worthy of its protections."[3] Such a notion of pluralism weakened the ability of groups to dissent because acceptable dissent could only ever be construed within a policy of overall agreement. Censorship of beliefs or actions determined to be outside of the American pluralist consensus could be justified on this basis.

Robert Dahl and David Truman were paradigmatic figures in the pluralist movement. Truman's 1951 book *Governmental Process* describes "the vast multiplication of interests and organized groups . . . [that] imply controversy and conflict, the essence of politics."[4] While pluralism permits conflict between groups, such conflict takes place with the understanding that these groups and interests balance each other.[5] In his 1967 book *Pluralist Democracy in the United States*, Dahl described American pluralism's conception of society as "multiple centers of power, none of which is or can be wholly sovereign."[6] Decentralized centers of power give people a plethora of opportunities to exercise their power. "Because one center of power is set against another, power itself will be tamed, civilized, controlled, and limited to decent human purposes."[7] Both Truman and Dahl appealed to Alexis de Tocqueville's *Democracy in America* and Madison's *Federalist* No. 10 to support their understanding of American pluralism. However, they misinterpreted both Tocqueville and Madison.[8] Madison's argument regarding factions was especially mangled. A "faction" for Madison was not a liberal interest group, as the pluralists would have it, but a group of people "who are united and actuated by some common impulse of passion, or of interest, adverse to the rights of other citizens, or to the permanent and aggregate interests of the community."[9]

What emerges from consensus pluralism is not a pluralism of associations that matter in their own right or that exist for ends beyond that of the political order, which is the goal of Nisbet's philosophy of pluralism. Rather, consensus pluralism conceptualizes associations that exist to support the political state. Such associations are exclusively intermediary institutions in the sense that they exist only to mediate between the individual and the state in order to facilitate the proper functioning of the democratic political order. Nonpolitical ends are subordinated to political ends. Inazu explains, "The imposition of a 'democratic mold' collapsed pluralism into a position similar to the state-centered idealism that pluralism had originally challenged: lurking behind a seemingly benign agreement of values was the normative (and coercive) association of the state."[10] This underlying ethos to consensus pluralism reflects what Nisbet describes as politicization, that politics is the highest goal of social existence and all other social goals must be appropriately submissive.

Egalitarian Liberalism: Individual Equality and the Limits of Association

Consensus pluralism prepared the way for the egalitarian liberalism of the 1970s. Because "undemocratic" groups could be considered beyond the pluralist pale and justly excluded, then the equality movement could simply bring attention to groups with discriminatory membership practices and apply the arguments from pluralism. John Rawls articulated the theoretical foundation of egalitarian liberalism, which became the uncited theoretical basis of later Supreme Court decisions regarding freedom of association. Inazu writes, "Legal academics eager to provide intellectual cover to the Warren Court's decisions and its recognition of fundamental rights not found in the text of the Constitution embraced [Rawls's] framework."[11] The liberalism of Rawls differed in some ways from consensus pluralism but placed at the center of political values "egalitarianism rooted in an individualist ontology [which] trumped and thus bounded difference."[12] At the heart of Rawls's liberalism was agreement about central liberal values. The notion of consensus and, for Rawls, stability influenced the understanding of groups. While Rawls was not cited in the case law, Inazu argues that these notions pervaded developments in legal theory and case law throughout this period.

Ronald Dworkin was the most prominent legal scholar influenced by Rawls's philosophy. His theory introduced an important nuance into consensus pluralism and egalitarianism. For Dworkin, "individual rights prevail over majoritarian democracy."[13] Consensus pluralism and egalitarianism should not be reduced to simple majoritarianism. But the assumption that individual rights are universally understood in a similar basic way undergirds both movements, and it informed other theoretical and legal developments. Democracy means rule by the people, but it assumes "democratic" social conditions "of equal status for all citizens."[14] The functioning of democracy, in order to be true democracy, must be done in such a manner "that collective decisions be made by political institutions whose structure, composition, and practices treat all members of the community, as individuals, with equal concern and respect."[15] Judges have a duty to enforce such dignity and respect.[16]

Egalitarian liberalism reinforced the limits that pluralism had set around freedom of association. Associations that affected individuals adversely, or even constrained them, were immediately suspect. The conditions of legal equality that prevailed in the polity at large were deemed necessary associational requisites in the smaller associations. Associations also had to reflect the value of equality that was essential to the democratic state. In this way egalitarian liberalism demonstrates Nisbet's idea of individualization. Individuals should be separated from their social context and considered only in their legal relationship to each other and to the state.

This process took place within the context of concern for the good of the larger polity, thus demonstrating the relationship Nisbet posits between politicization and individualization. Associations do not exist for their own sake or even for the sake of their members, but for the sake of the political entity as a whole. And associations must reflect democratic political values, especially equality, to facilitate the democratic ethos of the political order. This is in contrast to a different understanding of the purpose of associations I described in the last chapter, which is to produce meaningful community around shared beliefs and practices.

A BRIEF HISTORY OF FREEDOM OF ASSOCIATION

This brief introduction to the theoretical background of the Supreme Court's freedom of association jurisprudence is meant to alert the reader to the basic elements of the First Amendment Dichotomy in the case law. As the right of association developed within First Amendment jurisprudence, it reflected the processes of individualization and politicization inherent in consensus pluralism and egalitarian liberalism. From these processes, freedom of association does not emerge as a robust right to associate that Nisbet envisioned when he praised the creation of the right.[17] Instead it reflects the Court's conceptions of the individual and the state. The history of freedom of association is complex, but the Court ultimately located the right in the "First Amendment guarantees of freedom of speech and assembly and the Fourteenth Amendment protection that one cannot be denied life, liberty, or property without due process of law."[18]

This section examines how the idea of freedom of association emerged from the textual rights to assembly and speech and the penumbral right to privacy in such a way that it undermined the right to assembly as a textual right and the right to association as a right independent of the individual right to free speech. This development defined freedom of association as an aspect of the individual right to speech and the individual right to privacy that was *incidentally* associational rather than *intrinsically* associational. As the case law played out, the associational aspect that attached to freedom of assembly receded and the individual right that attached to freedom of speech subsumed freedom of association. While the justification for acts of association was the value to individual speech, individual speech was in turn only valuable insofar as it upheld the democratic political order.

Origins of Freedom of Association

Freedom of association arose in the historical context of the red scare of the early twentieth century and the rise of the civil rights movement. On the one hand, the federal government had an interest in suppressing communist groups for national security reasons; on the other, it sought to protect freedom of association for civil rights groups.[19] This led to a strange split in the case law where a robust understanding of freedom of assembly was suppressed and a related freedom, freedom of association, was created out of freedom of assembly and freedom of speech to justify the work of civil rights groups.

The Court first recognized freedom of association in *NAACP v. Alabama* (1958).[20] The NAACP was ordered by the state of Alabama to turn over its membership list, and the Court ruled that such a demand was a violation of the NAACP's freedom of association. Justice John Harlan, writing for the Court, argued that "freedom to engage in association for the advancement of beliefs and ideas is an inseparable aspect of the 'liberty' assured by the Due Process Clause of the Fourteenth Amendment."[21] His textual location of the right of association was ambiguous. Harlan cites freedom of assembly cases, but declined to find the freedom of association there, instead defining it as a freedom derived from both the freedom of speech and the freedom of assembly. He writes, "Effective advocacy of both public and private points of view, particularly controversial ones, is undeniably enhanced by group association, as this Court has more than once recognized by remarking upon the close nexus between the freedoms of speech and assembly."[22] Harlan's opinion was vague, probably a necessity to garner a unanimous opinion.[23] He never actually cites the First Amendment, although he states that rights of association and speech are protected by the Fourteenth Amendment and, citing *DeJonge v. Oregon*,[24] notes the "close nexus between the right to assembly and speech."[25] In the following paragraph, he discusses the rights to speech, press, and association as "indispensable liberties," but never links them directly to a textual location in the First Amendment.

Scholars have interpreted *NAACP* as both a First Amendment case and a Fourteenth Amendment case.[26] No less an eminent constitutional scholar than Thomas Emerson argued[27] that *NAACP* was a First Amendment case, despite the fact that Harlan does not once actually cite the First Amendment, but only refers to the rights located there. By citing the Fourteenth Amendment, Harlan leaves the textual location of the right open to interpretation. Was association derived from the "liberty" protected by the Due Process Clause, or was it located in a First Amendment textual right but incorporated against the states by the Fourteenth Amendment?

In *Bates v. City of Little Rock* (1960),[28] the Court dealt again with the question of whether a state government could acquire NAACP membership lists. Justice Stewart wrote for the Court and likewise appealed to the rights of speech and assembly found in the First Amendment, but, like Harlan, he referenced only the Fourteenth Amendment. Nonetheless, Stewart connects association to "advancing ideas and airing grievances," which connects association intimately with speech in a broad sense.[29] Justices Black and Douglas issued a joint concurrence noting that "freedom of assembly includes of course freedom of association; and it is entitled to no less protection than any other First Amendment right."[30] The concurrence argues that at the heart of the case is the First Amendment, but the fact that a concurrence had to be written indicates that this was not the argument the majority had actually made, and the authors of the concurrence were providing their own gloss on the opinion.

The same year, the Court ruled in *Shelton v. Tucker* (1960) that an Arkansas statute requiring teachers to disclose all memberships they held in any organization was a violation of freedom of association. Citing the Due Process Clause of the Fourteenth Amendment, the Court wrote, "To compel a teacher to disclose his every associational tie is to impair that teacher's right of free association, a right closely allied to freedom of speech and a right which, like free speech, lies at the foundation of a free society."[31] The dissent agreed on the fundamental framing of the issue even while disagreeing on its application in this particular case. Justice Harlan wrote for the dissent, "The legal framework in which the issue must be judged is clear. The rights of free speech and association embodied in the 'liberty' assured against state action by the Fourteenth Amendment are not absolute."[32] The whole Court agreed that the Fourteenth Amendment was the location of the right, and both the majority and the dissent wrote eloquently of the right to free speech, while not specifically citing the First Amendment. Important for our argument is that every Justice on the Court, whether voting with the majority or the dissent, closely connected the freedom of association with freedom of speech. We will see the same pattern in *CLS v. Martinez*.

In short, from the very beginning of the Court's articulation of freedom of association in its First Amendment jurisprudence, the Court was unclear where it actually derived the right. Was it implied in the liberty guaranteed by the Fourteenth Amendment, or was it found in the First Amendment and incorporated against the states by the Fourteenth? Inazu emphasizes the disagreement on the Court and among scholars commenting on these opinions as to where the right of association was to be found, evidence in itself of the Court's lack of consensus and clarity.[33] What was clear is that the Court linked freedom of association with political advocacy of some sort, which implied that association was only important for its role in democratic governance.

Association as a Form of Speech

The idea of freedom of association as simply an extension of freedom of speech, which was nascent in *NAACP*, *Bates*, and *Shelton*, became more explicit in the 1960s as the Court firmly established the right of association's link to the First Amendment. In *Louisiana v. NAACP* (1961) the Court struck down two Louisiana statutes, the second of which required disclosure of membership lists. Citing *Bates*, the Court wrote, "Freedom of association is included in the bundle of First Amendment rights made applicable to the States by the Due Process Clause of the Fourteenth Amendment."[34] In *NAACP v. Button* two years later, the Court struck down a Virginia statute banning "the improper solicitation of any legal or professional business" as applied to the activities of the NAACP on the grounds that the banned activities were "modes of expression and association protected by the First and Fourteenth Amendments which Virginia may not prohibit."[35]

While freedom of association had triumphed in five cases in five years, all regarding the NAACP, during the same period it was losing in a series of cases involving communist groups.[36] Organizations that the government considered subversive would not be granted the same rights of association as those en-gaged in political advocacy. A winning strategy for segregationists seemed to be linking the activities of the NAACP to communism. In *Gibson v. Florida Legislative Investigation Committee*,[37] the Court rejected this argument and overturned the conviction of an NAACP member who refused to relinquish the NAACP membership list to the state of Florida. At the time, the NAACP (among other groups) was under investigation by the state for potential com-munist infiltration. The Court ruled that the NAACP was not a subversive group, and therefore it was guaranteed the constitutional right of association. "Groups which themselves are neither engaged in subversive or other illegal or improper activities nor demonstrated to have any substantial connections with such activities must be protected in their rights of free and private as-sociation guaranteed by the First and Fourteenth Amendments."[38] Again the Court related freedom of association to freedom of speech writing, "The First and Fourteenth Amendment rights of free speech and free association are fun-damental and highly prized."[39]

The failure of communist groups to prevail indicates that associational rights were not nearly as secure as a reading of the NAACP cases would in-dicate. The Supreme Court was interested in the expressive activities of the NAACP insofar as the organization advocated democratic change. But the Court ruled against various communist groups because they were deemed subversive for their goal of overthrowing the U.S. government. This point is not intended to downplay legitimate national security concerns that steered members of the Court to rule against communist groups, but to point out that these circumstances demonstrate the link we are positing between speech and association in Court jurisprudence. The right of association as the Court understands it protects the right of advocacy within democratic consensus to the extent that it supports the proper functioning of the democratic state. The Court could have ruled against communist groups on the grounds of the As-sembly Clause, which requires "peaceable assembly," and protected freedom of association in the NAACP cases without tethering the right to the freedom of speech.

The connection between association and expression became even more ex-plicit in the 1970s. In *Runyon v. McCrary* (1976) the Court moved from simply denying constitutional protection to private discrimination when the state is involved to the conclusion that freedom of association is a matter of the *mes-sage* conveyed, not the *act* of association or exclusion. The case related to the right of private schools to practice segregation. Justice Stewart wrote for the Court,

> From [the principle of freedom of association] it may be assumed that parents have a First Amendment right to send their children to educational institutions that promote the belief that racial segregation is desirable, and that the children have an equal right to attend such institutions. But it does not follow that the practice of excluding racial minorities from such institutions is also protected by the same principle.[40]

The Court makes two assumptions in *Runyon* that form the basis of its later freedom of association jurisprudence: the compelled inclusion of members does not necessarily change the core of a group's expression, and there is a "distinction between the *act* of discrimination and the *message* of discrimination."[41] This distinction between status or immutable characteristics (such as race) on the one hand and belief on the other later defined the distinction between licit and illicit discrimination. While the Court was defining freedom of association in terms of status and belief, conduct associated with belief was ambiguous from the right's inception. As the doctrine was clarified over time, conduct associated with belief became an essential part of freedom of association.[42] But the group's right as such was not affirmed by the Court from the beginning of its definition of the right of association. The Court did not rely exclusively on the Assembly Clause as the textual location of the right in *NAACP* and eventually attached freedom of association entirely to freedom of speech, dropping any reference to the right of assembly.

The Court may have been right to restrict race discrimination in *Runyon* and similar cases, especially given the particularly ugly history of race relations in the United States. But what we are pointing out here is that the link the Court makes between association and message conveyed misses the fundamental nature of association. It would have been better for freedom of association jurisprudence if the Court had found an alternative argument to its holding in *Runyon* that did not reduce the constitutional right of association to its relationship to speech.

I have left a number of important cases out of the discussion in addition to the Civil Rights Acts of 1866, 1964, and 1991, all of which bear upon the relationship between individual equality, state action, and group autonomy. What my brief history is intended to show is that the Supreme Court has relied upon freedom of speech to ground freedom of association, because speech is a fundamental individual right and plausibly essential to democratic government, and therefore it fits nicely in the Court's dichotomous framework, whereas a right of association grounded solely in the right of assembly does not. The Court's increasing reliance on speech and a notion of penumbral rights anticipated an eventual bifurcation of freedom of association into an aspect of speech and an aspect of privacy. Both of these types of the right of association attach to the individual rather than to the group.

Association as a Form of Privacy

The discovery of the right to privacy in *Griswold v. Connecticut* (1965) took its doctrinal cue from the development of freedom of association. Privacy did not have any textual basis, but the appeal to rights that are implicit in the text, "penumbral" freedoms, matched the Court's earlier exposition on the right of association. In writing the *Griswold* opinion, Justice Brennan encouraged Douglas to advocate for the right to privacy by analogizing it to freedom of association to demonstrate how the Court could develop a right not found explicitly in the text of the Constitution. He pointed to *NAACP v. Alabama* and the notion that in freedom of association there is a realm of privacy that is expected to be beyond incursion by the government.[43] In the context of *NAACP*, privacy meant privacy in one's association with others, a concern later reduced to the privacy related to reproductive issues. Since freedom of association could be asserted as a constitutional right, despite lack of an explicit textual provision, then so could privacy.

Privacy and Expressive Association:
Roberts v. United States Jaycees

The right to freedom of association as a species of speech and the right to freedom of association as an aspect of the right to privacy emerged in two separate streams of case law and finally joined in *Roberts v. United States Jaycees* (1984).[44] There the Court coined the term "expressive association" to refer to the associational aspect of the freedom of speech, while considering whether the right of association included the ability of Jaycees to limit membership based on sex. Justice Brennan wrote the majority opinion, basing his reasoning on the two streams of cases discussed above as sources for the freedom of association. The privacy stream protected "intimate associations," an essential part of the personal liberty asserted in cases such as *Griswold v. Connecticut* and *Roe v. Wade*. The other stream defended "expressive associations," which protects groups that gather for the purpose of pursuing First Amendment rights such as freedom of speech and freedom of the press.[45] These two types of association reflect the "intrinsic and instrumental features of constitutionally protected association."[46] Both leave out the broad swath of associations that are neither expressive nor intimate.

The concept of intimate associations, while it existed implicitly in the privacy jurisprudence, was first defined in a 1980 article in the *Yale Law Journal* as "a close and familiar personal relationship with another that is in some significant way comparable to a marriage or family relationship."[47] It was based on the relational needs of the individual but focused on the intrinsic human bonds closely tied to a concept of family. Freedom of intimate association was more protected than expressive association because it touched the center of human existence and particularly the individual's perception of his own existence. Brennan based his case for intimate association in *Roberts* on this concept of the individual and the individual's relational needs. He wrote, "The Constitutional shelter afforded [intimate associations] reflects the realization that individuals draw much of their emotional enrichment from close ties with others. Protecting these relationships from unwarranted state interference therefore safeguards the ability independently to define one's identity that is central to any concept of liberty."[48]

In contrast to intimate associations, the freedom of association articulated by *Roberts* was dependent on the expressive activities of the group.[49] The Court coined the term "expressive association" to describe this right, treating association as if it were only freedom of speech and a group's exclusion or inclusion of members as only an aspect of expression. The Court based its decision solely on its own determination of whether exclusion of women from membership would harm the ability of the Jaycees to convey its *message*. The Court recognized that forced acceptance would be an egregious violation of a group's autonomy writing, "There can be no clearer example of an intrusion into the internal structure or affairs of an association than a regulation that forces the group to accept members it does not desire. Such a regulation may impair the ability of the original members to express only those views that brought them together. Freedom of association therefore plainly presupposes a freedom not to associate."[50] But the Court determined that the free speech rights of the individual members of Jaycees would not be affected by the presence of female members. The Court defended freedom of association on the basis that freedom of speech is "often exercised collectively and so entails a certain degree of freedom of association."[51] The expression of individuals can take the form of group expression, and that expression is protected by the same principle that protects the speech rights of individuals—but not by its own principle.

Inazu points out that the *Jaycees* Court effectively established four types of associations: intimate expressive associations, intimate nonexpressive associations, nonintimate expressive associations, and nonintimate nonexpressive associations. The Court's privacy jurisprudence from *Griswold* and beyond indicated that both types of intimate associations would have the most constitutional protection under the privacy jurisprudence, followed by expressive associations, insofar as the association in question could prove an expressive purpose, and provided no protection for nonintimate nonexpressive associations.[52]

Cases following *Roberts* recognized a similar dichotomy between expressive and intimate associations, although the category of "intimate association" was abandoned in favor of a broad privacy right derived from the "liberty" guaranteed by the Due Process Clause of the Fourteenth Amendment.[53] But the Court has kept the category of "expressive association" in subsequent freedom of association cases, considering only the value of association to expression. One scholar sums up the Court's position, "The Court will only find an expressive association violation when forcing the association to accept an unwanted person will produce a measurable impact on the association's speech."[54]

Expressive Association after Roberts

After *Roberts*, the Court continued to rule for the association in freedom of association cases only if the question were a matter of "expressive association," and that designation became increasingly speech-oriented. In the first two association cases after *Roberts*, the Court ruled against the associative rights of the groups in question. In *Board of Directors of Rotary International v. Rotary Club of Duarte* (1987),[55] the Court ruled that Rotary Club was not sufficiently intimate or sufficiently expressive to warrant constitutional protection for its freedom of association. In *New York State Club Association v. City of New York*

(1988),[56] the Court also found the collection of associations under scrutiny insufficiently expressive for protection under the *Roberts* standard. Individual members could still organize to express their viewpoints, but the Court decided that these associations were not explicitly expressive, and therefore they did not garner First Amendment protection.

While the associations in question lost the first three cases under the doctrine of expressive association, starting in the 1990s the Court ruled differently in two cases implicating associational rights. In neither did the Court offer a constitutional justification different from what it argued in *Roberts*. In *Hurley v. Irish-American Gay, Lesbian, and Bisexual Group of Boston* (1995),[57] the Court determined that the organizers of a Saint Patrick's Day parade in Boston could exclude groups from marching in the parade if, by their own estimation, the groups compromised or changed the message the organizers wished to convey. The Court framed the primary issue as the *message* of the parade organizers, which implicated the *speech* in which they wished to engage.

Five years later in *Boy Scouts of America v. Dale* (2000), the Court established that strict scrutiny would apply to the Court's consideration of expressive association. The Court wrote, "The forced inclusion of an unwanted person in a group infringes the group's freedom of expressive association if the presence of that person affects in a significant way the group's ability to advocate public or private viewpoints."[58] The case is significant because the Court understood the exclusion of an unwanted member not just for the message that member might convey but also for the example that member might set. The message of the group could reside not only in the explicit expression of the group but also implicitly in the conduct of its members. The Court did not consider the possible effects of "the forced inclusion of an unwanted person" on the associational dynamics of the group itself. Only *speech* by members of the Boy Scouts organization mattered for the Court's analysis.

The Court explicitly rejected the application of the *O'Brien* test,[59] which allowed government regulation of conduct "unrelated to the suppression of free expression" (in that case, burning a draft card) in *Dale* because the conduct in question was directly related to the message the Scouts wished to express. Given the close nexus between conduct and expression in *Dale*, the Court applied strict scrutiny, writing, "A law prohibiting the destruction of draft cards only incidentally affects the free speech rights of those who happen to use a violation of that law as a symbol of protest. But New Jersey's public accommodations law directly and immediately affects associational rights, in this case associational rights that enjoy First Amendment protection. Thus, *O'Brien* is inapplicable."[60]

Dale was not explicitly trying to convey a message that was deemed contrary to the Scout code. However, he disagreed with that message and was known to take a public stance contrary to that message, therefore his very presence in the Scouts would contradict the message the Boy Scouts desired to send to its members and the public at large.[61] The Court viewed an instance of the government forcing a group to accept an unwanted member as tantamount to compelled speech.[62] Freedom of association was not so much in question as was freedom of speech that would be affected by altering the members who associated.

In *Hurley* and *Dale*, the Court upheld a status/belief distinction that affirmed the ability of the group to discriminate in membership on the basis of belief, but not on the basis of status, immutable characteristics such as race or sex. However, the belief affirmed by the Court was necessarily a belief expressed by the group rather than simply a belief around which the group associated.[63] Protections for the associational aspect of the groups in question were not explicitly affirmed. Only the effect of association on expression mattered in the Court's analysis.

Speech, the Individual, and the Democratic State

The Court's reduction of freedom of association to freedom of speech is significant for its relationship to the two poles of the First Amendment Dichotomy: the individual and the political state. In these cases, the Court reduced freedom of association to freedom of expressive association because speech could be justified according to the interests of the individual and the state. Speech emanates from individuals as an expression of individual thoughts. Freedom of expressive association is individuals speaking in unison for the purposes of amplifying their individual voices. Speech also facilitates democratic governance because disagreement and discussion are essential to governing the political community in a democratic manner. However, speech is not protected on the grounds of its social, as opposed to political, value or for its communal, rather than individual, purpose. The divide between intimate and expressive associations articulated in *Roberts* and underlying the Court's later cases was based on the assumption that the associational aspects of all nonintimate associations are unimportant because they do not offer individuals the intrinsic value of intimate liaisons nor the instrumental benefit of speech amplification for democratic governance. In these cases, the Court ignored the communal nature of associations and their ability to integrate individuals into meaningful social bonds. Only the value of associations for freedom of speech mattered for constitutional analysis because of its enabling effect on individual self-expression and democratic governance.

The processes of individualization and politicization are evident here. For the purposes of judicial analysis, individuals are abstracted from their social context in associations, and associations are analyzed only for their value to the political order, not for their essentially associational nature. Political power is engaged in individualizing persons, separating them from their associational contexts, unless the state determines that the association can be politicized, justified for its ability to facilitate democratic dialogue. Judicial doctrine does not stand against these trends, protecting associations from political intrusions, but incorporates these conceptions into its doctrines. The process of dichotomizing freedom of association outlined above found its *reductio ad absurdum* in *Christian Legal Society v. Martinez*, to which we now turn.

CHRISTIAN LEGAL SOCIETY V. MARTINEZ

In *Christian Legal Society v. Martinez*, the Supreme Court upheld its long-standing designation of student organization programs at public universities as limited public forums, places that the government creates for the practice of First Amendment rights. But it refused to recognize a regulation restricting the freedom of association of student organizations at a public university as a threat to their First Amendment rights because, the Court reasoned, the free speech rights of individuals were uninhibited by the regulation. This move effectively excised associational freedom from the First Amendment. To explain how this happened, we will begin by outlining the facts of *CLS v. Martinez* and then explain the Court's reasoning, including its decision to collapse freedom of association into freedom of speech. Finally we will turn to a detailed discussion of the elements of the case organized according to the two exclusive concepts of the First Amendment Dichotomy, the individual and the state. We are primarily concerned here not with the Court's holding in the case but with its reasoning, the way it treated freedom of association.

Facts and Issues

The Christian Legal Society (CLS) was a Registered Student Organization (RSO) at Hastings Law School.[64] In the 2004–2005 academic year, the University of California, Hastings College of the Law rejected the application for official student group recognition to the campus chapter of CLS on the grounds that CLS was in violation of the university's nondiscrimination policy, which forbids discrimination on the basis of a variety of criteria including religion and sexual orientation.[65] CLS's bylaws contained a "Statement of Faith" requiring belief and practice in accordance with Christian moral teaching. In addition to a list of required theological beliefs,[66] CLS also included the following prohibitions:

> In view of the clear dictates of Scripture, unrepentant participation in or advocacy of a sexually immoral lifestyle is inconsistent with an affirmation of the Statement of Faith, and consequently may be regarded by CLS as disqualifying such an individual from CLS membership . . . [which includes] all acts of sexual conduct outside of God's design for marriage between one man and one woman, which acts include fornication, adultery, and homosexual conduct.[67]

While any student was allowed to attend meetings regardless of their beliefs or professed moral practices, CLS required all leaders and voting members to sign the Statement of Faith and adhere to its requirements.[68]

Under the antidiscrimination policy, Hastings enforced an "all-comers policy" that required every RSO to allow anyone to join its group, be allowed to vote, and even to run for office within the organization.[69] CLS's requirement that leaders and voting members sign the Statement of Faith was in apparent contradiction of this policy, and they were denied RSO status along with its incumbent benefits,[70] including use of school funds, facilities, and channels of communication, as well as Hastings's name and logo.[71] Specifically, the Hastings chapter of CLS was denied travel funds to attend the national CLS conference.[72]

CLS filed suit against Hastings for violating its "First and Fourteenth Amendment rights to free speech, expressive association, and free exercise of religion."[73] Hastings won at both the district and circuit levels. CLS appealed the decision to the Supreme Court, which granted *certiorari*. CLS had agreed to a stipulation during litigation that the all-comers interpretation of the non-discrimination policy was at issue and not the non-discrimination policy as written,[74] assuming that the Court would treat the case as a matter of freedom of association.[75] The Court refused to rule on the constitutionality of the non-discrimination policy.[76] The Court only ruled on "whether conditioning access to a student-organization forum on compliance with an all-comers policy violates the Constitution."[77] In a 5–4 decision authored by Justice Ruth Bader Ginsburg, the Court agreed with the lower courts' rulings that "Hastings's all-comers policy . . . is a reasonable, viewpoint-neutral condition on access to the student-organization forum."[78] The Court argued that the restrictions imposed on RSOs at Hastings were "reasonable in light of the purpose served by the forum" and viewpoint neutral.[79] The regulations applied to all RSOs, and therefore they met the purpose of the limited public forum, which exists to encourage "tolerance, cooperation, and learning among students" at Hastings Law School.[80]

The Court's Reasoning

The Court refused to analyze CLS's arguments on the basis of freedom of association because it did not distinguish between the arguments for association and the arguments for speech.[81] The Court wrote, "[CLS's] expressive-association and free-speech arguments merge: *Who* speaks on its behalf, CLS reasons, colors *what* concept is conveyed, . . . It therefore makes little sense to treat CLS's speech and association claims as discrete."[82] By conflating these claims the Court, in the words of one legal scholar, "executed a major legal maneuver" that bypassed nearly all of its previous jurisprudence regarding expressive association claims.[83] This allowed the Court to avoid strict scrutiny, which applies to expressive association,[84] and instead apply a rational basis test for speech claims in a limited public forum.

A limited public forum exists when the government "open[s] up property for certain purposes or certain groups."[85] The Court gave three reasons for deciding the case according to limited public-forum precedents. First, "speech and expressive-association rights are closely linked."[86] In other contexts the Court has allowed a lower level of scrutiny to speech restrictions in a limited public forum so it could apply the same lowered standards to expressive association.[87] Second, the state can restrict limited public forums to certain groups. Universities, for example, may limit student groups to students.[88] Third, "CLS may exclude any person for any reason if it forgoes the benefits of official recognition."[89] Hastings was not forcing CLS to admit other students, only refusing RSO recognition and benefits to them on that basis. The Court distinguished between the government's use of "the carrot of subsidy . . . [and] the stick of prohibition."[90] Effectively, if the CLS wanted to practice associational rights, it would have to exit the student organization forum. The Court's forum analysis is complicated, and it will be discussed in detail below.[91] But in general, the Court allows restrictions on freedom of speech in a limited public forum as long as the restrictions are reasonable and viewpoint neutral.[92] The Court found the policy reasonable on the grounds that the RSO forum was taking place in the educational context. It considered the RSO program an extracurricular part of the college's mission and an essential part of the educational process.[93] If the university decided that its educational mission was best served by allowing all comers into its RSOs, then, the Court reasoned, courts should defer to the university's judgment.[94]

The Court ruled that Hastings's policy was viewpoint neutral because it applied equally to all RSOs despite the fact that it unequally burdened some groups more than others.[95] Furthermore, the policy only aimed "at the *act* of rejecting would-be group members without reference to the reasons motivating that behavior."[96] So group members could continue to profess certain beliefs, but could not act collectively to exclude would-be members on the basis of whether would-be members held those beliefs. All individual students had an equal right to join any group on campus, whether the group wanted them there or not, and regardless of whether their presence affected the message that the group wished to convey.

The Court rejected three of CLS's arguments based on freedom of speech and freedom of association. First, the Court rejected CLS's argument that "there can be no diversity of viewpoints in a forum . . . if groups are not permitted to form around viewpoints"[97] on the grounds that Hastings's decision was constitutional, even if it was not advisable.[98] The university's position had its own reasoning even if it was not "the most reasonable" option. Second, the Court rejected the argument that the policy enabled hostile takeovers of unpopular groups on the grounds that such a possibility was "more hypothetical than real."[99] Third, the Court rejected CLS's argument that Hastings did not have a legitimate interest in encouraging religious groups to admit nonbelievers into the group.[100] The Court did not rule on whether the inclusion of unwanted members would affect the association as such.[101] The putative neutral language of the policy would not trigger a separate freedom of expressive association analysis.[102] The Court would only examine the case on the grounds of whether the policy was facially applicable to all student groups. It deemed that it was.

THE INDIVIDUAL AND THE STATE
IN *CLS V. MARTINEZ*

Several features of the *Martinez* Court's reasoning deserve emphasis at the outset to demonstrate that it is a First Amendment case on par with *NAACP, Dale,* and *Hurley* and that it is the case that effectively removes freedom of association from the pantheon of First Amendment rights, the direction in which I believe freedom of association case law was headed for some time. First, the case takes place in a *public* university, which the Court has repeatedly affirmed is an arena under the aegis of the First Amendment, writing on one occasion, "With respect to persons entitled to be there, our cases leave no doubt that the First Amendment rights of speech and association extend to the campuses of state universities."[103] We will discuss in more detail the importance of the public designation below. Second, First Amendment rights include the freedom of association in addition to the freedom of speech. The Court acknowledged that the First Amendment applied specifically in the student organization forum, but it refused to acknowledge freedom of association as applying to that forum.[104] It only considered First Amendment rights in terms of speech. This maneuver by the Court effectively removes the freedom of association from First Amendment protection. To sum up: a public forum, governed by the First Amendment and created by a public university for the express purpose of allowing groups to form, was not required by the Supreme Court to protect freedom of association for groups that formed there. I believe that the underlying theoretical reason for this maneuver is the First Amendment Dichotomy. The rest of the chapter is devoted to supporting this claim.

Scholars have focused on various aspects of the *Martinez* decision. Some hold that it is a narrow decision that applies *only* to an "all-comers" policy that existed *only* at Hastings Law School and apparently applied *only* to the specific instance in the case.[105] Some argue that it is much broader and that it will dismantle the doctrine of equal access,[106] change the understanding of limited public forums,[107] alter the understanding of student organizations at public universities,[108] affect state subsidy analysis,[109] and eliminate freedom of association as a separate First Amendment right.[110] Some see it as setting up a scenario where the Court can choose from several streams of jurisprudence that are all equally valid given the case history and achieve the outcome it wants based upon which stream of jurisprudential precedents it chooses to follow.[111]

My analysis uses the insights of much of the scholarship on the *Martinez* case cited in the previous paragraph to develop the First Amendment Dichotomy as a conceptual framework to understand the case and the Court's treatment of freedom of association. I organize the issues identified by these scholars according to what I take to be their fundamental theoretical origin in the Court's conceptions of the individual and the state. The scholars who have addressed the *Martinez* case are not wrong about the aspects of the case on which they comment. But by focusing on various particular features of the case, they fail to diagnose the fundamental theoretical framework at play in the *Martinez* case as a whole and, by implication, freedom of association jurisprudence more broadly. It should be further pointed out that the scholars cited above are not universally critical of the decision. Most are at least skeptical, but some simply note the changes that the decision will bring, and some are outright supportive of the decision.[112]

However, the opinions of these scholars on the soundness of the Court's holding in *Martinez* are not important for our analysis here. What concerns us is the fundamental theoretical issues undergirding the Court's decision which their scholarship helps to illuminate by describing the jurisprudential ramifications of various aspects of the case. I am criticizing the reasoning of the *Martinez* Court, how it got to its holding. One need not reject the Court's holding in *Martinez* to be troubled by its treatment of freedom of association in its reasoning. For example, Paul Horwitz accepts the Court's ruling on the grounds that CLS was a "nested institution." By its nature it operated under the aegis of the university, and in the name of First Amendment institutionalism the Court should defer to the presiding institution, in this case the university, rather than the institution nested within it.[113] But Horwitz admits that the Court's reasoning in *Martinez* is "half-hearted in its institutionalism." He writes, "Although [the case] pays lip service to the idea of deferring to universities, it is really driven by broad, acontextual doctrinal categories."[114] The *Martinez* Court ultimately fails to adequately develop a doctrine of First Amendment institutionalism along the lines he suggests.[115] Horwitz writes, "If the Court had examined *CLS* through a genuinely institutional lens, the outcome might not have been different. But the language would have been, and so would the ensuing public conversation."[116]

The rest of the chapter is devoted to a discussion of six aspects of the Court's opinion in terms of their relationship to the themes of the individual and the state. The first three—the way in which speech subsumed association, the dismantling of the status/belief distinction, and the Court's use of "reasonableness" and "viewpoint neutrality"—reflect the Court's concern with the individual. The latter three themes—the Court's instrumental view of groups and democratic politics, its treatment of state property and state action, and its support for restrictions on associational regulation of conduct—reflect the Court's concern with the state. The subject of state property and state action includes the Court's use of forum analysis, government property and government subsidy, and its application of restrictions on the government to private groups.

We focus our analysis on the majority opinion, but we will discuss concurrences[117] and the dissent[118] when relevant. Our point in doing so is to demonstrate that the First Amendment Dichotomy suffuses the thinking of all of the justices of the *Martinez* Court, not only the five who voted in the majority. While the holding in this case was closely decided, it would be a mistake to understand the First Amendment Dichotomy as only coloring the reasoning of a bare majority of Justices. The entire Court was implicated in this way of thinking to various degrees. Even if the Court's holding had been in favor of CLS, the First Amendment Dichotomy would have still permeated the Court's reasoning.

The Individual

This section explores the concept of the individual at the center of the *Martinez* decision as it is manifested in the Court's argument. In the introduction we defined the Court's conception of the individual as abstract, solitary, interchangeable with other individuals, and bereft of social attachments other than the rights it receives from the state. The individual encountered in each of the three aspects of the Court's reasoning discussed below fits this definition. Furthermore, each of these features contribute to the process Nisbet called individualization. Court doctrine treats individuals as separate from their communities of belief. Qualities that attach to the communal person or emerge from his interaction with others in the community are subsumed into the concept of the abstract individual. During the course of our discussion we will articulate and respond to two objections to our depiction of the individual in the *Martinez* decision.

Speech Subsumes Association

Recent First Amendment scholarship has harshly criticized the Court's treatment of freedom of association as a species of freedom of speech.[119] We take this point further to locate the *Martinez* Court's conflation of free speech and expressive association in an individualistic rubric.[120] Speech rights, unlike rights of association or assembly, are individual rights.[121] An individual can speak alone, as our example of the soapbox speaker, or he can speak in unison with others. The right to free speech encompasses both, but the locus of the right is the individual in that the right to speak does not emerge from the act of associating with other individuals. To the contrary, the Court has held that the act of associating with other individuals emerges from the individual right to speech.[122]

By locating the right of association in the right to speech, the Court effectively subsumed freedom of association into freedom of speech. The Court wrote that "expressive-association and free speech arguments merge: who speaks on its behalf . . . colors what concept is conveyed."[123] Rather than analyze the claims separately under each right's respective precedents, as the Court had done previously,[124] the Court stated that "it would be anomalous for a restriction on speech to survive constitutional review under our limited-public-forum test only to be invalidated as an impermissible infringement of expressive association."[125] Apparently, "the expressive association claim played a secondary role in support of the free speech claim, [so] the Court concluded that free speech analysis should control."[126] By merging the two rights, the Court eliminated independent protection for associations in a limited public forum and possibly beyond. The reduction of expressive association to speech demonstrates that the Court will only uphold the right of association if it amplifies the speech of individuals, but not if it reflects a group dynamic or an associational goal that cannot be reduced to individual speech. This move on the part of the Court eliminated freedom of association as a separate right and grounded it solely in freedom of speech. It is difficult to see how the speech of any individual in a group would be harmed by the presence of an individual who disagrees. Members of CLS or any other group may still express their *individual* views regardless of the presence of a dissenting person.

It has become unclear under what circumstances the Court will *ever* recognize an associational right.

Justice Kennedy's concurrence and even the dissent likewise saw the case through the prism of the individual right to free speech rather than the right of association. Justice Kennedy's concurrence displayed a disregard for associations similar to that found in the majority's opinion by describing the purpose of student groups as "facilitating interactions between students, enabling them to explore new points of view, to develop interests and talents, and to nurture a growing sense of self."[127] For Justice Kennedy, associations do not exist to cultivate camaraderie around shared values, but to encourage interactions with different points of view for the purposes of self-development.

The dissent arranged its objections to the decision on the grounds of speech and not association. It summarized the majority opinion as resting on the principle that there is "no freedom for expression that offends prevailing standards of political correctness in our country's institutions of higher learning."[128] While such a statement is critical of the majority's holding, it accepts the premise that the issue at stake is *speech*, not *association*. One of the dissent's main arguments drew from analogizing the case to *Healy v. James* (1972) in which a university rejected the application of a chapter of Students for a Democratic Society (SDS).[129] The opinion in *Healy* focused on the associational rights of the group in question and related them to speech. But when citing *Healy*, the dissent emphasized that the First Amendment meant the defense of *expression*. The dissent wrote, "The *Healy* Court was true to the principle that when it comes to the interpretation and application of the *right to free speech*, we exercise our own independent judgment. We do not defer to Congress on such matters . . . and there is no reason why we should bow to university administrators."[130]

A counterargument to what is presented above is that the Court needs a message-based analysis of associations to properly identify groups as First Amendment institutions. We have already noted that Paul Horwitz makes a variation of this argument. What we are pointing out here is that the Court in its entirety has collapsed freedom of association and freedom of assembly into freedom of speech. The Speech Clause has swallowed other freedoms that have historically been part of the pantheon of First Amendment rights.[131] While it is certainly true that there is a First Amendment right to associate for the purpose of speaking, it doesn't follow that the right of association grounded in the right of assembly[132] can be exercised only for the purpose of expression. A message-based approach to association misses that important point.

Dismantling the Status/Belief Distinction

For most of the freedom of association precedents prior to *Martinez*, the Court allowed discrimination in membership based on belief and conduct that accompanies that belief, but not based on immutable characteristics or status.[133] On the one hand, freedom of belief and freedom of speech are fully protected, and individuals can associate freely with those of like mind; on the other hand, invidious discrimination on the basis of race or sex is forbidden, so individuals are judged for what they choose to think, say, and do, but not for who they ineradicably are.[134] The status/belief distinction was operative in *Roberts* where the Court allowed an association to determine its message by restricting its membership.[135] Jaycees could not reject a potential member based on her *status* as a woman, but it could reject a woman—or a man—who disagreed with the Jaycees' *message* to advocate for the interests of young men in business. The Court made a distinction between discrimination based on status (in this case, sex), which is not an acceptable criterion for membership and cannot survive strict scrutiny, and discrimination based on belief, which is constitutionally acceptable.[136]

While I will argue in chapter 4 that the status/belief distinction is largely inadequate to protect fully the right of association, at least it locates the right of association *in the association*. It allows groups to have unique identities by limiting their membership to those who agree with the ideals of the group, and it maintains the potential for substantive ideological differences between groups. Under this concept of freedom of association, individuals are not interchangeable, but have diverse characteristics that find form and reinforcement in various associations. The associations in turn can police the borders of their groups so that each can maintain its distinctive identity—as long as the border of the group is based on belief, not status.

In *Martinez*, the Court dismantled the distinction between status and belief. Associations are allowed to express whatever discriminatory view they have, but they may not limit their membership on the basis of belief or conduct arising from belief.[137] The Court relied on its ruling in *Lawrence v. Texas* (2003) to eliminate the distinction between status and belief on the grounds that to discriminate on the basis of sexual acts that emerge from sexual orientation amounted to status discrimination on the basis of sexual orientation.[138]

The Court wrote, "When homosexual *conduct* is made criminal by the law of the State, that declaration in and of itself is an invitation to subject homosexual *persons* to discrimination."[139] Conduct, previously an aspect of *belief*, was transferred to an aspect of *status*. One scholar explained, "Discriminating against same-sex conduct constitutes discrimination against gays as a class of persons."[140] Rejecting someone who engages in same-sex conduct from membership in a religious group was tantamount to rejecting someone who has a same-sex sexual orientation.[141]

The Court reasoned that requiring Hastings to make a distinction between a status-based and a belief-based rejection would place too high a burden on Hastings to determine "whether a student organization cloaked prohibited status exclusion in belief-based garb."[142] However, the Court had never had a problem with this in the past, but based its past opinions on this very distinction.[143] "In the expressive-association context, private groups, who are not prohibited from discriminating by the Constitution and who do not possess the power of the state, often wish to select members who share their core values for the purposes of expression, not discrimination."[144] The Court had previously deferred to that associational prerogative when expression was at stake.[145]

The status/belief distinction was an attempt by the Court to eliminate invidious discrimination based upon immutable characteristics while maintaining the reality of stark differences of opinion and lifestyle among individuals. These differences include religious creeds, moral values, lifestyle choices, political views, and much else that characterizes an ideologically diverse populace. The status/belief distinction presupposed that association around belief was a meaningful association. The collapse of that distinction by the Court reduced all persons to discrete individuals in its jurisprudence and ignored profound ideological disagreements and lifestyle differences drawn from the complexity of their individual histories and dispositions. The Court considered these differences unimportant compared with persons' fundamental equality as *individuals before the state.*

A counterargument to the status/belief distinction discussed here is that the Court was simply recognizing homosexuality as a status rather than conduct associated with belief. Julie Nice is the scholar who most clearly and directly defends this aspect of the Court's opinion, writing, "By effectively refusing to conflate openly gay identity with any ideological expression, *Martinez* enhances liberty, making space for an individual to embrace any religious ideology regardless of his or her sexual orientation."[146] She situates the *Martinez* decision in the *Romer v. Evans* and *Lawrence v. Texas* line of jurisprudence.[147] *Romer* was the first case where the Court recognized equal rights of homosexuals, applying the Equal Protection Clause to strike down a state constitutional amendment that forbid state and local laws from protecting homosexuals as a group.[148] *Lawrence* relied on the Due Process Clause to strike down a state law outlawing homosexual sexual conduct.[149] Each case ruled that gays have an equal right to privacy and liberty in their sexual conduct as do heterosexuals.

What Nice's analysis ignores is the extent to which the individual liberty appropriately established in *Romer* and *Lawrence* is inappropriately applied in the *Martinez* case. The inapposite use of the *Lawrence* precedent and the Fourteenth Amendment to *Martinez* is addressed in detail below. Here it will suffice to point out that, unlike *Romer* and *Lawrence*, *Martinez* dealt with a *private association* and its ability to determine requirements for its leaders that align with its mission. Both *Romer* and *Lawrence* were striking down *state* enactments, either a state constitutional amendment (as in *Romer*) or a state law (as in *Lawrence*). In *Martinez*, the issue is not a state law or action but the liberty of an association to determine its own membership and the liberty of an individual to act corporately, to join a group that supports his or her viewpoint, and to commune with other individuals who support his or her lifestyle.[150]

Three additional points are worth making in response to Nice's argument. First, Nice downplays the synergy between the rights of religious groups and the rights of LGBTQ groups. The Court's defense of religious viewpoints and membership discrimination for campus religious groups in a case like *Rosenberger v. University of Virginia* was used by lower federal courts to defend the rights of LGBTQ groups on college campuses.[151] The right of association, including the right of membership requirements attenuated in *Martinez*, is the same right of association that protects the right of LGBTQ groups to associate. The right of CLS to exclude those who engage in acts it finds immoral is the same right that would allow a group like OUTLAW, the gay rights group at Hastings, to exclude conservative evangelicals who oppose one or all of the organization's goals. This concern was reflected incidentally in the bylaws of OUTLAW that required all of its members to have a commitment to gay rights.[152] Presumably, any member of CLS who signed the CLS statement of faith would be unwelcome in OUTLAW. Equality would require that CLS be granted the same associational liberty to determine the terms of its membership. What Nice sees as an expansion of individual rights for gays to join all student groups at Hastings is a shrinking of individual rights of all students there to act corporately, to act with others of the same ideological disposition. It affects the rights of gay students to associate with others of like mind just as much as it affects the right of conservative evangelical students to associate in CLS.

Second, associations with closed membership requirements are often the source of the sort of salutary social change that Nice praises.[153] What begins as a fringe dissenter opinion gains momentum as individuals associate around certain values, build internal consensus, support each other, and convince fellow citizens that their ideas have value. What was true for racial and sexual equality holds true for the success of gays in having their individual rights respected in *Romer* and *Lawrence*[154] and various legislative efforts. Early gay rights groups had trouble associating and advancing their agenda because their right to freedom of association was not recognized.[155] It was only with the Court's expansive treatment of expressive associations that gay rights groups were able to organize and achieve social change.[156] The individual rights for gay persons that Nice praises were made possible by the work of associations that had closed membership requirements around support for gay rights.[157]

Third, dismissing freedom of association after it has contributed to the achievement of a certain amount of social progress ignores the possibility of social *regress*. While current scholarly and public opinion, as Nice notes, is favoring gay rights, it is impossible to know if that will last. One gay scholar poignantly wrote after the *Dale* case, "In Germany, there were nightclubs for gays in the 1920s and concentration camps for them in the 1940s. The relative tolerance of pre-Depression New York gave way to the repression of the 1930s. Yesterday New Jersey declared us criminal; today it protects us from discrimination; tomorrow it may again find us wanting."[158] If such a reversal of recent social changes were to take place, a robust freedom of association would ensure that gays and their allies still had a place of refuge in their own associations and a starting point to engage once again in the fight for equality.

Here I am emphasizing the associational nature of groups, not their role in the individual and the democratic state. But this should not be taken as an argument that individual speech or well-being and democratic government are not positively affected by associations. Salutary social change in a democratic society, including an expansion of equality and individual rights, often starts with the work of dissident associations forming around viewpoints and discriminating in membership based upon those viewpoints. But in order for groups to achieve these salutary aims, they require a freedom of association that exists prior to and apart from individual speech and democratic governance. This is why I think the Court must refocus attention on the group itself. This refocusing of the Court's attention would have benefited gay associations of yesteryear as readily as religious groups like CLS today.

"Reasonable" and "Viewpoint Neutral"
The Court's definitions of "reasonable" and "viewpoint neutral" in the *Martinez* case are premised on the concept of the individual abstracted from social context. When arguing for the reasonableness of the decision, the majority wrote,

> CLS's analytical error lies in focusing on the benefits it must forgo while ignoring the interests of those it seeks to fence out. Exclusion, after all, has two sides. Hastings, caught in the crossfire between a group's desire to exclude and students' demand for equal access, may reasonably draw a line in the sand permitting *all* organizations to express what they wish but *no* group to discriminate in membership.[159]

The Court is concerned with exclusion of individuals from student groups, even though the potentially excluded individuals do not agree with the orienting mission of the group they may be joining and, while excluded from CLS, may join any other group whose ideas they agree with or even start their own student group. The Court's analysis focused exclusively on accommodating the individual's desire to join a group, ignoring the social context of a diverse student body manifested in a variety of cultural and religious student organizations.

The reasonableness of the policy depends on the Court's definition of individuals as largely interchangeable. On such an assumption of the nature of the individual, there is no reasonable justification for an individual's exclusion from a group on the basis of membership requirements around associational prerogatives that implicate an individual's ideological commitment to the group, as CLS argued. Individuals are virtually indistinguishable from each other and the Court finds no reason why groups would be able to make any distinctions in membership. This "reasonable" finding by the Court yields results that would be considered unreasonable if associations were treated by the

Court as a category of analysis independent of its conception of the individual. If students are allowed to form groups around certain ideas or ideologies,[160] then it would follow that they be allowed to restrict membership to those who agree with their ideas and will abide by conduct the group finds appropriate to its own ideology. The university established a forum for student groups to express views that then eliminated the very item, membership requirements, that allowed identifiable groups to form.[161]

The Court's argument regarding "viewpoint neutrality" likewise demonstrates an abstract individualism. The argument allows for the dismantling of differences between groups that ensure that all members of the Hastings community, as individuals, have equal access to student groups. The Court wrote, "It is, after all, hard to imagine a more viewpoint-neutral policy than one requiring all student groups to accept *all* comers."[162] A premise of this statement is that all students are the same or similar enough that it makes little difference that any student, no matter how different from another, may join any group, no matter how much he may disagree with the purpose of the group he wishes to join. The policy is neutral in that it purportedly applies to all groups. But, as constitutional scholar Erica Goldberg writes, "The ability to select members based on ideology in order to promote a group's expression, one of the primary purposes of the right to expressive association, is entirely eroded by Hastings's policy, viewpoint neutral, or otherwise."[163] Under the Court's understanding of viewpoint neutrality, a university could forbid the use of religious viewpoints in making membership decisions. This would hamstring only religious groups whose existence depends on certain religious viewpoints, but would have no effect on the chess club or most political or cultural groups. "Thus, a university could apply its nondiscrimination policy in a way that affects certain student groups—such as religious groups—differently from other groups— such as political groups—yet still comply with the Court's reasonable and viewpoint-neutral standard."[164] For the Court, "viewpoint neutrality" means neutralizing the viewpoints of groups and making the individual—conceived abstractly—the locus of ideas and action in its constitutional analysis.

The State

The previous section intended to demonstrate the presence of the concept of the individual in the *Martinez* decision. The other end of the First Amendment Dichotomy, the concept of the state, also loomed large in the Court's reasoning. The state is conceived here in Hobbesian terms as monolithic political power, sovereign and all-encompassing. Associations are regarded as part of the state's overall structure and denied the ability to pursue goals independent of state prerogatives. Defense of associations must take place within the context of their role in advancing state objectives. Even constitutional restrictions against state power over individuals are applied to restrict private associations' authority over individuals.

As a public university, the Court treated Hastings Law School as an extension of the state itself and activities taking place there as under the authority and responsibility of the state. This was reflected in the Court's assertion that CLS's discrimination in membership would amount to state discrimination. The Court wrote, "The First Amendment shields CLS against state prohibition of the organization's expressive activity, however exclusionary that activity may be. CLS enjoys no constitutional right to state subvention of its selectivity."[165] This statement was based on the notion that the activity of private groups in the student organization context at a public university constitutes state action. This was reflected in the Court's conception of the relationship between speech and the democratic state, its treatment of the university as government property, and any action taking place there as state action and its prohibition of associational regulation of conduct. Each of these topics demonstrates Nisbet's idea of the process of politicization, the state co-opting associational functions for political purposes, subsuming groups into its apparatus. I will explain each of these aspects of the Court's reasoning in turn to demonstrate the presence of the concept of the state in the *Martinez* decision. Along the way I will address two objections to my arguments.

Speech and the Democratic State

Above we discussed the Supreme Court's treatment of speech as an individual right. In this section we explore the Court's understanding of the importance of associational speech to the functioning of the democratic state. This understanding is found not only in the majority opinion but also in Kennedy's concurrence and the dissenting opinion. The justification for associations under Supreme Court jurisprudence is that they have instrumental value to the state insofar as they provide a means of dialogue to reach democratic consensus.[166] The *Martinez* Court wrote, "The Law School reasonably adheres to the view that an all-comers policy, to the extent it brings together individuals with diverse backgrounds and beliefs, 'encourages tolerance, cooperation, and learning among students.'"[167] These goals of the state university are important to a democratic society and worthy goals for a state educational institution to encourage and inculcate among students. Therefore, the Court reasoned, groups could be co-opted by the state university for these purposes.[168] The Court saw associations operating in a limited public forum as useful tools in democratic governance, but not entities that should have (and do have) their own diverse and pluralistic ends.

Justice Kennedy's concurrence demonstrated that his vote was swayed at least in part by his understanding of the link between associations and democratic governance. In his concurrence, Kennedy elaborated on the Law School's purposes for the forum, "A law school furthers [its] objectives by allowing broad diversity in registered student organizations. But these objectives may be better achieved if students can act cooperatively to learn from and teach each other through interactions in social and intellectual contexts. A vibrant dialogue is not possible if students wall themselves off from opposing points of view."[169] Kennedy believes that students are engaged in a cooperative endeavor and that groups exist only to facilitate cooperation, an important objective of the democratic state. But groups do not exist in their own right for their own purposes, which may be beyond the scope and purview of the state.[170] For Kennedy, forming an exclusive association is nothing but intellectual seclusion. Kennedy acknowledged that he would vote differently if "in a particular case the purpose or effect of the policy was to stifle speech or make it ineffective."[171] Speech, but not association, is important to democratic governance and therefore deserves heightened protection.

This notion that associations exist only to bolster the democratic state was also the primary justification for the dissent's defense of free speech. Justice Alito wrote, "Our country as a whole, no less than the Hastings College of Law, values tolerance, cooperation, learning, and the amicable resolution of conflicts. But we seek to achieve those goals through '[a] confident pluralism that conduces to civil peace and advances democratic consensus building,' not by abridging First Amendment rights."[172] Associations must be protected for the purpose of "democratic consensus-building," but not for the purposes for which they were created by their members. The importance of the group, the end for which it exists, was ignored by both the *Martinez* Court and the dissent. All of the justices, no matter their vote, focused on the student groups' role in facilitating democratic discussion, which reduced groups to their instrumental role in the democratic state.

State Property and State Actors

In a previous case that took place at a university, *Widmar v. Vincent* (1981),[173] the Court ruled that providing meeting space "does not confer any imprimatur of state approval on religious sects or practices . . . [or] dominate [the university's] open forum."[174] This changed in *Martinez*, where the state university in question was treated by the Court as state property. This understanding of the public university as state property where the state pursues its own objectives means that anything that happens at the university, including the activity of student groups, is considered state activity. This aspect of the Court's concept of the state was reflected in three areas: the Court's new limited public forum doctrine, its use of the idea of government property and subsidy, and its application of constitutional restrictions on the state (in the form of the Fourteenth Amendment) to private groups.

Forum Analysis. The Court chose to hear *CLS v. Martinez* as a matter of limited public forum doctrine.[175] The Court has articulated four types of forums, although it consistently claims it has only three, and some argue it has only two.[176] The four that appear in Supreme Court doctrine are traditional public forums,[177] designated public forums,[178] limited public forums,[179] and nonpublic forums.[180] The Court has not been consistent in how it defines each type of forum or in the name it uses for each type.[181]

Conventionally, a limited public forum is one where the Court opens up a public forum but limits it in a particular way, such as by who is permitted into the forum or what subject matter may be discussed.[182] "While the government is not required to open up these types of forums for First Amendment purposes, once it does, the forums are to be held to the same standards as the traditional public forum."[183] In *Widmar* the Court ruled that a university student organization forum is a limited public forum in that it is a public forum, a place where First Amendment rights are practiced, but one that is explicitly limited to students. The Court has made it clear that in these forums "students enjoy First Amendment rights of speech and association on the campus."[184] A public forum, whether traditional or limited, is a place where the state is not only *not* speaking or acting but is explicitly forbidden from restricting private groups and persons from exercising First Amendment rights. Restrictions on First Amendment rights in the context of the limited public forum must be reasonable and viewpoint neutral subject to strict scrutiny.[185] The Court has treated student groups at public universities as a matter of limited public forum doctrine since 1980,[186] and it confirmed the presence of First Amendment rights in the student group forum nearly a decade earlier[187] What is disputed here is the Court's novel application of this category, which permits the state to co-opt private groups operating in the forum. I am especially concerned that the Court insisted that it was using public forum doctrine while simultaneously providing justification for the public university to determine the associational prerogatives of groups that enter the forum.

The *Martinez* Court relied on a recently redefined limited public forum that differed substantially from how the forum was described in *Widmar* and the other public forum cases. In *Pleasant Grove City v. Summum* (2009)[188] the Court defined three categories of public forums: traditional public forums, designated public forums, and a third less protected category, which, while not labeling it a limited public forum, the Court defined as "a forum that is *limited* to use by certain groups or dedicated solely to the discussion of certain subjects."[189] However, the Court did not indicate that there were nonpublic forums, which seemed to conflate a limited public forum with a nonpublic forum as the third and least-protected category. This changed the limited public forum from a category similar to a public forum, except for an explicit limitation on content or participants, to a forum where the government has wide latitude to regulate First Amendment rights for its own purposes. This move dramatically altered the Court's treatment of speech and action within the limited public forum. "While the designated and limited public forums have at times been treated synonymously, under this bifurcated system courts will apply strict scrutiny in cases involving a designated forum and the much less restrictive reasonableness standard in cases involving the limited public forum."[190] A limited public forum went from a place where First Amendment rights are practiced to a place where the government accomplishes its own purposes, just as it does in a nonpublic forum.

The Court cited *Summum* in its decision to use forum analysis in *Martinez* and listed the three types of forums described in *Summum*: traditional public forums, designated public forums, and limited public forums.[191] Note the absence of nonpublic forums, implying, as it did in *Summum*, that limited public forums are the Court's lowest category for the purpose of forum analysis. The Court's conception of a limited public forum in *Martinez* was more akin to a nonpublic forum than to the middle category of designated public forum or the pre-*Summum* definition of limited public forum, both of which were more protective of First Amendment rights by providing more strenuous requirements on government regulation than what is found in *Martinez*. The new definition of a limited public forum the Court established in *Summum* made it little more than a state-sponsored nonpublic forum, which means that when the state declares a limited public forum, it is only required to abide by standards of reasonableness and viewpoint neutrality subject to rational basis scrutiny.[192] Whereas the student organization forums were previously places where "students enjoy First Amendment rights of speech and association,"[193] the *Martinez* definition of a limited public forum reduced the student groups of Hastings to little more than state appendages, private entities acting at the government's behest and for the government's purposes.

The dissent accepted limited public forum analysis on the grounds that the requirements of reasonableness and viewpoint neutrality would favor a contrary ruling on the case. Its opinion assumed the pre-*Summum* understanding of limited public forums.[194] The dissent was careful to point out that the use of religion and sexual orientation fall under the viewpoint category, and any effort by the Law School to exclude organizations because of the group's membership requirements would be textbook viewpoint discrimination subject to strict scrutiny.[195] Hastings Law School allowed political, social, and cultural groups to discriminate in membership on the basis of viewpoint so they must allow religious groups the same latitude or demonstrate a compelling government interest to justify the disparate treatment.[196]

In sum, the Court's forum analysis dubs limited public forums essentially forms of *state* speech and *state* action. Groups are allowed to enter the forum insofar as they accomplish state objectives. The change in forum analysis imported the state into group activities in this context. By doing so it subsumed group activity into state activity and made it subject to state prerogatives.

Government Property and Subsidy. The Court's emphasis on the government as property owner implicated a notion of government subsidy and state action. The Court wrote, "We are persuaded that our limited-public-forum precedents adequately respect both CLS's speech and expressive-association rights, and fairly balance those rights against Hastings's interests as *property owner* and educational institution."[197] Constitutional scholar Jesse Hill remarks, "By applying forum analysis in CLS, the Court reminded us that the government is not just a regulator—it is also a property owner that exercises dominion, control, and exclusionary rights over its domain."[198] As a property owner, it may do what it likes and exclude who it will from its property. In addition to a much lower standard for reasonableness and viewpoint neutrality, the Court's move to consider public universities as public property bolstered the government's right as a property owner in the context of expressive association, which "empower[ed] the government to exclude unwanted speakers, mostly under conditions that the government itself is free to define."[199]

The Court's argument is dubious on its face. The government as "property owner" does not accurately capture the state's relationship with traditional public forums such as public parks and public sidewalks, despite the fact that the government owns the property. On the contrary, government ownership of public forums renders these locations uniquely open to the practice of First Amendment rights and uniquely binds the hands of government in those spaces. As Hill notes, the "use of property is problematic when First Amendment values are at stake."[200] It is doubly problematic when the right of *association* is as stake because this conception of government property makes all activities of private associations on public property effectively acts of the state. Rather than private institutions that act according to their own ends, under this doctrine, associations are considered nothing more than state actors whose otherwise private actions and speech are rendered effectively state sponsored.

This government property analysis was further exacerbated by the Court's claim that CLS's application for RSO status was "seeking what is effectively a state subsidy."[201] The Court distinguished between compelling "a group to include unwanted members, with no choice to opt out," as was the case in *Dale*,[202] and simply denying a group government benefits. The Court wrote, "Through its RSO program, [Hastings] is dangling the carrot of subsidy, not wielding the stick of prohibition."[203] The description of university benefits as "subsidy" means that when the state university subsidizes, the state university speaks. Under this understanding, groups operating at state universities are effectively channels of government speech and government action. The Court placed subsidy analysis in the context of Hastings's claim that it was simply incorporating California state law into its nondiscrimination policy,[204] and therefore it was acceptable for a public university to forbid the use of "public money" to subsidize conduct that the people of California had determined was discriminatory.[205]

The primary problem with the Court's subsidy analysis is that the "subsidy" for student groups is not a state subsidy but *funding for a public forum*, which requires the public university to distribute funds to student groups in a reasonable and viewpoint neutral manner, subject to strict scrutiny. In this way, funding for student groups is just like reserving a room on campus or accessing the student organization listserv. As one scholar explains, "In the student organizational context, the Court has never considered a university's lending of its facilities or funding to be a governmental subsidy in the same way it has in other contexts."[206] Funding for student groups is not government subsidy subject to government restraints on the recipients, but funding for the forum in which groups form and act. Furthermore, the very presence of a forum implies precisely the opposite of government speech. As one scholar wrote, "When a university sets up a forum for speech, that speech is considered entirely private and not attributable to the school."[207] The Court has ruled this way repeatedly regarding benefits in the university forum, including funding.

In *Healy* (1972), the Court wrote,

> The primary impediment to free association flowing from nonrecognition is the denial of use of campus facilities for meetings and other appropriate purposes. . . . Petitioners' associational interests also were circumscribed by the denial of the use of campus bulletin boards and the school newspaper. If an organization is to remain a viable entity in a campus community in which new students enter on a regular basis, it must possess the means of communicating with these students.[208]

The important point for the *Healy* Court was that a student group's First Amendment right to freedom of association included access to all aspects of the public forum including campus media, bulletin boards, meeting space, and so forth. While funding was not part of *Healy*, it highlights the Court's treatment of the student organization forum as a First Amendment forum, a place where First Amendment rights are practiced, regardless of the fact that these actions take place on government property or implicate government resources.

Nearly a decade later, in *Widmar* (1980), the Court dealt with the presence of a religious group in the student organization forum. The Court wrote, "The Establishment Clause does not bar a policy of equal access, in which facilities are open to groups and speakers of all kinds. . . . The 'primary effect' of such a policy would not be to advance religion but rather to further the neutral purpose of developing students' *social and cultural awareness as well as [their] intellectual curiosity.*"[209] The fact that the university was not required to create the forum does not mean that its doing so gives it special authority in that space. The state university is still restricted by the First Amendment, as the *Widmar* Court further wrote: "The Constitution forbids a State to enforce certain exclusions from a forum generally open to the public, even if it was not required to create the forum in the first place."[210] The Court made it clear that groups operating in the forum are not receiving the official approval of the state, writing, "An open forum in a public university does not confer any imprimatur of state approval on religious sects or practices . . . [or] commit the University . . . to the goals of the Students for a Democratic Society, the Young Socialist Alliance, or any other group eligible to use its facilities."[211] The Court was clear that a public university could not discriminate in the distribution of "general benefits" to student groups such as meeting space and funding. Such a prohibition, the Court explained, would be like the police and fire department refusing to protect a church or the city refusing to repair the sidewalk in front of a religious building.[212] The benefits accorded to student groups, including funding, by public universities are akin to the generally available resources in a public forum.

Subsequent cases involving student fee funding supported the *Widmar* Court's conclusions and insisted that funding for student groups in the student organization forum was part of the category of "public benefits" attached to the public forum, and the university was denied discretion in the disbursement of such benefits. In *Rosenberger*, (1995), after acknowledging that the government may subsidize in order to spread its own message, the Court wrote, "It does not follow, however, and we did not suggest in *Widmar*, that viewpoint-based restrictions are proper when the University does not itself speak or subsidize transmittal of a message it favors but instead expends funds to encourage a diversity of views from private speakers."[213] With this understanding the Court distinguishes between subsidies for things the government supports and funding for a public forum—and it explicitly places the student organization forum and its funding in the latter category. Likewise, in *University of Wisconsin v. Southworth* (2000), the Court wrote, "In the instant case, the speech is not that of the University or its agents. It is not, furthermore, speech by an instructor or a professor in the academic context, where principles applicable to government speech would have to be considered."[214] Constitutional scholar Tracey explains, "The University of Wisconsin's activity fees were fostering private speech from student groups. As such, the university had to allocate those fees in compliance with the principle of equal access."[215] Tracey further writes,

"The Court had always categorized a school's recognition of student groups as the creation of a forum for private speakers. Schools are accommodating the student groups' private expression, not using the student groups to send their own message."[216]

According to the Court's analysis of public universities as public property in *Martinez*, the messages expressed in that context are the government's messages. Private groups can now be subsumed into the state when they associate in a public forum on "government property." The Court's dubbing of funding for a limited public forum as a government "subsidy" to specific groups fundamentally changes the nature of the forum from one that is public, and therefore under the strictures of the First Amendment, to one where the government is speaking and acting. It allows a public university to dictate the associational requirements for groups that form in a public forum as if it were a nonpublic forum while insisting that the forum remains public. This development is a radical departure of the *Martinez* Court from its precedents regarding the status of the student organization forum and one that I believe is a grave threat to freedom of association. Benefits for groups in the student organization forum have never been treated by the Court as a subsidy as such, an expenditure of government funds for its own purposes. The reason the Court has not done so is clear: the student organization forum is a public forum, a place where First Amendment rights are practiced. It is a blatant contradiction to declare the student organization forum a public forum (with all of the generally available benefits attached to it) and then to grant the state university full control over who enters that space.

I believe three options would have left freedom of association better protected. First, the Court could have vindicated the right of association in the student organization forum and insisted that Hastings as a public university respect the First Amendment right of association for all student groups. I prefer this outcome because I think that the Court was right to "leave no room for the view that, because of the acknowledged need for order, First Amendment protections should apply with less force on college campuses than in the community at large"[217] and that it was right when it repeatedly acknowledged the student organization forum as a First Amendment forum in the cases I discussed above. The formation and activities of a plethora of political, social, and religious groups looks a lot more like the practice of First Amendment rights to association, press, religion, and speech than it does the creation of colleges, academic departments, and administrative offices. The public university creates the student organization forum, but it doesn't create the groups themselves. This action resembles government creation of a public forum rather than government activity to accomplish its own legitimate purposes. But I do think this is a point on which reasonable people may disagree. The Court could have reached the same ruling but better protected freedom of association than it did in *Martinez*.

Second, the Court could have overturned *Rosenberger* and separated funding from all of the other benefits of the public forum, allowing public universities to discriminate in who they give funding to but not in who has access to the forum. The public university in *Rosenberger* insisted that its actions in denying funding to a religious group was constitutional precisely on this basis: it allowed equal access to the student organization forum per the First Amendment rights of the religious group, but refused to fund it on Establishment Clause grounds.[218] This movement by the Court would create some tensions in the forum and confusion over the nature of benefits attaching to the forum. The Court would also need to revisit its ruling in *Southworth*. There it held that the use of student fees to fund groups in the student organization forum was not compelled speech on the grounds that the public university was not using funding from student fees for its own purposes but distributing it in a viewpoint neutral manner to which all students had access.[219] If the Court wants to declare funding in the student organization forum as government speech, then it seems like the use of student fees would be compelled speech just as the *Southworth* respondents had argued. It would further mean that a federal appellate court was wrong to insist that a LGBTQ group receive funding on an equal basis with other student organizations.[220] Those problems aside, at least this option would have acknowledged freedom of association as a First Amendment right on par with freedom of speech in the limited public forum.

Third, the Court could have declared the student organization forum a nonpublic forum, a place where the government is acting and speaking and not a place where First Amendment rights are practiced. If it wishes to change the status of student group forums to a matter of government property and subsidy, then I think it's only fair to insist that the Court be clear about what it is doing which requires that it admit it was wrong in dubbing the student organization forum a public forum in the first place. This means it was wrong to question the decision of Central Connecticut State College to reject a chapter of Students for a Democratic Society from its student organization forum;[221] that it was wrong to require the University of Missouri to open its facilities to religious student groups on the grounds of equal access;[222] that it was wrong to require the University of Virginia to fund a religious student paper on an equal basis as other student papers;[223] and that various lower federal courts were wrong to require Texas A&M, the University of Southern Mississippi, Virginia Commonwealth University, and the University of Southern Alabama to admit a variety of LGBTQ groups to their student organization forums.[224]

My argument on the *Martinez* case does not hinge on the Court either ruling that the student organization forum is a First Amendment forum or that it isn't. What is dangerous for the freedom of association is the Court's reasoning that upheld the student organization forum as a public forum, a place where First Amendment rights are practiced, and then permitted a public university to dictate the associational prerogatives of groups in that forum. Since the student organization forum is a place the state university creates so that groups may form it seems obvious that freedom of association is the primary right at issue. The Court's complete dismissal of that concern in a First Amendment forum is a grave threat to the status of freedom of association as a First Amendment right. As constitutional scholar Ashutosh Bhagwat writes, "Granting the state the power to dictate access to its property by fiat is essentially the power to denude [the rights of assembly and association], a result surely forbidden by the First Amendment."[225]

A counterargument to what is argued here regarding the role of associations in a limited public forum that implicates state property and state subsidy is that, regardless of the above analysis, CLS is still seeking RSO status and therefore state recognition and approval of its views.[226] As the majority in *Martinez* notes, CLS had the freedom to meet off campus without state recognition with all the rights of exclusion that entails.[227] The problem for the Court is that CLS sought "state subvention of [its] selectivity."[228] If CLS, or any group, does not seek state recognition, then they have full freedom "to exclude any person for any reason."[229]

The issue of state recognition confuses state recognition as state appropriation and state recognition as a securing of rights. While the issue of subsidy and student fees in the limited public forum was addressed in the previous sections, it is worthwhile to note here that entering a public forum is *not* seeking state recognition of one's views or of one's association. But when persons enter a public forum, such as a public park, to practice First Amendment rights they *are seeking government recognition of those rights.* The state is obligated to recognize their rights by refraining from censorship and even offering protection, no matter the content or viewpoint of the speech or other First Amendment acts.[230] An important implication of the First Amendment is precisely that these persons have a right to enter the forum, a right the government must, by definition, recognize. In terms of a limited public forum, a person has a right to the forum as long as he meets the specific limitations of the forum. In the case of student groups, the person or persons in question must be students of that university, but otherwise the logic of government recognition of their rights applies. CLS was not seeking "state subvention" of their group, but its members, as students of a public university that had established a student organization forum, were seeking only state recognition of their First Amendment right to freedom of association.

The subsidy issue and its relation to state recognition is similarly refuted. Subsidy, as it pertains to this case, is not state recognition. Some government "subsidy" is inevitable in any public forum. Inazu writes, "The public forum does not appear out of nowhere, with free meeting space for the forum and free electricity to keep the lights on. Government dollars pay for the spaces, the utilities, and the employees who make public forums possible. Facilitating pluralism means funding pluralism."[231] Inazu is arguing here that government funding for a First Amendment forum, whether a public park or a student organization forum, means inevitably funding for a diversity of groups and voices. In addition to the necessity of some government funding for public forums is the simple fact of "the ubiquity of government dollars in today's regulatory state."[232] If the state is allowed to claim that the use of all public dollars is government speech or government action, including student fees at public universities, then the work of many private groups becomes state-sponsored.

Inazu further argues, "We might be especially concerned when government constrains *generally available* funding in settings that welcome and encourage a diversity of viewpoints and ideas."[233] While this part of the argument would extend beyond the student organization funding issue to all generally available government funding, it is an important point that undergirds the proper use of funding for the student organization forum. The state can use resources to advance its own agenda through the use of "government speech."[234] But it should not discriminate based on a group's viewpoint in distribution of generally available resources. Funding for the student organization forum is this sort of government funding. It is funding for the forum, not funding for state-approved groups. This applies to Hastings in that a public university should not be allowed to refrain from extending generally available resources in the form of campus meeting space and student organization funding to any student group that meets the basic requirements of the limited public forum (i.e., being students at Hastings). This was the logic of the student fee cases such as *Healy, Widmar, Rosenberger,*[235] and *Southworth*. Inazu writes, "Public colleges and universities that establish forums for student organizations must welcome student organizations without regard to viewpoint or ideology. That includes extending generally available funding to them."[236]

The Fourteenth Amendment and the Extension of Restrictions on the State to Private Groups. The third area in *Martinez* where the Court treats a private group as a government entity is in its application of Fourteenth Amendment restrictions on the government to student groups.[237] The Court argued that CLS's conduct policy, which forbade "sexual conduct outside of . . . marriage between one man and one woman,"[238] was a veiled attempt to discriminate based on status.[239] The Court referenced *Lawrence*, which struck down a state law that prohibited homosexual conduct.[240] The Court explicitly cited a constitutional limitation on government—the Fourteenth Amendment proscription on discrimination grounded in the Due Process and Equal Protection Clauses—and applied it to private groups. Private groups are not state actors and are not supposed to be subjected to the strictures of the Fourteenth Amendment in the same manner as the state. The Court's extension of limits on state discrimination against private groups regarding beliefs demonstrates the theme of politicization: the Supreme Court defines private groups as essentially subdivisions of the state, subject to its restrictions, and works to make them primarily political units. Rights granted to individuals against government encroachment are expanded to protect individuals against private belief-based discrimination. The Court applied the principle that the state must treat citizens equally to private groups to ensure that they, like the state, cannot treat individuals unequally. The action of a private group was treated as state action.

The concurrences of Justices Stevens and Kennedy similarly reflect the idea that private associations are subject to constitutional proscriptions aimed at government action. Neither Kennedy nor Stevens referenced the Fourteenth Amendment, but their concerns tracked the majority's logic and concerns and applied constitutional restrictions on the government to private groups. For both justices, if a group acts in a student organization forum at a state university, it acts in the name of the state. Discussing the antidiscrimination policy of which the all-comers policy was part, Justice Stevens wrote, "The policy's religion clause was plainly meant to promote, not undermine, religious freedom."[241] His reasoning is that "all acts of religious discrimination are equally covered. The discriminator's beliefs are simply irrelevant."[242] Stevens was correct under the premises of the First Amendment Dichotomy. Individuals who hold religious beliefs may continue to hold those beliefs as individuals, but they may not form a cohesive group around their beliefs and enforce practices and lifestyle choices consistent with them. A restriction on government power over individual conscience was used to justify the requirement that private groups abide by the same restrictions as the state in their treatment of individuals.

Justice Kennedy's concurrence demonstrated a similar disregard for groups and a conflation of restrictions on nonstate associations with those that apply to the state. He wrote, "The era of loyalty oaths is behind us. A school quite properly may conclude that allowing an oath or belief-affirming requirement, or an outside conduct requirement, could be divisive for student relations and inconsistent with the basic concept that a view's validity should be tested through free and open discourse."[243] Like the Fourteenth Amendment issue, the proscription on loyalty oaths applies to the government but not to private groups. Churches may have creeds, and social groups may be arranged around loyalty to certain ideas, but liberal constitutional states may not.[244] Under Kennedy's conception, religious groups are not allowed to make a claim on their members by requiring adherence to certain belief-based tenets in order to be a part of the group. Such a neutral policy should apply to the state, but not to nonstate associations.

A response to the argument articulated above regarding state property and state action is that the Court was simply granting the university institutional independence. Rather than ignoring associational rights, the Court was recognizing the associational autonomy of the university to define for itself what sorts of lesser groups it allows within its domain. When the university dictated the terms of its student organization forum, it was doing so not as a state institution but as an institution independent of state control.[245] Under this view, the Court was wrong to take the case as a matter of limited public forum doctrine because this case simply does not implicate the First Amendment at all.

Both Paul Horwitz and Jacob Levy take this position on the case. Horwitz argues that CLS should be understood as a "nested institution" a smaller social entity that owes its existence to a larger institution.[246] When this happens, courts ought to defer to the highest institutional level. If there is a dispute between the Catholic Church and a Catholic university, the courts should allow the Catholic Church to resolve the dispute internally. The Catholic university is an institution nested within the larger institution of the Catholic Church itself.[247] It would be inappropriate for courts to intervene in such a dispute. Similarly, according to this argument, student groups are nested within the university, and courts should defer to the university.[248] Levy similarly describes "complex associations,"[249] which are associations that contain smaller associations within them. For Levy, the relationship between student groups and the university is a prototypical example of this type of association.[250] Like Horwitz, Levy would have courts defer to the highest level of the association. The basis of both Horwitz's "nested institutions" and Levy's "complex associations" is an explicit rejection of a firm distinction between public and private in the university context.[251] Both would treat particular categories of institutions and associations as having their own character and autonomy regardless of whether a specific institution is public or private. So courts would consider the category of the institution (i.e., library, university, voluntary association) and assign institutional rights based upon the categorical nature of the particular institution. Public libraries and private libraries, public universities and private universities would be treated the same by the courts with the same institutional rights appropriate to the category of library and university, respectively. Therefore, public institutions would not be constrained by the First Amendment but treated as First Amendment institutions with the same deference given to private institutions in the same institutional category.

Whatever the merits of that position as a whole, there is no need to abandon the traditional liberal demarcation between public and private in the case of universities.[252] When the state creates an institution and acts through it, as the Court believes it is doing in the case of public universities, then the Court should not grant institutional rights to the public institution in the same way it would to a private institution. This does not mean that the Court should not distinguish between types of public institutions. Certainly a public university ought to be treated differently than the post office, and public university professors ought to be recognized as having different rights and responsibilities than those of postal workers. But it means the Court ought to apply a nuanced analysis to public institutions and enforce the First Amendment where appropriate. Public universities should have the autonomy to carry out their educational mission but nonetheless be constrained in certain activities by the First Amendment. The organization of academic departments and administrative offices would be under the discretion of the university while the university's organization of a student organization forum would be constrained by First Amendment concerns. The simple reason for the distinction is that the former are not public forums, places where First Amendment rights are practiced, and the latter is. Regarding *Martinez*, I think that a pre-*Summum* limited public forum analysis is the most appropriate judicial treatment of the student group forum in a public university. This coheres with how the Court treated student group forums for several decades prior to *Martinez*.

Private Authority and the Regulation of Conduct

The Court's rejection of conduct as an aspect of speech was discussed above as part of the Court's theme of the individual and its role in associational expression.[253] This section examines how the Court refused to acknowledge the authority of a private group to regulate the conduct of its members. The Court's treatment of conduct reflected a deeper violation of group autonomy than simply an imposition on the speech rights of the group's individual members. It was a rejection of the collective (albeit limited) authority of the group over individuals within the group. In a sense, this is a combination or culmination of the Court's dichotomous conception of the individual and the state. By refusing to allow a group to determine membership based on conduct associated with the group's mission, the Court was denying a group's ability to maintain an existence independent of the state and the state's goals. Individuals should think of themselves only as individuals, not members invested in and loyal to a group and its ideals. State institutions should consider associations only as state appendages, not independent associations with their own prerogatives drawn from the ends for which the associations came into existence. The Court wrote, "The Law School's policy aims at the *act* of rejecting would-be group members without reference to the reasons motivating that behavior. . . . CLS's conduct—not its Christian perspective—is, from Hastings's vantage point, what stands between the group and RSO status."[254] The Court acknowledged that the internal motivations, beliefs, and thoughts of each individual member of CLS remain intact, and it justified its ruling on that basis.[255] But the *Martinez* ruling hindered group conduct, the ability of groups to exercise authority over their members in a manner that provides functional value by concretizing their belief system. The enforcement of rules regarding conduct through exclusion makes an association's presence felt to its members to a greater degree than if it merely forbade through exhortation. This element is important for an association's existence and activity independent of the state and for its importance in the lives of its individual members.

The dissent also did not understand the importance of this element of the case. While the dissent rejected some aspects of the Court's concept of the state, its treatment of group regulation of conduct indicated that it understood conduct simply as an aspect of expression and did not understand its role in the internal associational dynamics and identity of groups. The dissent wrote,

> This Court has held, however, that the particular conduct at issue here constitutes a form of expression that is protected by the First Amendment. It is now well established that the First Amendment shields the right of a group to engage in expressive association by limiting membership to persons whose admission does not significantly interfere with the group's ability to convey its views.[256]

The dissent's defense of group regulation of conduct was based on the role of conduct in expression, not on its role in group cohesion that is essential to group identity or on its importance to individuals through the concept of social role. As we discussed in the section above on "Speech and the Democratic State," the Court considers groups valuable for their effect on the state in terms of promoting dialogue. But groups do not matter in terms of their own purposes apart from bolstering the state, however democratic it may be. Once again, the dissent is indistinguishable from the majority in its fundamental theoretical orientation that identifies only the state and the individual in its analysis of First Amendment rights.

In the last chapter we discussed in detail how authority is an essential part of associations. By rejecting group authority, the Court was allowing a state university to participate in the process of individualization, separating group members from the cohesion of group authority. The Court was simultaneously permitting a public university to engage in the process of politicization by allowing the assertion of state prerogatives to trump the purposes of a social group. Nisbet believed that individualization and politicization often work in tandem to dichotomize the qualities of association toward the individual on one side and the state on the other. The Court's rejection of conduct-based requirements for nonstate associations demonstrates this point.

CONCLUSION

The First Amendment Dichotomy is the Court's theoretical framework consisting of the state and the individual as the exclusive categories of analysis of First Amendment rights, ignoring the role of associations in freedom of association. This framework forms the background to the Court's rendition of freedom of association in *CLS v. Martinez*, the latest installment of its freedom of association jurisprudence. The Court based its reasoning in *Martinez* on how Hastings's all-comers policy relates to individuals, understood as abstract, solitary entities bereft of social context and basically interchangeable, and the state university as a concretization of the political state and the primary source of identity and purpose for all individual students. This bifurcated hermeneutical framework warps the Court's understanding of freedom of association. When the associational right comes into play, the Court will defend it only on the basis of its value to the individual or to the state, and it will allow its restriction when the right of association does not explicitly serve the interests of either component of this dichotomy. The Court's theory, its way of *seeing* freedom of association, is determined by the First Amendment Dichotomy, which excludes groups from its analysis.

You need not agree with my critiques of the holding in *Martinez* or any of the other cases discussed in this chapter to agree that the Court simply does not have adequate theoretical tools to treat the freedom of association as a First Amendment right equal to freedom of speech. I think that it makes sense for the Court to treat a student organization forum at a public university as a First Amendment forum because it looks a lot more like a public forum where freedom of association and other First Amendment rights are practiced than it looks like a collection of academic departments or administrative offices. This leads me to think the Court should have ruled differently in *Martinez*. I could be wrong. Maybe the Court should overturn *Healy*, *Widmar*, *Rosenberger*, and *Southworth* and define the student organization forum as a nonpublic forum. Regardless, my primary critique is aimed at the *Martinez* Court's inability to treat freedom of association as a substantive First Amendment right, a theoretical shortcoming that was manifested in the Court's reasoning in freedom of association cases long before *Martinez*. This deficiency in the Court's jurisprudence is what I wish to remedy.

In the previous chapter I focused on political sociology and Nisbet's analysis of the category excluded from the First Amendment Dichotomy, the social group. My goal was to unpack the characteristics and identity of the particular type of social group at issue in *Martinez*, the voluntary association. In the next chapter I will turn again to political sociology to explain the specific qualities of associations that must be protected for voluntary associations to operate effectively. If we wish to correct the dichotomizing treatment of associations in the Court's jurisprudence, we will have to understand better the contours and extent of autonomy that ought to be granted to associations under First Amendment Pluralism.

4. First Amendment Pluralism: Authority, Allegiance, and the Functional Autonomy Test

First Amendment Pluralism is my alternative to the First Amendment Dichotomy as a framework for talking about First Amendment rights. It is based on a "theory of the social," a way of perceiving First Amendment rights that recognizes the reality of the social. This way of seeing in the judicial context constitutes First Amendment Pluralism, and it is precisely what is necessary for a healthy Supreme Court jurisprudence of freedom of association. I will now delve more deeply into the idea of First Amendment Pluralism, working out in detail the qualities that must characterize an effective freedom of association to protect the realm of autonomy appropriate to the voluntary association, to protect the particularly social elements of these social groups.

At the heart of this discussion are the concepts of authority and allegiance and their relation to function. These concepts accrue certain nuance as they apply specifically to voluntary associations within the context of liberal democracy. Here I will further explain these concepts with three compound terms, "functional integrity," "limited authority," and "conditional allegiance." These terms elucidate the nature of these concepts with regard to voluntary associations and show how various properties of associations work together. These concepts demonstrate the importance of the judicial test and sample legislation I develop later through which the Supreme Court can reintroduce the concept of the social group into its doctrine on freedom of association. My concern is to preserve the properties that voluntary associations must possess to be associations, to cement the social bond that effectively integrates members into groups, and to put the "social" into freedom of association.

FUNCTION, LIMITED AUTHORITY, AND CONDITIONAL ALLEGIANCE

Every group exists for some end, a function it performs, and it articulates that function as a dogma, "some transcending function," that constitutes the purpose of the group.[1] The dogma is the central tenets, the locus of shared beliefs that was the impetus for forming the group in the first place. Along with central tenets are the group's prescribed practices, which are collective and individual activities that the group agrees are inferred by the central tenets. This is the core of any community worthy of the name. The other five qualities that Nisbet attributes to community—authority, hierarchy, solidarity, status, and sense of superiority—are in service to or derivative of these two fundamental qualities. In this section I will explain how Nisbet's philosophy of pluralism allows voluntary associations to form and to thrive. Two elements, authority and allegiance, can be distilled out of Nisbet's four elements of pluralism that enable voluntary organizations to achieve functional significance and to maintain functional integrity, which are key to the value they hold for individuals. The free interaction of authority and allegiance demonstrates how the seven attributes of community can be achieved.

Imagine group and member as two poles of the association. The seven characteristics of a functional community emanate from one pole and connect it to the other, composing the substance of the interaction between the two. We can describe the relationship between group and member in terms of the authority proceeding from the group toward the individual and the allegiance flowing from the individual toward the group. Each characteristic of a functional community operates to facilitate that interaction, originating either in the authority of the group or in the allegiance of the individual member. The exercise of authority implicates function, dogma, and hierarchy. Through authority the hierarchy enforces its dogma, the central tenets, and prescribed practices of the group. Thereby it is able to perform its function. Allegiance is the response of the individual to the functional value the group bestows through execution of its function. It is what the individual gives to the group in return for the status, solidarity, and sense of superiority conferred by membership in the association.

Status connotes belonging. The need for status is fulfilled in voluntary associations because of their ability to achieve functional integrity around a shared mission, which allows an individual to belong to a group organized to achieve a purpose the individual believes to be important. All members of the group achieve solidarity around their central tenets and prescribed practices. Communing together according to particular practices and specifically defined beliefs give members a sense of community, solidarity with others in the group. Since each member devotes himself to the central tenets of the group and agrees to abide by its prescribed practices, the group has a sense of superiority in that each member believes the group's central tenets are worth believing and its prescribed practices are worth doing over and above tenets and practices of other groups. Any individual member could devote himself to a different set of central tenets and prescribed practices, but he does not do so because he believes his group's tenets and practices are superior. Authority and allegiance define both sides of the reciprocal, interactive relationship between association and individual member.

Further nuance is required to understand the interplay of these elements. To be a functional community, an association must be able to maintain its functional integrity, its ability to remain true to its function. The interaction of authority and allegiance are best understood by the use of two compound terms, limited authority and conditional allegiance, to further elucidate how each concept operates in the context of voluntary associations. The tentative nature of the words "limited" and "conditional" is intended to highlight the voluntary nature of these associations and head off criticisms from those who find in a defense of associations and the autonomous social realm composed of voluntary associations a lurking authoritarianism that would subject the individual to oppression. The freedom of association that I am advocating here is fundamentally liberal in this sense.

Functional Integrity

Functional integrity is the ability of a group to function in the manner in which the group claims to function, according to its central tenets and prescribed practices. Authority and allegiance matter for their role in maintaining a group's functional integrity. Only by preserving its functional integrity, actually functioning according to a group's professed central tenets and prescribed practices, may it perform the function it does in the lives of individual members. Functional integrity is the source of value that groups hold for individuals. This requires that associations exert authority, a hierarchy of role and function in their structure, to enforce the continued functional relevance of the association to individuals. And it is only on the basis of this functional integrity that associations are able to demand allegiance from their members.

Limited Authority

Voluntary associations, like other social groups, require a hierarchy to organize the group, to determine its purposes, to establish its central tenets, and to define and promulgate the means to accomplish its purposes. A group functions as a psychological support for individual members, providing reinforcement for their beliefs and practices, or as an expressive association providing unitary form to the members' collective voice, by exercising authority and enforcing the central purposes of the association.[2] The authority practiced by the hierarchy of voluntary associations is a limited authority, which means that the authority is limited to the purposes of the association, such as enforcement of belief in its central tenets and obedience to its prescribed practices. The use of the term "limited authority" implicates our discussion of the conditionality of authority discussed in chapter 3. Authority should not be confused with sovereignty. Sovereignty is by definition a total, absolute, and unlimited power, but authority is always limited according to the purposes of the group.

Conditional Allegiance

The corollary to limited authority in the relationship between association and member is the allegiance the individual gives to the association's authority, which is essentially the allegiance the individual gives to the association's central tenets and prescribed practices. The individual's allegiance to the group is a conditional allegiance. It is conditional upon his continued allegiance to the purposes of the group, its central beliefs and associated practices, as well as perpetual agreement with the means the hierarchy is implementing to accomplish its purposes.

The psychological and functional effect in the life of the individual member depends upon both the individual's continued alignment with the purpose of the group and the ability of the group to function meaningfully in the life of the individual by pursuing its purposes through collective assertion of its central tenets and enforcement of prescribed practices. This is the crux of the relationship between allegiance and authority. The ability of the association to function in the life of the individual relates directly to the limited authority of the hierarchy to enforce the rules associated with the group's purposes. The group functions meaningfully by being able to uphold the central tenets and enforce the prescribed practices of the group, which are the very conditions under which the individual offers allegiance to the group in the first place.

Exit and Exclusion

The inverse of authority and allegiance is exit and exclusion. If interaction between group and member ceases to function appropriately, then exit or exclusion results from the nature of limited authority and conditional allegiance. Just as there is reciprocity represented in the interaction between authority and allegiance, so there is a reciprocal relationship between the right of exit and the right of exclusion.

If the association no longer functions for the individual in the manner described above, the individual has the right of exit. This could happen for several reasons. The individual may cease to believe in the central tenets of the group's purpose or choose not to follow the incumbent practices the hierarchy requires. The individual could retain belief in the central tenets of the group but cease to believe that the required practices are inferred by the central tenets in the manner enforced by the hierarchy. It is also possible that the individual could retain belief in the central tenets of the group as well as its prescribed practices, but the group itself has evolved away from those beliefs and practices in such a manner that the individual no longer desires to offer allegiance to the group. In other words, the hierarchy has exerted authority in a manner so as to alter or undermine the founding dogma of the group, or it has refused to enforce the central tenets and prescribed practices in a way that would have maintained the functional integrity of the group for the particular individual. Given the voluntary nature of these types of associations, the right of exit is inherently secure for individuals who either cease to support the purpose of the group or who no longer receive the benefit of the function of the group.

The reciprocal right of exit for the individual member is the right of exclusion, which is the association's right to omit from its membership individuals who do not agree with the purposes or the inferred practices of the association but who have not exercised the right of exit and left the group on their own. The right to exclude is exercised by the hierarchy of the group that has the limited authority to enforce its own association's purposes and practices through, among other things, the exclusion of individuals from membership based on the purposes of the group.

The right of exclusion is an essential exercise of the authority of the group. The functional integrity of the group depends on its ability to effectively pursue its purposes through the means it finds appropriate. This requires a membership dedicated to the group's purposes. The association's continued fidelity to its purposes through the exercise of its authority depends on the exclusion of individuals from the group who do not support the purposes or means implemented under the limited authority of the hierarchy. Only on the basis of its functional integrity, its ability to operate meaningfully in the lives of the individual members, can the association claim the conditional allegiance of its members.

Recall that the notion of "exclusion" was precisely what was at issue in *Christian Legal Society v. Martinez*. This discussion indicates that exclusion is essential to the functional integrity of a group. Without the right of exclusion, a group does not have the ability to pursue its function, the purpose of its existence, by enforcing adherence to its central tenets and prescribed practices. Without the right of exclusion, neither CLS nor any other group at Hastings would have been able to maintain their functional integrity, along with all that entails for their members.

APPLICATION

Above I introduced two concepts, limited authority and conditional allegiance, to explain the relationship between association and member. The compound nature of the terms highlights the tentative and restricted nature of the voluntary association. In this section I will apply these concepts to an uncontroversial student group, a chess club, to demonstrate the importance of the principles of pluralism in allowing student groups to function adequately according to their purposes in the lives of individual members. Then I will apply the principles of pluralism to a religious student group, the type of voluntary association at issue in the *Martinez* case, before explaining their application specifically to CLS.

In order for a chess club to function meaningfully, it must have the ability to enforce the purpose of the group, which is to play chess, by exercising its authority to require its members to play chess and not other games, such as backgammon, at association events. A student who disagrees with this central tenet, that chess playing is valuable and ought to be done during club events, and who would rather play backgammon, either because he finds the game more appealing or comes to think that his time would be better spent playing backgammon, has the full right of exit to leave the group and to join a backgammon group.

By the same token, the chess club, to function meaningfully for the members who continue to believe that their time is best spent playing chess, must be able to exclude members who insist on playing backgammon. The chess club must have the limited authority over its members to enforce the purpose of the group in order for the members to be able to play chess unimpeded by members who think their time is better spent playing backgammon. In this way, the chess club would maintain its functional integrity and operate meaningfully in the lives of its chess-loving members. It would continue to provide the time and space for its members to play chess as well as the psychological support of camaraderie in a shared activity. The chess club's authority is limited to the purposes of the group, which is playing chess, and does not extend into other spheres of life. However, there may be prescribed practices, behavioral requirements that take up further time or affect its individual members outside of association events. For example, the chess club might require a certain amount of home practice each week, reading articles about chess or other items associated with chess playing.

If an individual objects to the prescribed practices, he may withdraw his allegiance. If a member believes that the prescribed practices do not further the central goals of the group or if he simply does not value them as appropriate practices, the member may refuse to give allegiance to the group by exercising the right of exit. If an individual does not desire to put in the prescribed amount of chess playing, then he may refuse to attend meetings. Such an individual's allegiance to the group is conditional upon its continued functioning in the individual's life for the purposes of which the individual joined the group. If the association's required practices do not function in such a manner, then the individual may withdraw his allegiance. The association may exercise a right of exclusion and expel such an individual from the group on the grounds that the individual is not sufficiently dedicated to the central tenets of the group to follow the group's required practices. If a member fails to put in the allotted hours of practice time, for example, the chess club may expel him from the group, finding his refusal to practice irrefutable evidence of a lack of devotion to chess playing. The allegiance of members to the group is conditional upon the purpose of the group, chess playing. The individuals take on the responsibilities of membership with the understanding that they will play chess and not backgammon or any other game at association events. The chess club, as a voluntary association, relies on this understanding of authority and allegiance in order for the group to function in the lives of its members in a meaningful way limited to the purposes of the group and to the means that accomplish those purposes.

The question of how strong a relationship should be between the functional integrity of the group and its central tenets and prescribed practices will differ from group to group. Some groups may have loose restrictions on only a few core tenets and provide only tepid advisory positions on prescribed practices, and others will be stricter when requiring its members to adhere to its central tenets and prescribed practices, and such a group may put a strong premium on the relationship between the two. The point is that each group will determine over time through its internal processes whether it is strict or lax in the enforcement of its central tenets and prescribed practices. A particular chess club may insist on members practicing at least a minimum prescribed amount of chess during the week between meetings. A different chess club may merely advise a certain number of hours.

There may be a dissonance between a group's claims regarding central tenets and prescribed practices and its actual functioning. Such a group may function in the lives of its members for socializing purposes and only superficially around central tenets such as the importance of playing chess. A chess club may require five hours of weekly practice but never actually enforce the requirement. Members may attend club meetings largely for the social aspects of the club and ignore the practice requirement of their membership responsibilities. By the same token, the value a particular individual receives from socializing with other members may be precisely that such socializing is with other individuals who adhere to the group's central tenets and prescribed practices. The weakening of shared belief in those tenets or the importance of those practices will then hinder the social value of the group to its members. Members of a chess club may have little in common other than playing chess, but to those who love playing chess, socializing is valuable because it takes place around that activity.

A chess club is unlikely to be a Gemeinschaft group for the majority of its members, since it only involves them in the practice of playing a board game. However, the friendships that arise around the playing of chess, especially to those who find intrinsic value in the game, may endow the group with the quality of Gemeinschaft. If the club facilitates this development, it will involve its members in much more than simply playing chess. The group will involve them in deep friendships around a shared love and camaraderie that will involve their whole person to a greater extent than it appears at first blush.

The concept of a reference group is also implicated in this discussion. The chess club may be the group to which an individual "refers" in terms of primary identity. This could be because the person may be very good at chess or have some other reason to value the intrinsic goods of chess. For whatever reason, the chess club is a reference group because it represents and reinforces the individual's identity as a chess player. The ability of the group to maintain its functional integrity is connected to the ability to operate as a reference group for this particular member whose identity is bound up with chess.

To put this discussion in slightly different terms, individuals may pursue membership in the chess club for intrinsic or extrinsic goods that they receive from group membership and participation.[3] Goods intrinsic to the practice of chess, such as exercising chess strategy, as well as concentration, competition, and comradery, are found within a club that provides the context for those goods. Extrinsic goods, such as resume padding or networking may also result from membership in the group.

The idea of intrinsic and extrinsic goods is essential to the definition of function. The function of a group may be the delivery of goods intrinsic to the purpose of the group and intimately related to its dogma. But another function may be provision of goods extrinsic to the purpose of the group. While in some moral sense the provision of extrinsic goods may be less significant than delivering intrinsic goods, such a judgment about the value of that particular group can only be made from within the group itself. What those intrinsic goods are and whether they are being achieved by their members can only be determined from within the practice itself, from those who are participating in the association.[4] The argument that a group is failing to deliver goods intrinsic to its function and dogma does not undermine the necessity of an association's functional autonomy even if the group is ultimately less morally significant to its members for that reason.

Nisbet's ideas of decentralization and tradition are applicable here. Each group decides whether it is a strict group or a lax group—and to what extent it is strict or lax—and it decides this over time through its own practices. In the same manner, each group decides to what extent it desires to deliver intrinsic goods or extrinsic goods. Individuals in need of stricter groups will congregate in those groups, with full right of exit if their needs or wants change, and others will congregate in laxer groups. Individuals in pursuit of intrinsic goods will join groups where such goods are available, and those in pursuit of extrinsic goods will join groups that enable such pursuits. Of course, these goods may be found in the same group. Nonetheless, each group will establish its own tradition, its own way of being that is appropriate to its purposes and the function it performs in the lives of its members and determine whether that function is the delivery of intrinsic goods or extrinsic goods. Each group must do this for itself, without centralized direction. These groups' functional autonomy and functional integrity depend upon their ability to develop their own character around the needs of their members through the development of traditions that emerge from interactions in that particular group. In such a way a group's intrinsic or extrinsic goods are provided in a manner appropriate to the members of that group.

Through the exercise of limited authority, a chess club is able to maintain itself as a functional community in Nisbet's terms. It has a dogma or a central tenet (chess playing), function (providing a forum for chess playing), limited authority exercised by a hierarchy that enforces chess playing, solidarity garnered by shared allegiance to chess playing, status by virtue of membership in a chess club, and a sense of superiority in that chess playing is more valuable, at least for these members, than playing backgammon or any other game at club events. While this discussion primarily implicates the intrinsic goods of chess playing, it bears repeating that such a judgment can only be made from within the association, by those who are participating not only in the practice of chess but in the practice of chess in that particular chess club.

Application to Religious Groups

The above example of a chess club is intentionally banal to demonstrate in an uncontroversial context the importance of functional autonomy and functional integrity and the relationship between authority and allegiance in securing the elements of a functional community in something as simple and seemingly trivial as a club organized around chess. Limited authority and conditional allegiance operate in the same manner for political and religious groups, although more controversially. The function of a religious group in the lives of religious believers, for example, is dependent upon the authority of the group to enforce beliefs and practices in keeping with the religious orientation of the group. Communal worship and fellowship valued by religious believers depend upon a certain agreement regarding central tenets of doctrine and prescribed moral and social practices that correspond to the needs and expectations of the members. The allegiance of the members to the group is conditional on the function of the group in their lives, on the delivery of these intrinsic goods, which in turn is dependent upon the limited authority of the group and its leadership to enforce the group's purpose and practices.

To demonstrate the application of these principles to a religious group, let's look at a group of Shakers, a sect of radical Protestant dissenters who believe that practicing celibacy is required of all people, not just a class of ordained people. A group of Shakers must be able to require that all members believe in its central religious tenets and prescribed practices, which include universal celibacy. Persons who believe in the central tenets of the Shakers regarding eschatology, pacifism, and equality of the sexes, but reject the practice of universal celibacy, could be justly excluded from the group on the grounds laid out above. The Shaker community has determined that universal celibacy is a practice essential to their central tenets and requires this practice of all members. The prescribed practice of universal celibacy is essential and not peripheral to a good Shaker life. The Shakers may then exercise the limited authority inherent in their association to exclude an individual who rejects an essential practice of the Shaker community.

This exercise of limited authority in the practice of exclusion is essential to creating the communal context for Shaker members who agree with the central religious tenets and adhere to its prescribed practices. The allegiance these individuals give to the Shaker community is conditional upon the community maintaining its Shaker values. Individuals who believe in the importance of universal celibacy and practice it in their own lives must be allowed to worship with those of like mind. It is essential to the functional value of the Shaker association in the lives of its members that it provides the context for a joint exercise of the prescribed practices. The ability to associate exclusively with those who agree with the particular practice of celibacy helps to reinforce its importance to the individual as well as to provide the context that will help all members live by the practices that they collectively believe are essential to a good Shaker life.

An individual excluded from the Shaker community would be free to join a group whose central tenets and prescribed practices were better in keeping with his own beliefs and practices. The authority of the group is limited to the beliefs and practices of the group itself. Reciprocally, an individual Shaker who comes to disagree with the practice of universal celibacy, or any of the other beliefs or practices of the group, may exercise the right of exit. The allegiance a member offers to the group is conditional upon the person's continued belief in the central tenets and prescribed practices of the group.

The qualities of Nisbet's functional community are much easier to discern in a religious community such as the Shakers because the dogma of such a group is explicit and often referred to in religious groups by the term "dogma." The Shakers have dogma, or central tenets, derived from Shaker theology, including belief in the importance of universal celibacy, as well as a function that is providing a forum for the practice of Shaker values, including the practice of universal celibacy. Limited authority is exercised by a hierarchy that enforces Shaker values and beliefs, and solidarity is garnered by shared allegiance to Shaker theology. Status exists in the Shaker group by virtue of membership in the Shaker community, and members have a sense of superiority in that they believe Shaker theology is true and the Shaker way of life is better than the alternatives.

A religious or a political group is much more likely to operate as a Gemeinschaft group and to serve as a reference group for an individual than is a chess club, although the fundamental principles at issue regarding functional autonomy and the other principles of pluralism are the same. Given the small nature of a Shaker commune and the great sacrifices and high standards that membership requires, individuals are much more likely to devote their whole personality to their Shaker identity. Indeed, the demands of the Shaker life requires the involvement of the whole personality of its members. The Gemeinschaft quality of the Shakers is related to the fact that religious organizations often demand a suffusion of religious influence throughout an individual's life. They further serve as reference groups because they provide a set of doctrines and a prescribed lifestyle to which persons may "refer" for their core identity. The same is true of nonreligious ideological groups such as political parties. Both religious and political groups offer ideological positions that strike much deeper to the core of a person's identity than hobbies like chess.

The importance of the functional integrity of the Shakers is bound inextricably to the exercise of limited authority through the right of exclusion and to its ability to function as a reference group for individual members. A person who sincerely believes in Shaker theology regarding eschatology, pacifism, equality of the sexes, and universal celibacy and seeks to exemplify a good Shaker life can offer allegiance that is conditional upon the group functioning in a way that maintains the integrity of the Shaker community around Shaker values. The allegiance of the individual and the individual's ability to "refer" to the Shaker group as central to his identity are conditional upon the group operating in a manner consistent with its central tenets and prescribed practices. The value of the group to the individual member is bound up with the exercise of the limited authority of the Shaker hierarchy, such as it is, to enforce belief in Shaker theology and lifestyle.

This example makes the application of extrinsic goods difficult. Most of what the Shaker community does must be intrinsically valuable to the individual member. But potentially the sacrifices of Shaker communitarianism would carry a certain prestige for a particular member. His temporary association in a Shaker commune may bring fame or legitimacy to him in some way later in life, say, if he were to write a book on the experience. He may join for a time for that reason. If he abides by the prescribed practices in a manner that the Shaker community considers acceptable to its functional integrity, then it may allow him to remain a member. It is possible that a member joins for an extrinsic good, such as the fame garnered from a book on the Shakers. However, over time, the pursuit of the extrinsic good gives way to intrinsic goods as the person becomes submerged in the Shaker lifestyle and community. Perhaps his initially insincere presence disrupts other members' devotion to Shaker teachings and practices, or maybe they appreciate the opportunity to demonstrate the value of their lifestyle to outsiders by accepting him into their community. Either way, the point is that only the group itself can determine whether such a member is—or is not—a threat to its functional integrity.

Application to Christian Legal Society

I applied the principles of pluralism to the Shakers in the thought experiment above for a similar reason that I used the chess club as our first example. Very few would object to the Shakers' right to maintain their principles, possibly because the Shakers have so few adherents that they do not offer a serious alternative idea-system to the ruling cultural paradigm. I doubt a group of Shakers has ever sought recognition on a university campus. However, these same principles apply to the Christian Legal Society. CLS has dogma, central tenets, derived from evangelical Christian theology.[5] As part of the prescribed practices that accompanied its dogma is the belief in the statement of faith that "a person who advocates or unrepentantly engages in sexual conduct outside of marriage between a man and a woman is not considered to be living consistently with the statement of faith." Such a person would be excluded from leadership and voting membership in the group. If a student believes in the dogma of CLS and agrees to abide by its prescribed practices, namely, refraining from "engag[ing] in sexual conduct outside of marriage between a man and a woman," then the student can be a voting member or a leader in the group.

The group clearly states in the statement of faith that its hierarchy will exercise its limited authority over the group to enforce its central tenets and prescribed practices. The purpose of the group derives from membership around shared dogma. The function of the group is to provide the context for shared worship and for a reinforcement of shared values. The allegiance offered to the group by its members is conditional upon the group enforcing its central tenets, drawn from evangelical dogma, and prescribed practices, including proscriptions on certain sexual behaviors. The right of exclusion exercised by the CLS hierarchy preserves the elements of functional community in the same manner that it preserves them for the hypothetical group of Shakers. In order for CLS to preserve a forum where CLS members could hold to their central tenets and engage in their prescribed practices, they would need to enforce the bounds of membership that hold to the same standards through the exercise of limited authority and the exclusion of would-be members who do not hold to the tenets of the group. Only in such a manner could the group maintain its functional integrity. The functional integrity of the group is the basis of its claim on the conditional allegiance of its members.

Individuals who find in CLS a reference group, meaning that they primarily identify as evangelical Christian lawyers, find an important source of reinforcement for their primary identity by being involved in such a group. In order for CLS to function as a reference group for these individuals, it must preserve its functional integrity as a group dedicated to evangelical Christian beliefs and values. Those beliefs and values serve an orienting function for particular individuals. In the eyes of those who adhere to them, these evangelical doctrines strike at the heart of what it means to be a human being. In a similar manner CLS may operate as a Gemeinschaft group. CLS implicates both religious and professional aspects of its members' lives, which is an expansive claim on their identity. It is a small, close-knit group that asks much of its members in terms of belief and practice and thus has potential to involve the whole personality of its members.

The analogue to the group's right of exclusion is the individual's right of exit. If a member disagrees with a tenet of evangelical dogma held by CLS or if the individual disagrees with the prescribed practices at issue with CLS, either because the member believes that CLS's central tenets are wrong or the member does not believe that the proscription on certain sexual practices is inferred by CLS's central tenets, that member would have the full right of exit. They could cease attending meetings and supporting the group. They could then join another group, or start their own group through the Registered Student Organizations process at Hastings Law School.

A Note on the Expressive Association

I have been critical of the idea of the "expressive association," spending considerable time on the problems associated with limiting freedom of association to its expressive component. I provided an alternative account of freedom of association. The problem with the doctrine of expressive association is that the dogma of a group, the core function for which it exists, may not be expressive or, at least, it may not be explicitly or primarily expressive. For example, the practice of universal celibacy by members of the Shaker community has an implicit message: that this way of life is good, and it is superior to others. However, the primary purpose of that practice is right living according to Shaker theology and the value that practice holds for members of that particular community in terms of their concept of right living.

The last point is the crux of the distinction between the inclusion of the social group as a conceptual category under First Amendment Pluralism and the Court's current doctrine of expressive association under the First Amendment Dichotomy. The goal of protecting the social group in terms of Nisbet's "functional community" is to preserve the value of dogma and function for the individuals who compose the group. This means guarding the associational context where dogma and function are instantiated. In contrast, the goal of the doctrine of expressive association is to protect individual speech for the purposes of the democratic state.

This criticism of expressive association is not intended to diminish its protections in First Amendment law. It has an important role in making the Speech Clause relevant to groups. But rather than understanding expressive association as the purpose of freedom of association, the Court should understand expressive association as one possible function of autonomous and constitutionally protected groups. The point of functionally autonomous groups is to preserve the realm wherein individuals may flourish, but it also serves as the realm wherein individuals may speak in unison with others and be strengthened for the purposes of democratic government.

The main flaw of consensus pluralism and current Court doctrine is that it reverses these priorities. The goal of freedom of association is the preservation of the social group. One benefit of preserving the social group is what the social group does for democratic government through the expressive association. But what the social group may do for democratic government as an expressive association is not the goal of freedom of association as such. It is simply one benefit. To put this in the textual terms of the First Amendment: individuals may exercise the right of assembly for any peaceful purpose, one of which is the exercise of freedom of speech. But speech is not the only reason, or even the most important reason, for which individuals may assemble. Regarding the *Martinez* case, the important point is that the CLS chapter is able to preserve its functional autonomy, not that it serves as an "expressive" medium for its members' views on religion or sexuality. Even if the doctrine of expressive association would have caused CLS to prevail in the case, Court doctrine would still miss the heart of the matter: freedom of association is the right to associate around shared dogma and to preserve the functional integrity of the group so that it may serve as a "functional community" for its members.

THE FUNCTIONAL AUTONOMY TEST: CREATING THE JUDICIAL CONTEXT FOR A LAISSEZ-FAIRE OF GROUPS

The theoretical underpinnings of the voluntary association implicate the manner in which groups integrate individuals into their membership and act as functional communities providing individuals with functional value around shared beliefs. Three terms demonstrate this property: functional integrity, limited authority, and conditional allegiance. Even a chess club needs limited authority to maintain its functional integrity and garner the conditional allegiance of its members. The final step is to determine how Nisbet's understanding of pluralism and the laissez-faire of groups may be made concrete in judicial doctrine to instantiate First Amendment Pluralism and to protect freedom of association. The social presence of voluntary associations as functional communities needs an analogue in constitutional law. Where the association exists in society, it should have a category of constitutional protection: a properly defined freedom of association protected by the Assembly Clause.

Nisbet's goal with a laissez-faire of groups is to "create conditions within which autonomous groups may prosper."[6] He emphasizes that the use of the word "create" is purposeful. He believes the state created the context for the old laissez-faire of individuals through the planned destruction of groups and that public policy and federal jurisprudence can "create a laissez-faire in which the basic unit will be the social group."[7] Writing in the preface to the 1970 edition of *Quest*, Nisbet closes with a discussion of the need for this type of social planning. He writes that planning "is indispensable in the kind of world that technology, democracy, and high population bring. Conservatives who aimlessly oppose planning, whether national or local, are their own worst enemies."[8] What he means by "planning" is "planning that contents itself with the setting of human life, not human life itself."[9] If properly informed by Nisbet's social perspective, a certain planning on the part of the state, including a jurisprudence of freedom of association, may help to secure the context within which groups may flourish in modern society. Broader public policy prescriptions are beyond the scope of this book, although the argument I present here has broad ramifications for the debate over faith-based organizations and the like. While Nisbet did not discuss specific reforms for any branch of government to create the context for a laissez-faire of groups, he hoped for large political reforms along the lines he suggests.

I will use the four principles of Nisbet's philosophy of pluralism to craft a judicial test and sample legislation to guide the Court toward recognizing the voluntary association in First Amendment law and respecting its autonomy. The goal is to create the context for groups to flourish within judicial doctrine by securing freedom of association (grounded in Assembly) as a "right cognate to those of free speech and free press, and . . . equally fundamental."[10] Such a freedom of association will provide a plurality of voluntary associations with the requisite autonomy to serve as functional communities for their individual members. It provides a practical means for the Court to expand its theory of the First Amendment to account for the presence of the voluntary association in its social fullness—to put the "social" into freedom of association.

Judicial Solution: The Functional Autonomy Test

First Amendment Pluralism is a theoretical paradigm that allows the Court to see associations in addition to individuals and the state for purposes of judicial analysis. Below I propose a test to provide a way for the Court to incorporate First Amendment Pluralism into its jurisprudence. This judicial test is a practical means of removing the blinders from Supreme Court analysis that blocks associations from view and instituting a judicial mechanism that secures freedom and functional autonomy for voluntary associations. It adapts the four principles of pluralism into a four-part test to guide the Court. Most Supreme Court tests are named after the cases in which they are articulated. For now, I will call this the functional autonomy test, since its goal is to secure Nisbet's first principle of pluralism, functional autonomy, for the association under judicial analysis. This test applies strict scrutiny through the "compelling interest test" to any restrictions on freedom of association, even restrictions taking place within a limited public forum.

When a government entity, including a state university, enacts a policy that restricts freedom of association, it must consider the following:

1. *Does the policy inhibit the functional autonomy of the group?* In a free society, groups should be allowed to form around a plurality of dogmas, central tenets, and prescribed practices that organize and provide meaning to individuals. A plurality of functions is necessary for a healthy society that recognizes the "variety [that] extends into the many directions of man's interests."[11] In order to inhibit the functional autonomy of an association, a government entity must meet two criteria: the proposed restriction must be driven by a compelling government interest, and the means it pursues must be narrowly tailored to accomplish that end.[12]

2. *Does the policy inappropriately centralize power?* A state entity generally should not take action in a way that arrogates social authority from its location in a voluntary association without compelling justification. A helpful way to articulate this prong is to consider it from the vantage point of individual allegiance. The question could be formulated as follows: through the proposed policy does the state improperly appropriate the allegiance of individuals from a nonstate social group?

3. *Does the policy improperly inhibit exercise of the association's rightful authority to uphold the association's central tenets and prescribed practices?* A government entity may not impede an association's exercise of authority except where the right of exit is placed in jeopardy.

The government may not force inclusion of unwanted members or otherwise impede the exercise of an association's authority over its members. Just as the right of exit is an essential individual right, so the right of exclusion is an essential associational right necessary to the functional integrity of a voluntary association.[13]

4. *Does the policy inappropriately interfere with the tradition of a group?* Every association develops its own internal norms. This is true of all groups, from romantic couples to multinational corporations to nation-states. Each develops its own culture and way of conducting associational activities that are essential to the life of the group and to its ability to maintain its functional integrity. Government entities must take into consideration the tradition of the group and the way in which an association's particular culture may have grown organically from the ends to which the association was established and to which members of the group have consented, if not endorsed through the principle of interaction. Interference with tradition, the internal norms and ways of being, is an interference with the functional autonomy of the group. As always with voluntary associations, members may exit at any time, and the government must enforce the individual right of exit.

If the association is formed within a limited public forum, the government may generally only limit the functional autonomy of the group according to the clear and specific limitation of the forum. A limited public forum is not a nonpublic government forum. The practice of First Amendment rights in this context is not government action. A public university may limit its student group forum to students at its own university, but it may not limit associational prerogatives beyond that without triggering the functional autonomy test.[14]

The goal of each of these prongs is to preserve a plurality of groups of all sizes, especially the small groups that are essential to a person's well-being. As one scholar comments on Nisbet's understanding of the purpose of groups, "Associations must . . . be very small because it is essential that interactions be face-to-face. However, it is also necessary that these small associations carry out significant functions so that the interactions . . . operate meaningfully in people's lives."[15] Student groups very nearly fit this description for their student members. But to maintain their distinctiveness of function in the lives of students, they require the ability to police their membership.

Legislative Solution:
The Freedom of Association Preservation Act (FAPA)

A judicial remedy is helpful but not necessary to secure First Amendment Pluralism. The context for a laissez-faire of groups could also be implemented through properly designed legislation. Below I sketch out a legislative proposal called the Freedom of Association Protection Act (FAPA). Much like the bipartisan Religious Freedom Restoration Act (RFRA) passed nearly unanimously by Congress in 1993, FAPA would aim to protect an essential First Amendment right that federal courts have devalued. Just as RFRA was a congressional response to the Supreme Court's decision in *Employment Division v. Smith*,[16] which it rightly saw as an egregious threat to religious liberty, FAPA would be a congressional endeavor to protect the freedom of association as it was threatened by the Court in *Martinez* and previous cases in the same line of expressive association jurisprudence.

In *Smith*, the Supreme Court upheld the denial of unemployment benefits to two Native Americans who were fired for using peyote in a Native American religious ceremony. The Court argued that laws of general applicability could be enforced against religious institutions, despite the fact that this particular law interfered with a Native American religious rite. In *Martinez* the Court similarly upheld a policy that was "reasonable" and "viewpoint neutral," despite the fact that its content disproportionately affected the membership requirements of a particular group. The goal of RFRA was effectively to reverse the *Smith* decision, requiring federal courts to use strict scrutiny when considering laws and policies affecting religious liberty, even those of general applicability. In *City of Boerne v. Flores, Archbishop of San Antonio*,[17] the Supreme Court struck down the aspects of the law that applied to state laws and provisions, ruling that Congress exceeded the scope of its enforcement power. In response, a number of states have passed state level RFRAs to similarly restrict the ability of their own legislatures and localities to implement ordinances of general applicability that restrict religious liberty. The language of FAPA is intended for use at both the federal and state levels, so the wording of particular clauses would need to be altered to account for its context.

The Freedom of Association Protection Act advocated here requires that federal courts treat the freedom of association as an essential First Amendment right, one that is located in the textual right of assembly and on par with the freedom of religion, speech, and press that the Court has effectively protected from government interference at the federal, state, and local levels. I do not call it the Freedom of Association Restoration Act, because the Court's jurisprudence on freedom of association has never been particularly protective, and it has not effectively explored the potential for protecting association in the Assembly Clause. It would not be adequate to return to *Roberts* or even to *NAACP*, because of the Court's connection between speech and association in those cases. My proposals are intended to secure freedom of association as an independent First Amendment right, one that is located in the Assembly Clause and untethered to speech but equally protected and treated as "equally fundamental."[18]

Below is the sample FAPA. Most of the language is lifted directly from RFRA, but it is adapted to the essential purposes and protections necessary to freedom of association.

Freedom of Association Preservation Act
  a. Findings
    The Congress (or state legislature) finds that—
    1. The framers of the Constitution, recognizing the freedom of association as an essential right, secured its protection in the right to peaceably Assemble in the First Amendment to the Constitution;
    2. Laws or policies "neutral" toward associations may burden the freedom of association just as surely as laws or policies intended to interfere with the freedom of association;
    3. The textual restriction on assembly and association—that they be peaceable—forbids governments from substantially burdening freedom of association without compelling justification;
    4. The limited public forum is an important category of constitutional protection especially in places that carry out specific types of government activity, such as public universities;
    5. In *Christian Legal Society v. Martinez* (2010) the Supreme Court virtually eliminated the requirement that the government justify burdens on the freedom of association imposed on laws or policies neutral toward the association in a limited public forum; and
    6. The compelling interest test as set forth in prior Federal court rulings is a workable test for striking sensible balances between First Amendment rights, such as freedom of association and competing governmental interests.

b. Purposes

The purposes of this chapter are—

1. To require the compelling interest test as set forth in *Sherbert v. Verner*, 374 U.S. 398 (1963) and *Wisconsin v. Yoder*, 406 U.S. 205 (1972) and to guarantee its application in all cases where freedom of association is substantially burdened; and

2. To provide a claim or defense to persons or associations whose freedom of association is substantially burdened by government.

a. In General

Government shall not substantially burden a person's freedom to associate or assemble with others for any peaceable purpose; nor shall the government substantially burden the functional autonomy of any association; nor shall it centralize power in a manner that transfers the allegiance of persons from an association to itself; nor shall it improperly inhibit the exercise of an association's authority to uphold its central tenets and prescribed practices; nor shall it inappropriately interfere with the traditions, the internal norms, of an association.

b. Exceptions:

Government may burden the exercise of a person's or group's freedom of association only if it demonstrates that the application of the burden to the functional autonomy of the association

1. Is substantially interfering with an individual's right of exit; or

2. A. Is in furtherance of a compelling government interest; and
   B. Is the least restrictive means of furthering that compelling governmental interest.

c. Judicial Relief

A person or an association may assert a violation of freedom of association as a claim or a defense in a judicial proceeding and obtain appropriate relief against the government. Standing to assert a claim or defense under this section shall be governed by the general rules of standing under Article III of the Constitution.

As used in this chapter:

1. Government includes a branch, department, agency, instrumentality, and official (or other person acting under color of law) of the United States (or of a state), or of a covered entity;

2. The term "covered entity" means the District of Columbia, the Commonwealth of Puerto Rico, and each territory and possession of the United States;

3. The term "freedom of association" means both the freedom of a person to associate with others for any lawful and peaceable purpose and the right of an association to establish boundaries of membership according to its own internal articulation of central tenets and prescribed practices that do not threaten the public peace. Freedom of association is a right required by the Assembly Clause of the First Amendment.
4. The term "central tenets" refers to fundamental beliefs, no matter how profound or mundane, that guide an association and that form its founding purpose, the end for which it exists.
5. The term "prescribed practices" refers to actions or prohibitions from acting required of members by the organization that it asserts are associated or important to its central tenets.
6. The term "traditions" refers to the ways and means, written or unwritten, that guide the internal workings of an association in ways sometimes opaque to outside observers.

Applicability
   a) In general
   This chapter applies to all federal (or state) law, and the implementation of that law, whether statutory or otherwise, and whether adopted before or after date passed.
   b) Rule of Construction
   Federal (or state) statutory law adopted after date passed is subject to this chapter unless such law explicitly excludes such application by reference to this chapter.
   c) Other First Amendment Rights Unaffected
   Nothing in this chapter shall be construed to affect, interpret, or in any way allow the federal (or state) government to prohibit freedom of speech or infringe upon the free exercise of religion or otherwise affect rights that adhere to expressive associations and religious organizations.

I noted earlier that the account of freedom of association given in this book was nonperfectionist. Neither the functional autonomy test nor FAPA is intended to solve all problems related to freedom of association in First Amendment law. The purpose of these two remedies is to provide the judiciary with a means of securing the existence of functional communities, especially in the form of the voluntary association, against government intrusion in a variety of contexts. They are designed to provide the Court with a way of seeing the social group so that it can recognize associations in judicial doctrines and jurisprudence. The language above is tentative, using such qualifiers as "inappropriately" and "improperly," because the Court will need to interpret in context the meaning of each prong. The Court will further have to balance and blend doctrines of the social group with existing First Amendment doctrines, which will include some doctrinal pruning. The point is that where the First Amendment Dichotomy of state and individual form the conceptual underpinnings of freedom of association doctrine, I want a First Amendment Pluralism to take its place, one that recognizes not only the category of association in addition to the individual and the state, but also the inherent plurality of functionally autonomous associations.

Alternatives to the Functional Autonomy Test and the Freedom of Association Protection Act

Others have wrestled with the problem of the vanishing freedom of association and offered their own solutions to the challenges presented by the *Martinez* case. Some of these are judicial remedies, and at least one is an explicit legislative remedy. Below I compare those solutions to the functional autonomy test required by FAPA. Fundamentally, the criticism of each of these proposed solutions is that they fail in one way or another to conceptualize the social group and to offer a theory of associations, a way of seeing associations, that properly reorients judicial doctrine and public policy, which is the primary goal of my proposals.

John Inazu proposes a revival of the First Amendment right of assembly, which he argues functioned like a right of association without the baggage of attaching association only to its intimate or expressive functions. Inazu writes, "The right of assembly protects the members of a group based not upon their principles or politics but by virtue of their coming together in a way of life."[19] He encourages lawsuits under the Assembly Clause rather than under the doctrine of freedom of association.[20] Inazu points out that the Assembly precedents, while unused for more than three decades, would provide better ground for protecting group rights than the anemic freedom of association precedents.

The functional test proposed above would not be at odds with Inazu's proposal. If anything, they are mutually supporting strategies. While Inazu is focused on the textual support for the right of associations to exist for their own sake, the goal of social group analysis on the basis of functional autonomy and the like is to provide the conceptual framework for the same right. The functional autonomy test provides the judiciary with a means of determining whether or not the state is impinging upon the functional autonomy of the group, an autonomy that Inazu believes (and I agree) is protected under the Assembly Clause.

Erica Goldberg proposes an independent test for expressive association that would constitute "a separate standard . . . that appreciates the differences between speech rights and associational rights."[21] She offers two versions. In the first, she argues that the Court should treat expressive association as an independent right in a limited public forum by applying the standards of *Roberts* and *Hurley*, but using "intermediate scrutiny" instead of rational basis when the government policy applies to a limited public forum. The government would need to prove that its policy was reasonable and narrowly tailored in such a way that the policy does not hinder expressive association. If the government objectives of tolerance and cooperation could be achieved in a fashion less onerous to expressive association, then the state would be obliged to pursue those alternatives. Goldberg's second proposal is to apply the free speech test in a limited public forum, which would require viewpoint neutrality, but modify the requirement of viewpoint neutrality so that it would not "target the inclusion or exclusion of certain viewpoints" by student groups.[22]

Both proposals would help the judiciary protect expressive associations. They have the further benefit of working within existing Supreme Court case law on expressive associations. However, that benefit is at the same time a drawback in terms of the broader right of association at issue. By focusing on the expressive viewpoints of groups, the tests for expressive association still renders the associational right of the group dependent on the individual right of expression. The functional autonomy test aims to direct the Court's attention to the right of association of the group itself, apart from whether it is primarily an expressive association.

Jack Willems argues that every expressive association claim the Court considers must "pass both the freedom of speech and the freedom of association tests because any rule that restricts expressive association necessarily discriminates against the viewpoint that expressive association is a valid means of conveying one's message and thus cannot be viewpoint neutral."[23] The virtues and drawbacks of this proposal are the same as for Goldberg's proposal.

Working within the case law on freedom of association as it has been rendered by the Court (i.e., as expressive association) limits the existing test's ability to adequately protect the functional autonomy of groups, which is the aim of any freedom of association worthy of the name.

David Brown proposes a "Higher Education Equal Access Act" that would essentially overturn the *Martinez* decision through legislative directive by "requir[ing] a school to tolerate speech and expressive association."[24] This proposal calls for a piece of federal or state legislation that mandates equal access to university facilities "for student groups regardless of the groups' religious, political, or philosophical speech and associational activities."[25] The act would recognize the university's power to maintain order but "require the application of strict scrutiny analysis to any restrictions imposed on access to a student-group forum."[26] This proposal would correct the errors of the *Martinez* decision through legislative action, similar to FAPA described above. But our proposed legislation is broader, aimed at correcting *Martinez* not just in its application to student groups but in its potential application to freedom of association more generally, including its exercise in limited public forums beyond the university.

One of the most interesting proposals is to apply the "ministerial exception" established in *Hosanna-Tabor Evangelical Lutheran Church and School v. EEOC* 565 U.S. 171 (2012) to religious student organizations. Kyle Cummins argues that courts should treat groups like CLS as "religious organizations and treat their leaders as 'ministers.'"[27] If courts do so, they would then apply the same exception that applies to the employment decisions for ministers to the process of choosing leaders of religious student groups. We need not explore the arguments for how CLS would fit the Court's definition of a "religious organization" to accept the merit of the proposal for the particular CLS case. Where this option is not helpful is in the protection of freedom of association beyond that of religious groups. My proposals would protect the right of secular associations that form functional communities around central tenets and prescribed practices to maintain their functional autonomy, no matter their goals and ideological orientation.

A proposal by Rene Reyes would change the analysis for *Martinez* to a question of Free Exercise.[28] While an interesting proposal, it also would not apply to nonreligious groups. It has the same limitation as the "ministerial exception" proposal. The issue of functional autonomy for associations that are not explicitly religious would remain a problem in Supreme Court doctrine.

Because my proposals are derived from a "social" perspective, they would protect the right of association for secular as well as religious groups, providing a theoretical foundation to the First Amendment that would help the Court to see groups of all sorts for First Amendment protection.

Points of Clarification: Large Organizations and the Indeterminacy of Dogma and Function

There are two points of clarification that I wish to make about my application of Nisbet's principles of pluralism to judicial doctrine through the functional autonomy test and FAPA. These points have been covered previously, but if missed I think they would cause my proposals to be misapplied in First Amendment jurisprudence to the considerable detriment of freedom of association. The first is the appropriate application of freedom of association to large organizations, and the second is the indeterminate nature of dogma and function at the heart of associations.

The fundamental argument of this book is that the American state is constrained by the First Amendment in its relationship to associations. But what sort of associations? I suggested that there are a variety of associations that would be protected under this understanding of freedom of association but that in a liberal society groups often take the form of the voluntary association. One important point to emphasize is that freedom of association applies to the relationship between the state and both large and small associations, those that are Gemeinschaft as well as Gesellschaft. The defense of small associations as the plausible location for the personal allegiance associated with the concepts of Gemeinschaft and reference group should not be taken as an implicit argument that freedom of association does not apply to large organizations.[29] It would be a grave violation of freedom of association for the state to interfere in the inner workings of large organizations even on behalf of embattled small groups within them. The seven characteristics of functional community apply to large organizations as well as to small ones. Large organizations are psychologically effective in integrating individuals precisely through the small groups contained within them. It is essential that members devoted to the central tenets of the large organization are able to instantiate and participate in those tenets through prescribed practices in the functional context of small groups established for that purpose by the large organization. The small group provides the sense of solidarity and belonging associated with status and makes concrete the authority of the umbrella organization in the individual's life. However, the sense of superiority and the status of the member is derived from membership in the large organization. In Nisbet's "social" terms, the large organization is the "reference group," the one whose central tenets are the point of reference for the individual member.

Interference on behalf of the liberty of these small groups, what Horwitz called "nested institutions," would make impossible the ability of large organizations to be effective in enforcing their central tenets and prescribed practices. The functional autonomy of large organizations depends upon their control over the constituent groups nested within them. The value individuals get from these sorts of small groups is that they are repositories of the dogma of the large organization, making it concrete in members' lives. The ability of the large organization to exercise authority over the smaller groups is essential to the functional integrity of the organization and to its ability to function effectively in the lives of its myriad members.

Consider the example of the Roman Catholic Church. It is an enormous organization with very defined dogma in the teachings of Catholic theology and clear function, the reconciling of its adherents to the Christian God through its sacraments. It is a "complex association," to use Jacob Levy's term, composed of many parishes, universities, cloisters, religious orders, and the like.[30] My argument should not lead one to challenge the authority of the Catholic hierarchy on behalf of the lesser associations embedded within it. Catholic universities do not have a First Amendment freedom of association claim against the Catholic hierarchy. Rather, I want to emphasize that the purposes of the Catholic Church are made concrete to its individual adherents through these lesser associations and that protection for such large organizations follows the same logic as that for small associations. For many adherents, the goods the church provides are not identified with the smaller association per se, but they are considered important because the smaller association is an integral part of the large organization. The Roman Catholic Church is the reference group, the entity the individual refers to for personal identity as a Roman Catholic. The value such an individual derives from association with the local parish or monastery is that these institutions are explicitly connected to the larger organization of the Church. The Roman Catholic Church cannot serve as an effective Gemeinschaft organization because of its size in terms of truly integrating members into its values. But through the establishment of smaller groups in the form of local parish churches, it is able to provide the personal, face-to-face interaction that encompasses the whole person to an extent not possible if the Catholic Church could not establish and exercise authority over these lesser associations. The same applies to other large associations.

Let's return for a moment to the facts of the *Martinez* case. Why doesn't the "larger organization" principle hold for public universities and their relationship to student groups? Doesn't it make sense that student groups are smaller associations nested within the larger organization? This principle certainly applies at a private university. As a nongovernment institution, a private university is not constrained by the First Amendment in how it treats its student organization forum. Such decisions are a matter of internal policy. Many private universities do accord their students and faculty members corollaries to First Amendment rights and therefore may be contractually required to uphold those rights, including those claimed by student groups, but they are not required to do so as a matter of the First Amendment.[31]

The Court has held repeatedly and (I believe) rightly that the public university is a government entity constrained by the First Amendment in some ways, one of which is its treatment of private groups of students that enter the student organization forum. In other ways, the "larger organization" principle does apply to public universities, such as in their relationship to colleges, academic departments, administrative offices, and the like because these are all nonpublic forums, spaces that the public university creates to carry out its academic mission with no relationship to First Amendment rights. No one could plausibly argue that faculty members have a First Amendment right of association to create a new academic department at a public university. But, as I argued contra Horwitz and Levy, student groups in the public university are not governed by this "larger organization" principle, which Horwitz and Levy describe in terms of "nested organizations" and "complex associations." Rather, student organization forums at public universities are governed by public forum doctrine. When the state university creates a student organization forum, it is creating a public forum, a place where First Amendment rights are practiced.[32] It does not have to create that forum, but once it does, it is constrained by the First Amendment in how it treats groups in that space.[33] This includes protections for freedom of association.

The second potential problem with my description of groups is that my emphasis on dogma and function at the heart of associations makes group identity too propositional and implies that the judiciary should consider whether an organization is "sincere" or even sufficiently clear in its assertions and adherence to dogma and function. By "propositional," I mean that a group's purpose is tethered to a clearly defined dogma, a set of tenets laid out in what amounts to a written constitution. Often a group's dogma is clarified and articulated over time as a group identifies ideas and would-be members that fall outside of the group's functional purview. This can take place in fits and starts. A propositional view of groups would imply both that a group's central tenets are clearly defined from the outset and that the connection between central tenets, function, and prescribed practices is easily identified.

As implied in the discussion of intrinsic and extrinsic goods and the analysis of the relationship between central tenets and prescribed practices, the precise nature of dogma and function can sometimes be determined only from inside the association. Furthermore, members may receive great value from a group through external goods or in ways that are not discernible to the outside observer or not easily connected to the claimed dogma and function of the group. As Inazu writes, "A group's protections shouldn't turn on whether its purposes or activities are sincere or wholesome from an outsider's perspective."[34] The goods of association can only be realized and judged as adequate from within the association itself. When considering associations' functional autonomy, the judiciary must not ignore this fact and take great thought before it substitutes its own judgment in these matters for that of the group.

Race and Functional Autonomy

I have described the purpose of social groups, especially the voluntary association, and applied Nisbet's principles of pluralism to judicial doctrine. But so far I have avoided the application of these principles to the issue of race. How would the principles of pluralism undergirding the functional autonomy test apply to a voluntary association that had a dogma asserting racial separation and a function of gathering people of one race together? I suspect this is the most controversial issue surrounding freedom of association. Below I lay out what I see as the contours of potential applications of my theory to this question. Underlying this issue is the context of public forum doctrine. The application of any theory, including my own, is complicated, and even the author can remain unsure of how his theory plays out. Through this discussion I don't want to lose sight of the fundamental insight of this book: the necessity of the "social" perspective to any analysis of freedom of association.

In this book I am discussing voluntary associations such as CLS. My argument would not apply in the commercial context or to educational institutions' tax exemption status or to quasigovernmental groups.[35] What I have to say here would not affect the Court's analysis on *Runyon v. McCrary*[36] or *Bob Jones University v. United States*.[37] Even if federal courts implemented my theory and further decided that it allows racial discrimination in voluntary associations, the functional autonomy test or FAPA need not permit businesses to discriminate on the basis of race or educational institutions with racist policies to receive tax exemption status. International corporations, hotels, restaurants, and the like would not be able to claim the functional autonomy test as constitutional protection for rejecting patrons or refusing to hire employees on the basis of race (or any other protected status). Furthermore, I do not think this would apply to a private neighborhood association, which takes on a quasigovernmental role in regulating land use and the like.[38] There would be no need for amendments to the Civil Rights Acts or anything like that. We are only considering whether and in what context a voluntary association might set its membership boundaries on the basis of race. We will specifically ask whether a group practicing the right of association in a limited public forum in an educational institution may have such membership requirements. There are three ways to look at this issue: status is different, race is different, and what John Inazu calls "confident pluralism."[39] Each has its problems, but I think the third is the most consistent and takes most seriously the constitutional reality of freedom of association grounded in an independent First Amendment clause. That said, I think in certain contexts, the second strikes an acceptable balance between competing concerns.

The first is the "status is different" approach. This means that a group could exclude on the basis of belief in racial separateness but not on the basis of race itself. In other words, my theory protects the formation of groups around dogma, central tenets of belief, but not necessarily a particular static criterion like race or, for that matter, gender, sexual orientation, and the like. Under this standard, "discrimination on the basis of one's conduct or belief is permissible but discrimination on the basis of one's status is not."[40] Problems emerge from both sides with this perspective. On the one hand, it's not clear "why conduct-based discrimination is any less harmful or less problematic than status-based discrimination from the perspective of those who are excluded from a group."[41] If the harm of exclusion is the problem, then exclusion on any basis is problematic. On the other hand, whatever the harm is to the excluded person, this approach is underprotective of groups in a pluralistic society. I have explained at length the necessity of exclusion to the functional integrity of the group and the association's ability to act upon its members in an important way. This approach would not protect an LGBTQ social club or a sorority or, for that matter, CLS.

Think about it this way. While it would seem to be an advance for LGBTQ persons that sexual orientation is considered a status and not a belief or associated conduct and therefore not a valid criterion for discrimination in a voluntary association,[42] the ability to discriminate on the basis of status is what allows LGBTQ groups to close membership around sexual orientation. The first gay rights group in America had precisely this requirement, and some early LGBTQ student groups did as well.[43] Allowing for a broad right of functional autonomy, which includes discrimination on the basis of status, would protect rights of status minorities (including sexual orientation minorities) to form groups around their status.

The second option is what Inazu calls the "race is different" approach. This holds that racial discrimination alone may be excluded from the terms of freedom of association. This too runs into a similar difficulty as the status-based model. Inazu writes, "The standard objection in this approach is the difficulty with articulating why racial discrimination is worse (constitutionally, morally, or otherwise) than discrimination on the basis of gender or sexual orientation."[44] What is the difference in terms of harm to the excluded persons between allowing a group to establish membership criteria on the basis of gender and sexual orientation but not on the basis of race? Other groups have suffered discrimination on bases other than race. Why does the criterion of race get singled out? From the other side, why is it that membership requirements on the basis of some static characteristics are allowed but not on the basis of race? Don't all of the benefits of association to persons that accrue around any dogma and function also accrue around race?

The third approach to this issue is to acknowledge that the function of the particular racial group is gathering together those of a particular race and that an ability to discriminate on the basis of race is essential to the group's functional integrity. This description fits with what Inazu calls "strong pluralism" or "confident pluralism."[45] This approach suggests a need for rethinking the ban on tax exemption status for educational institutions with race-based policies. This application would seem most consistent with the robust nature of my account of freedom of association, and it rightly points out that the "race is different" account fails to take seriously the plural nature of freedom of association and essential protections for the authority and independence of associations, as I have said we should.

However, a balancing must take place between the prerogatives of state, individual, and association. The primary impetus for my inquiry into freedom of association is that the needs of the association have been understudied and underprotected and that the Court exhibits a fundamental conceptual inability to talk about associations as such. Some interests of the state may be allowed to infringe upon those of the association. I think in general Inazu's confident pluralism approach makes sense. Certainly, my discussion of the importance of associations would lend itself to an expansive and robust protection for associations represented by that view. Add to this the notion that the freedom of association is grounded in the Assembly Clause of the First Amendment and therefore on par with the rights of religion, speech, and press, and it strongly suggests that the right of association ought to be equally protected in First Amendment jurisprudence.

Where I would provide one caveat to confident pluralism is regarding limited public forums in educational institutions. There I am open to the "race is different" approach. This would not allow a government ban on race-based groups. In the great wide world of civil society, such groups may exist, and the government may not seek them out and forbid their racial membership requirements without violating a number of provisions in the Bill of Rights. There is wide agreement on that point. Where their presence becomes controversial is when they enter various public forums, especially if government funding or tax exemptions are involved. Such groups may enter traditional public forums, government-sponsored places open to the exercise of First Amendment rights. Consider protests in public parks and other areas termed traditional public forums. Race-based groups can form and assemble in these areas.[46] There is also wide agreement on that point. Furthermore, these groups would also have access to designated public forums, those spaces which the government has indicated are public forums with the same restrictions on government censorship and suppression as traditional public forums.

Where the analysis changes is in a limited public forum. Through these mechanisms, the state allows a plethora of groups and viewpoints but in a more involved way. This discussion is essential to my analysis of *Martinez*, a case that took place in the limited public forum of student organizations at a public university and implicated student fee funding. Limited public forums are still First

Amendment forums, places the government designates for the practice of First Amendment rights even though they may implicate state funding and some explicit limitations (such as limiting student groups to students at public universities). Some support for the *Martinez* ruling hinged on the concept of state funding, that the resources given to student groups were a matter of government support for a particular viewpoint, not government censorship. As the Court wrote, the university was "dangling the carrot of subsidy, not wielding the stick of prohibition."[47] I explained why I disagreed with that argument and argued that the funding in question was better seen as a benefit attached to the public forum, similar to reserving a room or accessing a listserv. Furthermore, I pointed out that treating funding in that way complicated the nature of the forum as a public forum, a place where First Amendment rights are practiced. How can it be that the student organization is a public forum if the state can dictate entrance based upon funding? The discussion is relevant to the point I am making now about race-based groups and the analogy I see between tax exemption status and the limited public forum of student group organizations.

The tax exemption status is essentially a limited public forum; it is a way that the government has established to promote the exercise of First Amendment rights by a variety of groups. The government is not required to fund public forums any more than it is required to establish them. It could get rid of the tax exemption for donations to religious, educational, and other organizations, just as a public university could get rid of its student organization forum. But as a general rule the government must treat tax exemptions as a matter of First Amendment law. The same principle applies to how the government must treat associations in limited public forums, such as student organization programs at public universities. Until *Martinez*, the Court held that student fee funding was one benefit of the public forum. To understand why this is the case we must return to our discussion in chapter 3 where I posited that there are two categories of government funding directed to private groups.[48] The first is generally available funding for any group. The tax exemption given to various groups is considered a government subsidy,[49] as indirect as it may be, to various nongovernmental groups. The government is entitled to the money, but it has permitted through legislation and administrative regulation for some of the tax money to be directed to a variety of organizations of taxpayers' choosing. It is a type of funding that is generally available to every group, even explicitly religious organizations like churches, mosques, and synagogues.[50] Few consider this an Establishment Clause violation because government funding is directed to religious organizations. Through this type of government funding or subsidy, the government encourages pluralism by removing financial barriers, such as taxes, to private organizations and encourages private support for nonprofit organizations of all types. The Internal Revenue Code is deliberately vague, giving the government very little leeway in denying what it considers the subsidy of tax exemption. To note but two examples, "religion" is undefined,[51] and the requirement that charitable organizations provide a "public benefit" is likewise vague.[52] It essentially means that you cannot establish a charity solely to avoid income taxes. Your charitable organization must actually do something in the world. In addition to tax exemption, there are other ways in which government funding may promote First Amendment Pluralism by facilitating the practice of various First Amendment rights. Consider the funding that makes possible traditional public forums such as public parks, sidewalks, and streets. Inazu writes, "The public forum does not appear out of nowhere, with free meeting space for the forum and free electricity to keep the lights on. Government dollars pay for the spaces, the utilities, and the employees who make public forums possible. Facilitating pluralism means funding pluralism."[53] Or consider the categories of designated and limited public forums. The government does not need to create them or fund them, but it does so on a regular basis at its own expense because they enable the practice of First Amendment rights. Once these forums are created, the government has little say in who uses the forums or the resources attached to them.

The second category of government funding is discretionary through government contracts and grants. The government speaks and expresses approval for certain groups through this second means. Government actors may literally speak in support of certain ideas, persons, or programs, and the government may provide funding for these things to signal its approval. The Court has held that government contracts do not have to be given on a viewpoint neutral basis.[54] The government in those cases is acting as speaker, and the First Amendment requirement of government neutrality is irrelevant.

I think we want to avoid a situation where the mere presence of government funding implies government endorsement or government speech, where all government funding is considered discretionary spending. This is dangerous if for no other reason than that in the modern administrative state, government funding is everywhere, including in the public forum.[55] This is not an argument against the administrative state but an argument for clearly distinguishing between state funding that promotes the First Amendment (such as tax exemptions and funding for public forums of various types) and state funding that constitutes government speech. It is also a warning about what it means for First Amendment freedoms if we allow the latter type of government funding to swallow the former.

Student fee funding and access to the benefits of the student organization forum have not been considered government subsidy in the second meaning of that term. The Court has explicitly called student organization programs public forums,[56] arenas where First Amendment rights are practiced and denied that student fee funding is a government subsidy of the latter sort. The Court wrote in *Rosenberger v. Rectors of the University of Virginia*, a case that explicitly dealt with student fee funding for a religious group, "We have held that the guarantee of neutrality is respected, not offended, when the government, following neutral criteria and evenhanded policies, extends benefits to recipients whose ideologies and viewpoints, including religious ones, are broad and diverse."[57] The Court further compared student fee funding to the tax exemption subsidy to demonstrate that this type of government funding is not government speech.

> When the government disburses public funds to private entities to convey a governmental message, it may take legitimate and appropriate steps to ensure that its message is neither garbled nor distorted by the grantee. It does not follow, however, and we did not suggest in *Widmar*, that viewpoint-based restrictions are proper when the University does not itself speak or subsidize transmittal of a message it favors but instead expends funds to encourage a diversity of views from private speakers.[58]

The Court acknowledged that "the Government is not required to subsidize the exercise of fundamental rights," but that it is forbidden to "discriminate invidiously in its subsidies in such a way as to aim 'at the suppression of dangerous ideas.'"[59] The *Rosenberger* Court's reasoning is similar to that made several years earlier by a federal appellate court forbidding a public university to discriminate in funding for an LGBTQ group on First Amendment grounds.[60]

The exception the Court has recognized to these two categories is tax exemption for some educational organizations with race-based policies. While tax exemption is generally available funding and therefore does not connote government approval, the government has been allowed by federal courts to deny tax exemption status to educational institutions with race-based policies.[61] This issue came to the fore in *Bob Jones University v. United States.*[62] I take the legitimacy of this exception as my guide for the state's ability to limit associational rights on the basis of race in the limited public forum attached to an educational institution such as a student group forum. I will give an overview of the *Bob Jones* case and then turn to a discussion of whether my concerns over the "race is different" exception should also apply to the "status is different" exception.

In 1971, the IRS created a policy denying tax exemption to institutions that practice racial discrimination.[63] Bob Jones University and Goldsboro Christian Schools both had racially discriminatory policies. Bob Jones forbade interracial dating, marriage, or advocacy of interracial dating and marriage, and Goldsboro restricted admissions mostly to white students. The schools filed suit arguing that the IRS's policy was a violation of their religious freedom because it discriminated against them based upon their racially discriminatory policies, which they argued were required by their religious belief. The Court upheld the IRS's policy change on the grounds that it comported with the common law understanding of charity for public purposes and that racial discrimination even in private schools was "contrary to public policy."[64] The Court wrote, "The Government has a fundamental, overriding interest in eradicating racial discrimination in education—discrimination that prevailed, with official approval, for the first 165 years of this Nation's constitutional history. That governmental interest substantially outweighs whatever burden denial of tax benefits places on petitioners' exercise of their religious beliefs."[65] The Court further explained in a footnote, "We deal here only with religious schools—not with churches or other purely religious institutions; here, the governmental interest is in denying public support to racial discrimination in education."[66] This is a significant point. The institutions that lose tax exemption status under the IRS rule are educational institutions.[67] They are uniquely linked to the concerns of *Brown v. Board of Education* and the ability of African Americans to overcome the lingering social and economic effects of slavery and generations of subsequent discrimination through access to education.[68] It bears further noting that the IRS has never expanded its exclusion of groups from tax exemption beyond those with race-based discrimination.[69]

I see this as potentially applying to student group programs as limited public forums that take place in the educational context. If I'm right, then in addition to the limitation that members be students, public universities could also prohibit organizations from implementing a racially discriminatory membership policy because of the fact that the student organization forum exists in an educational institution and therefore has this limited link to its educational mission. A potential objection to this exception is that I am allowing public universities to impose on student groups a policy regarding racial discrimination that is justified as applied to educational institutions because of their role in economic and social advancement. Can it really be said that student groups are as essential to their potential members' economic advancement as educational institutions with which they are associated through a limited public forum? Some would argue that isn't so. But I think this is an acceptable compromise that corresponds to the Court's concern over continued racial discrimination against African Americans in education and employment, but it allows a great deal of freedom of association in the limited public forum, which is an area where First Amendment protections apply. It offers freedom of association more protection than what we find in *Martinez* or even in *Roberts*.[70]

Given what I have said here about the history of racial discrimination justifying a caveat to freedom of association, could it be that as more cases and legislation accrue regarding sex and sexual orientation that they too would be added? I don't think so. I think that race discrimination against African Americans and the legacy of slavery are standards that would be nearly impossible to reach for status-based classes. Even within the category of race, federal courts have tended to interpret the exception as narrowly as possible. For example, in 2006, a federal court refused to apply the principles of *Runyun* to a race-exclusive private school in Hawaii on the grounds that the policy did not specifically exclude African Americans, which was the specific historical context of *Runyun*.[71] The justification for stripping Bob Jones University of its tax exemption status was that it perpetuated what in effect was a racial caste system by denying educational opportunities to African Americans. After the integration of public schools in *Brown v. Board of Education* (1954),[72] there was a migration of white students to private schools. The fear was that the economic and social discrimination against African Americans would continue if whites defunded public schools and sent their own children to segregated private schools.[73] So in *Runyun* the Court ruled that racial discrimination in private schools was not protected by freedom of association,[74] and in *Bob Jones* the Court ruled that religious liberty interests did not outweigh the government's compelling interest in eradicating racial discrimination in society at large.

Furthermore, the Court has indicated that its treatment of the racial exceptions to constitutional clauses may be historically contingent and that it may revise its rulings on race issues as racial equality improves. In *Grutter v. Bollinger* (2003), the Court upheld the use of race in admissions policies at public educational institutions based on the state's compelling interest in racial diversity in its student body. But it noted that as the economic and social differences between African Americans and white Americans disappeared, the necessity—and constitutionality—of such admissions policies would come into question. The Court wrote, "It has been 25 years since Justice Powell first approved the use of race to further an interest in student body diversity in the context of public higher education. Since that time, the number of minority applicants with high grades and test scores has indeed increased. We expect that 25 years from now, the use of racial preferences will no longer be necessary to further the interest approved today."[75] The state's compelling interest in racial equality may begin to lose out against other constitutional values such as Equal Protection (as in the case of *Grutter*), and public universities may lose their ability to use race as a factor in admissions.

The exception accorded the IRS's treatment of race-based educational institutions may follow a similar logic. By analogy, this might mean that the state's compelling interest in refusing admittance to a limited public forum for race-based groups may disappear as more racial economic and social equality is achieved. Inazu makes an argument along these lines, pointing out that the justification for the *Bob Jones* decision was the legacy of slavery and the state's compelling interest in ending continued racial discrimination. As that legacy recedes into the past and conditions of racial equality improve, it may be that future federal courts will abandon the holding on that basis. I don't believe that as a society we have achieved a level of racial equality where *Bob Jones* or even *Grutter* should be abandoned. But I could be wrong. This country recently elected a two-term African American president who governed with a reasonable level of popularity, and a record number of racial minorities were elected to national office in recent congressional elections.[76] These achievements indicate a salutary increase in social equality, and it becomes less clear that restrictions on freedom of association are necessary to achieve the state's compelling interest in racial equality.

What about the state's compelling interest in equality associated with status-based categories like sex and sexual orientation? The state has a compelling interest in removing barriers from African Americans achieving economic and social equality, one of which is access to higher education even in private schools. Does the state have a comparable interest in achieving equality between the sexes and between persons of various sexual orientations? I think it does. However, I don't see the state having a compelling justification for eliminating sex-based association requirements in the limited public forum in the educational context. The government may infringe upon explicit constitutional protections only when it has a compelling interest and when the means it implements are narrowly tailored to achieve that interest. The state would have to argue not only that it has a compelling interest in women receiving an equal education but also that there is a broad failure to provide women with equal opportunities (or even equal outcomes) in education. Women, however, have not only achieved parity but have surpassed men in rates of both enrollment and graduation in higher education.[77] If it were true that higher education continued to exhibit the lingering effects of sex discrimination even after the Nineteenth Amendment and various legislative efforts to achieve social and economic equality for women such that women still lagged behind men in educational achievement, then I could understand the argument for a ruling on sex discrimination analogous to the *McCrary* and *Bob Jones* rulings on race and therefore consonant infringement upon freedom of association in the student organization forum.

A similar argument applies to sexual orientation discrimination. Higher education is the place most protective and accepting of LGBTQ persons and often on the cutting edge of recognizing new variations of sexual orientation. Which is why it is not surprising that LGBTQ persons appear to be more likely to graduate from college than non-LGBTQ persons.[78] Furthermore, I have referred a number of times to the case law on gay rights groups and pointed out that it is far from clear that sexual orientation discrimination as an essential part of freedom of association is detrimental to gay rights groups in this context. To the contrary, it is precisely the right to associate in a group with the practice of excluding non-LGBTQ persons that allows these groups to grow and to thrive, especially in the social context where such a group faces social discrimination. For these reasons I don't see the necessity of an analogous ruling to *Bob Jones* and *McCrary* in this context either. If the state's compelling interest in broad social and economic equality has been achieved, then the government may lose its justification for infringing on First Amendment rights. Given the place accorded to higher education in our present economic and social environment and the apparent success of women and LGBTQ persons in higher education, I don't see how restricting freedom of association in the context of higher education can be considered necessary to the compelling government interest in equality.

There are some additional concerns with the status-based approach. Let's consider what it would mean if we extended the *Bob Jones* ruling on race and tax exemption status to sex and sexual orientation and the IRS was constitutionally permitted to strip tax exemption status from educational institutions that engage in sex-based or sexual orientation–based discrimination. This means that my former employer, Wellesley College, an elite women's liberal arts college, may no longer restrict its admissions to women, and Wabash College, an all-male college in Indiana, may no longer restrict admissions to men without losing tax exemption. Private religious colleges would not be able to discriminate in admissions based upon adherence to religious requirements on sex and marriage, some of which implicate sexual orientation issues.[79] Taken together I think there is sufficient reason to separate race from status in the context of freedom of association protections.

All that said, I will point out some problems and concerns with my own approach of applying the "*Bob Jones* exception" to the student organization forum. First, this policy limitation on the limited public forum participates in the suppression of what Robert Cover called a nomos, an association's ability to generate its own laws. Through the IRS policy change and the Court's decision in *Bob Jones*, the government is suppressing a particular way of being, of associational self-understanding, by pushing it to the fringes of society and making its institutions difficult to maintain by stripping them of tax exemption status. Cover's argument is that our constitutional system protects a plethora of norm-generating institutions and associations. If the state through brute force is going to shut down a particular norm-generating institution, it needs to give a very clear reason for why that institution and that norm are beyond the constitutional pale. In Cover's opinion, the Court failed to do so in *Bob Jones*. He writes that the university "deserved a constitutional commitment to avoiding public subsidization of racism."[80]

There is a distinction between a court's holding and its reasoning. Many, including myself, agree with the Court's holding in *Bob Jones*, but want something more from its reasoning. Our government singled out a particular nomos for exclusion from a constitutionally protected public forum and then failed to provide an adequate account of why that was an acceptable reason to violate religious liberty. This isn't a reason to think the Court was wrong. But it does mean that it should at least be clear about what it is doing with government power. A number of objections to *Bob Jones* rested precisely on this point: the Court was morally right but conceptually wrong,[81] and it needed a better argument for its holding or at least an acknowledgment of the difficulty of the constitutional question before it. As one law review article put it at the time, "Justice required, not a different result from that reached by the Court, but only an acknowledgment of the difficulty."[82]

Second, I have gone to great pains to explain the importance of pluralism, of tolerance for a variety of groups, even those we hate, and then I turn around and make an exception for groups that I hate. Inazu writes, "We cannot begin with the premise that the public forum is open to all groups and then start excluding those groups we don't like."[83] It may be that my conflation of the limited public forum to tax exemption status and my support for the *Bob Jones* ruling is doing exactly that.

Third, whenever we impose a membership requirement, we always imagine it in the worst possible context. So when we say we will not allow racially discriminatory groups on campus, we imagine we are excluding a KKK chapter from receiving student fees or Bob Jones University from receiving tax exemption status. But we fail to recognize that this also may apply to racial minorities who will not be allowed to associate on the basis of race in this limited public forum. Such groups have a role in bringing together members of particularly embattled racial minorities and providing them with all the benefits that accrue from association, especially a sense of solidarity derived from status in such a group. This may be essential to their members' educational success, and we are making that effect more difficult through this policy.

Fourth, my analysis of the importance of groups to their members' psychological well-being implies that even groups with unsavory dogmas may have value as groups for their members. The Harvard political theorist Nancy Rosenblum makes this point in her book *Membership and Morals: The Personal Uses of Pluralism*. She points out that often the sort of people who join neo-Nazi and white supremacist groups have few other social attachments, which is why they are amenable to adopting Nazi myths.[84] By membership and participation in these groups, individuals are freed from anomie and alienation, at least for a time. Despite the hateful basis of the group's dogma, associating with others may socialize and even moralize its members to a certain extent. In these groups members learn cooperation and garner social attachments that otherwise have eluded them. Rosenblum writes, "The significance of association depends on the experiences individuals bring to it, including the unique obstacles we each face in cultivating and exhibiting partial competencies or dispositions. So I caution against the unwarranted assumption that the effects of an association on members can be predicted on the basis of a group's formal purpose or system of internal governance. The moral valence of group life is indeterminate."[85] From the outside it seems that cultivating allegiance to the dogmas associated with white supremacism is an unmitigated moral evil. But Rosenblum's argument is that the moral evil may be diminished by the social nature of the groups in question regardless of their sinister purpose. As I have said, the social and moral value of membership is hard to determine ahead of time or from the outside.

Additionally, beyond the potential value to individual members there may be benefits to the rest of society from such groups. Those who may have channeled their social disengagement into socially destructive forms are instead part of groups that may exercise a restraining effect upon such people. A person prone to hate-inspired violence may find when he joins a white separatist group that many members are, rhetoric notwithstanding, prone to caution in actually carrying out violent acts. Ironically, such a person may be restrained from socially destructive acts of violence by membership and participation in a hate group that advocates violence. This benefits the rest of society in that we do not become victims of their destructive behavior, no matter how loathsome we find the central beliefs of the groups they join. These groups serve as a sort of "safety valve" in a liberal democracy, even though their central tenets are contrary to the values of liberty and equality.[86] In such a way these groups may actually bolster political stability by giving outlet to unstable elements, and they may uphold the political legitimacy of liberal democracy by demonstrating that liberalism does in fact follow through on its promise to allow freedom for all ideas.[87] This point is true for society at large, but the benefits pointed out here would apply to the limited public forum as well.

Fifth, as Inazu points out, it will prove difficult to limit the exception to race. As I noted above, once there is an exception to freedom of association, it is hard not to see analogous criteria on a host of bases.[88]

I write these concerns to acknowledge accusations of inconsistency in my position. Nonetheless, I think the compromise I have sketched out here for the limited public forum in the education context is one that makes sense in our circumstances. We have had the *Bob Jones* exception for nearly forty years, and we have not expanded it.[89] I think it is a workable compromise in the student organization forum as well.

Conclusion: Back to a Theory of the Social

I have been discussing why I think that freedom of association ought to be quite robust, protecting groups we normally regard as beyond the pale. The importance of associations as communities of belief and action strongly suggests that for associations to retain their functional integrity they must have wide latitude to determine their own membership requirements. But even those who find my arguments unconvincing for a freedom of association that adheres to Inazu's "confident pluralism" or even for a "race is different" approach in educational institutions will still find helpful my application of a "theory of the social" to freedom of association. The social perspective that I advocate provides a way we might approach freedom of association from the association's perspective, and it demonstrates how we can better protect freedom of association in First Amendment jurisprudence beyond what the Court has dubbed "expressive associations." It allows us to understand the importance of membership requirements around central tenets and prescribed practices and the connections of conduct, belief, and the functional integrity of the association. So even those who would adhere to the "status is different" understanding will find my argument helpful for protecting belief and conduct-based organizations. We can amend the functional autonomy test and FAPA with language excluding race- and status-based associations, but better protect the associational prerogatives of groups than what the Court gave us in *Martinez* and its "expressive association" jurisprudence more broadly.

Both the functional autonomy test and the Freedom of Association Protection Act serve the same purpose: to provide the Court with a "social" perspective and thus to open the Court's analysis to the presence of social groups and institutions. This change in Court doctrine would breathe new life into freedom of association as well as bolster religious liberty. In other words, it would put the "social" into freedom of association.

Conclusion: First Amendment Pluralism and the Freedom of Association

When Harry Potter and his friends established their student organization at Hogwarts School of Witchcraft and Wizardry, they were seeking to place their allegiance in something other than the Ministry of Magic. Students who joined the group sought out Harry Potter's authority to teach them "Defense against the Dark Arts." The allegiance students gave to the group was conditional upon it providing them with the functional value of learning a particular set of spells they were not learning in their normal classrooms. The authority of the group in their lives was limited to providing that functional value. When the Ministry of Magic placed a moratorium on student organizations, it sought to suppress the functional autonomy of associations that might operate according to a set of central tenets not endorsed by the Ministry of Magic, including the prescribed practices of learning and practicing spells for the Defense against the Dark Arts. It sought to centralize authority within the Ministry, forbidding a hierarchy of values and organizational officers not explicitly endorsed and appointed by Ministry officials. Various traditions associated with different Houses and organizations at Hogwarts were suppressed under the centralization schemes of the Ministry of Magic. In short, the Ministry violated the freedom of association of Hogwarts's students and disrupted the social bonds between students in the manner described in this book, ignoring the reality of the social at Hogwarts.

I defined "theory" as a way of seeing something. To have a theory on the First Amendment is to have a way of seeing First Amendment rights. First Amendment Pluralism is a theoretical paradigm that aims to provide the Court with a theory of the First Amendment that would allow it to see associations and institutions in addition to the individual for the purposes of constitutional analysis. It is important to emphasize the breadth of my critique based on political sociology. While I applied it only to freedom of association, this viewpoint has implications for the entire pantheon of First Amendment rights. Addressing these issues of constitutional interpretation raises questions about the need for rethinking the dichotomy that characterizes most modern political thought.

I opened this book with the problem of the vanishing freedom of association as emerging from the Court's theoretical framework of what I called the "First Amendment Dichotomy." This consists of the state and the individual as the two analytically exclusive units of constitutional analysis. This means that the Court understands First Amendment rights as negotiating the relationship between the state and the individual to the exclusion of associations and institutions that cannot be either reduced to their individual members or subsumed into the state for purposes of constitutional analysis. This dichotomy constricts the Court's constitutional vision when it applies its analysis to freedom of association. When examining First Amendment claims, the Court can only see the individual and the state.

Against the backdrop of the problem of the vanishing freedom of association, political sociology is a helpful perspective in understanding the *social*—as distinguished from *political*—entities at issue. The work of the political sociologist Robert Nisbet is a valuable source of insight into both the problem of the First Amendment Dichotomy and a means of expanding the Court's vision of First Amendment rights. While Nisbet was not a constitutional scholar, his work on political sociology diagnosed a dichotomous framework as a constricting vision in political and social thought. The lack of recognition of the social group in First Amendment law has an analogue in its absence from historiography and political philosophy. Nisbet writes, "We should no doubt know a great deal more than we do about [voluntary associations] were it not for a historiography in the West that has been anchored for so long in the political state on the one hand and the individual on the other."[1] This same quote could be rewritten to apply to constitutional law. "We should no doubt know a great deal more than we do about [voluntary associations and their role in the American constitutional system] were it not for a [jurisprudence] in [America] that has been anchored for so long in the political state on the one hand and the individual on the other."

Just as the voluntary association is not well understood in historiography, according to Nisbet, so is it not well understood in jurisprudence. The reason the social group is missing in both areas is that the theoretical dichotomy of state and individual is the primary conceptual paradigm for scholars and jurists. This theoretical dichotomy forms the backdrop for the First Amendment Dichotomy.

In addition to a diagnosis of the problem of a dichotomous theoretical framework, Nisbet offered a solution that he called a "laissez-faire of groups," an arrangement in which social groups, including voluntary associations, compete in a social market for the allegiance of individuals. He did not advocate replacing the dichotomy of state and individual in political and social thought with the dichotomy of state and social group, dichotomizing the qualities of the person between the state and the social group. Rather, he supported the idea of a plural society, one composed of state, individual, and social groups in political and social philosophy. These three categories are triangularly related to each other, each interacting with the other two. In the First Amendment context, this means assigning First Amendment rights of religion, speech, press, and assembly to both individuals and associations. These two entities are appropriately protected from state interference.

The goal of this book has been to investigate the efficacy of this plural conception for freedom of association jurisprudence by using Nisbet's political sociology to illuminate the ignored third point of the triangle, the social group, and its manifestation in liberal democratic society as the voluntary association. The voluntary association can serve as a "functional community," providing the individual with a real sense of belonging and counteracting the perils of alienation. Through the application of limited authority, these groups provide functional value to individuals and rightfully garner their members' conditional allegiance.

Applied to constitutional law, Nisbet's plural conception helps to construct the paradigm of First Amendment Pluralism as a way to conceive of the triangular relations of First Amendment rights of individuals and associations and their relationship to state power and to provide a means of recovering the vanishing freedom of association in Supreme Court jurisprudence. Out of Nisbet's principles of pluralism intended to undergird a diverse and plural society we developed both a judicial and a legislative solution. The functional judicial test is a practical means of helping the Court to see associations and institutions when associational rights are under review. Since the functional judicial test is intended precisely to protect a plural society, which means the protection of a plurality of functionally autonomous groups, Nisbet's four principles of pluralism can be translated directly into the four prongs of the functional judicial test. Likewise, a legislative remedy, the Freedom of Association Protection Act (FAPA) translated Nisbet's principles of pluralism into a piece of legislation modeled after the Religious Freedom Restoration Act (RFRA).

While my critique is broad, I should also emphasize the modesty of my proposal for a scheme of individual rights. First Amendment Pluralism and the functional judicial test aims not to diminish the rights of individuals or to substitute the First Amendment Dichotomy of state and individual with the First Amendment Dichotomy of state and social group. The constitutional protection of groups advocated here does not mean that individuals who do not fit into a particular existing group have no recourse. The *Martinez* Court wrote, "CLS's analytical error lies in focusing on the benefits it must forgo while ignoring the interests of those it seeks to fence out: Exclusion, after all, has two sides."[2] Freedom of association, interpreted according to Nisbet's theory of a laissez-faire of groups, means that associations can be formed by anyone for any reason. Indeed, the great value of freedom of association to individuals and to society at large is its capacity to provide the context for *social inventions*, the development of new associations that provide the communal context for novel functions and cutting-edge dogmas, upheld by a newly recognized authority and all adapted to the needs of their members. Students who are excluded from a student group have the freedom to form their own group around whatever dogmas and functional needs unite them with other students.

The intent of First Amendment Pluralism is to instantiate a proper relationship between the three conceptual pillars of the First Amendment—individual, state, and association—to revive freedom of association and to undergird the pantheon of First Amendment rights. Freedom of association includes both the right of the association to police its borders and the right of individuals to act corporately. Other First Amendment rights deserve a similar plural treatment. The rights of religion, speech, press, assembly, and petition should have both associational *and* individual components in Court jurisprudence. Each of these rights protects both individuals and associations. In adjudicating these rights, the Court will be negotiating the relationship between state and individual, between state and association, and between association and individual to ensure both the individual's right of exit and the association's right of exclusion. The point is that First Amendment Pluralism, as a theoretical paradigm, allows for the triangular relationship between state, individual, and association to come into appropriate judicial and legislative focus. When using this paradigm as a lens to assess a challenge to the right of association, courts may recognize the appropriate autonomy of associations through an application of the functional judicial test.

If the Court were to see the right of association through this lens in some future iteration of the *Martinez* case, it would implore university administrators and students not to fear a variety of associations with a diversity of dogmas and a plethora of practices. Such a Court may write, "Do not seek to stifle those who differ from you. If you find yourself excluded from a group for reasons of belief or practice, your rights are not violated. You are free to join another association that suits your own beliefs and practices. If you cannot find one, start your own. Freedom of association means the freedom to associate—and to disassociate—as you will." Then the Court could quote, as Nisbet often does with approval, the radical pluralist Pierre-Joseph Proudhon and adjure the university and its students, "Multiply your associations and be free." With that, the Supreme Court of the United States could put the "social" into freedom of association.

Notes

CHAPTER 1. POLITICAL SOCIOLOGY AND
THE PROBLEM OF THE VANISHING FREEDOM
OF ASSOCIATION

1. J. K. Rowling, *Harry Potter and the Order of the Phoenix* (New York: Scholastic, 2004), 351. The Hogwarts policy restricting students' freedom of association reads as follows:

By Order of the High Inquisitor of Hogwarts

All Student Organizations, Societies, Teams, Groups, and Clubs are henceforth disbanded.

An Organization, Society, Team, Group, or Club is hereby defined as a regular meeting of three or more students.

Permission to re-form may be sought from the High Inquisitor (Professor Umbridge).

No Student Organization, Society, Team, Group, or Club may exist without the knowledge and approval of the High Inquisitor.

Any student found to have formed, or to belong to, an Organization, Society, Team, Group, or Club that has not been approved by the High Inquisitor will be expelled.

2. Rowling, 303.

3. Aristotle, *The Politics*, trans. Ernest Barker (London: Oxford University Press, 1946), 1313b1.

4. *Christian Legal Society v. Martinez*, 561 U.S. 661 (2010).

5. See chapter 3 for a discussion of this jurisprudence. See John D. Inazu, *Liberty's Refuge: The Forgotten Freedom of Assembly* (New Haven: Yale University Press, 2012) and Timothy J. Tracey, "*Christian Legal Society v. Martinez*: In Hindsight," *University of Hawaii Law Review* (Winter 2012).

6. "Expressive association" is the formulation developed by the Supreme Court in *Roberts v. United States Jaycees*, 468 U.S. 609 (1984). Some of the scholars who accept this formulation will be discussed in chapter 3 to elucidate the issues involved with the *Martinez* decision and in chapter 4 in contrast to my proposal.

7. The Court did not originally place the right of association in the First Amendment, despite citing its relation to the rights of speech and assembly. See chapter 3.

8. See John D. Inazu, "The First Amendment's Public Forum," *William & Mary Law Review* 56 (2015): 1159, 1169. "One can speak alone; one cannot assemble alone."

9. Inazu uses similar examples to mine: "a gay social club, a prayer or meditation group, and a college fraternity." Inazu, *Liberty's Refuge*, 3n5. I chose these examples because as a non-Catholic, heterosexual male I would be excluded from all of them.

10. Dale Carpenter, "Expressive Association and Anti-Discrimination Law after *Dale*: A Tripartite Approach," *Minnesota Law Review* 85 (2001): 1515 at 1550.

11. Brief for Gays and Lesbians for Individual Liberty as Amicus Curiae in Support of Petitioner," *Christian Legal Society v. Martinez*, no. 08-1371 (February 4, 2010), at 10–11.

12. See *Chi Iota Colony of Alpha Epsilon Pi Fraternity v. City Univ. Of N.Y.*, 502 F.3d 136 (2007). The Second Circuit Court of Appeals overturned an injunction against a college for applying its nondiscrimination policy, which forbade sex discrimination, to a fraternity.

13. *Employment Division, Department of Human Resources of Oregon v. Smith*, 494 US 872 (1990).

14. We will discuss religious liberty and freedom of association in chapter 4. In *Smith*, the Court applied the constitutional test of rational basis scrutiny to general laws of neutral applicability. It is not likely that the nonexpressive activity of religious groups is as protected under current Court doctrine as is commonly believed. Even the Court's holding in *Hosanna-Tabor Evangelical Lutheran Church and School v. EEOC*, 565 US 171 (2012) where the Court ruled that the ministerial exception applied to employees performing religious functions would not necessarily apply to the gay Catholic club in our example above. The collapse of the freedom of association into the freedom of speech places the freedom of religious institutions as well as other nonreligious institutions in a constitutionally ambiguous position.

15. Inazu notes in his book that his "lack of direct theoretical engagement should not be mistaken for a lack of awareness or concern." He is aware of the theoretical shortcomings of the *Martinez* decision and freedom of association jurisprudence more broadly, but focuses in his book on the textual and historical concerns of freedom of association. Inazu, *Liberty's Refuge*, 18. What Inazu does have to say about the theoretical problem will be discussed in chapter 3 on "The Legal Theory Background" of freedom of association.

16. Nisbet wrote extensively on the history of sociology, the origins of sociological concepts in nineteenth-century conservatism, and the proper methodology of the social sciences. He received all of his degrees and taught in the Department of Social Institutions at the University of California at Berkeley, served as dean at the University of California at Riverside, taught briefly at the University of Arizona, and served as the Albert Schweitzer Professor at Columbia University. At the end of his career, he was granted emeritus status by Columbia and held a resident and then visiting fellowship at the American Enterprise Institute in Washington, DC. Summaries of Nisbet's career appear in Robert Perrin, introduction to Robert Nisbet, *Twilight of Authority* (New York: Oxford University Press, 1975). Reprinted by Liberty Press in 2000 with a new preface by Robert G. Perrin (all quotations are from latest edition); Constance N. Field, "My Father, Robert Nisbet," *Society* 52 (2015): 344–350; and Luke C. Sheahan, "Robert Nisbet: Reappraisal of a Political Sociologist," introduction to symposium on Robert Nisbet, *Political Science Reviewer* 42, no. 2 (2018). Nisbet offers his own short professional biography in the introduction to Robert Nisbet, *Making of Modern Society*

(Liverpool: Wheatsheaf Books, 1986), 1–22. For a discussion of Nisbet's work on the history of sociology see Luke C. Sheahan, "Conservative, Pluralist, Sociologist: Robert Nisbet's Burke," *Studies in Burke and His Time*, vol. 28 (2019). For his work on developmentalism in social thought and its relation to the rise of the modern state, see Luke C. Sheahan, "The State as Historical Necessity: Robert Nisbet's Critique of Developmentalism," *Political Science Reviewer* 42, no. 2 (2018).

17. Robert Nisbet, *The Quest for Community: A Study in the Ethics of Order and Freedom* (New York: Oxford University Press, 1953). Republished in 1962 by Galaxy Book, New York, under a new title: *Community and Power*. Reissued in 1969 under original title: *The Quest for Community*. Reprinted by Institute for Contemporary Studies, San Francisco, with a new preface in 1990, and by ISI Books, Wilmington, with a new introduction in 2010. All quotations are from the latest edition.

18. Robert Nisbet, *The Social Philosophers: Community and Conflict in Western Thought* (London: Heinemann, 1973), 110.

19. Nisbet, 109.

20. Nisbet, 110.

21. Nisbet, 135–136.

22. Nisbet, 140. Nisbet lifted the following discussion directly from *The Quest for Community*. See Nisbet, *Social Philosophers*, 140n26.

23. Nisbet, 142.

24. Nisbet, 145.

25. For a discussion of Nisbet on Rousseau, see Bradley J. Birzer, "Leviathan, Inc.: Robert Nisbet and the Modern Nation-State," *Political Science Reviewer* 42, no. 2 (2018): 471–476.

26. Nisbet, 145.

27. Robert Nisbet, *Tradition and Revolt* (New Brunswick: Transaction, 1999), 9.

28. Nisbet, *Social Philosophers*, 148.

29. Nisbet, 149.

30. Quoted in Nisbet, 150.

31. Robert Nisbet, *The Social Bond* (New York: Alfred A. Knopf, 1970), 372.

32. Nisbet, 373.

33. Nisbet, 373–744.

34. Nisbet, 381–382.

35. Nisbet, 385.

36. Nisbet, 383.

37. I discuss the processes and individualization and politicization in Luke C. Sheahan, "Antidote to Alienation: The Voluntary Association in the Work of Robert Nisbet," *Perspectives on Political Science* 48, no. 4 (2019): 2–3.

38. William A. Galston, *Liberal Pluralism: The Implications of Value Pluralism for Political Theory* (Cambridge, UK: Cambridge University Press, 2005), 21.

39. Nisbet, *Quest*, 2.

40. William A. Galston, *The Practice of Liberal Pluralism* (Cambridge, UK: Cambridge University Press, 2005), 2.

41. Nisbet, *Quest*, 28. "It is the image of community contained in the promise of the absolute, communal State that seems to have the greatest evocative power."

42. Nancy Rosenblum, *Membership and Morals: The Personal Uses of Pluralism in America* (Princeton, NJ: Princeton University Press, 1998), 36.

43. Many issues arise in the case, such as state subsidy, forum analysis, and the like. These issues are discussed in detail in chapter 3.

44. For the classic statement of the importance of free speech in a democracy, see Alexander Meiklejohn, *Free Speech and Its Relation to Self-Government* (New York: Harper, 1948).

45. Chapter 3 contains a critique of the consensus pluralism of Truman and Dahl drawing from John Inazu's work.

46. Nisbet, *Social Philosophers*, 420–421.

47. Alexis de Tocqueville, *Democracy in America* (Indianapolis: Liberty Fund, 2012), 898.

48. Nisbet explains this argument in detail in *The Quest for Community* and *The Social Philosophers*.

49. Nisbet, *Modern Society*, 25.

50. Robert Nisbet, *The Social Group in French Thought* (PhD diss., University of California, Berkeley, 1939. Reprint, New York: Arno, 1980).

51. Stephen V. Monsma, *Pluralism and Freedom: Faith-Based Organizations in a Democratic Society* (Lanham: Rowman & Littlefield, 2012), 54–55.

52. *Citizens United v. Federal Election Comm'n*, 558 U.S. 310 (2010).

53. Marion Crain and John Inazu, "Re-Assembling Labor," *University of Illinois Law Review* 2015:1791, 1801.

54. Most discussions of rights follow this paradigm.

55. Bruce Frohnen, "Individual Rights, Corporate Rights, and the Diversity of Groups," *West Virginia Law Review* 107 (2005): 805.

56. *Wisconsin v. Yoder*, 406 U.S. 205 (1972).

57. *NAACP v. Claiborne*, 458 U.S. 886 (1982).

58. *Boy Scouts of America v. Dale*, 530 U.S. 640 (2000).

59. *Hurley v. Irish American Gay, Lesbian, and Bisexual Group of Boston*, 515 U.S. 557 (1995). *Dale* and *Hurley* will be discussed in chapter 3.

60. *Roberts v. United States Jaycees*, 468 U.S. 609 (1984).

61. *Uphaus v. Wyman*, 360 U.S. 72 (1959), *Barenblatt v. United States*, 360 U.S. 109 (1959), *Communist Party v. Subversive Activities Control Board* (SACB) 367 U.S. 1 (1961), and *Scales v. United States*, 367 U.S. 203 (1961). The communist cases are complicated by the fact that they implicated national security. But that further indicates the presence of the First Amendment Dichotomy and that the state and the individual are the primary justifications for freedom of association. It was determined in the communist cases that the state was not served and the individual right of dissent was not adequately infringed, so the associations in question could be censored.

62. See *Chi Iota Colony of Alpha Epsilon Pi Fraternity v. City Univ. of N.Y.*, 502 F.3d 136 (2007).

63. See Inazu, *Liberty's Refuge*, 3.

64. *Holder v. Humanitarian Law Project*, 561 U.S. 1 (2010).

65. The most prominent recent commentator is probably Robert D. Putnam, *Bowling Alone: The Collapse and Revival of American Community* (New York: Simon & Schuster, 2001).

66. Robert Perrin refers to Nisbet as "one of America's most cited *public intellectuals*." Robert Perrin, "Introduction to the Transaction Edition," *Tradition*, viii.

67. Nisbet references freedom of association only twice, once in *Twilight of Authority* (249–250) regarding its origin as a constitutional right in *NAACP v. Alabama*, 357 U.S. 449 (1958) and once in *The Social Philosophers* (428) in a discussion of Tocqueville's idea that unfettered freedom of association is the only barrier to tyranny of the majority. While Nisbet's first book, *The Quest for Community*, predates the NAACP cases, the rest of his books came after the Court's primary decisions. Furthermore, his reference to *NAACP v. Alabama* in *Twilight* (1975) indicates that he was familiar with this jurisprudential development.

68. As Nisbet writes in the preface to the 1970 edition of *Quest*, "I would . . . preclude any possible supposition on the reader's part that there is in this book any lament for the old, any nostalgia for the village, parish, or other type of now largely erased form of social community of the past. Rereading the book today, I am frank in saying that I cannot find a nostalgic note in the entire book. It is not the revival of old communities that the book in a sense pleads for; it is the establishment of new forms: forms which are relevant to contemporary life and thought." Nisbet, xxii.

69. Nisbet, 11. Nisbet cites Emile Durkheim's groundbreaking 1897 book on suicide numerous times throughout his work. See Emile Durkheim, *Suicide: A Study in Sociology*, trans. John A. Spaulding and George Simpson (New York: Free Press, 1979).

70. Nisbet, *Quest*, 64.

71. For an argument that the voluntary association could solve the modern problem of social alienation, see Sheahan, "Antidote to Alienation."

72. I get this apt characterization of First Amendment law from Paul Horwitz, *First Amendment Institutions* (Cambridge, MA: Harvard University Press, 2013), 5.

73. Steven D. Smith, *The Rise and Decline of American Religious Freedom* (Cambridge: Harvard University Press, 2014).

74. Inazu, *Liberty's Refuge*, 6.

75. Inazu, 21–22.

76. Inazu, 164.

77. Inazu, 166. Historically, the first appeals to Freedom of Assembly came from Democratic Republican societies opposing the Federalists then in power. See Inazu, 26.

78. Inazu, "Public Forum," 1169.

79. Smith, *Religious Freedom*, 9.

80. Smith, 49.

81. Smith, 108.

82. Smith, 33.

83. Smith, 35.

84. This is an important distinction for Smith. See Smith, 9.

85. Smith, 70.

86. Smith, 170.

87. Most prominently by Richard Schragger and Micah Schwartzman, "Against Religious Institutionalism," *Virginia Law Review* 99, no. 5 (September 2013) and John Inazu, "The Freedom of the Church (New Revised Standard Version)," *Journal of Contemporary Legal Issues* 21, no. 335 (2013).

88. Schragger and Schwartzman, "Against Religious Institutionalism," 928.

89. Inazu, "Freedom of the Church," 337.

90. Schragger and Schwartzman, "Against Religious Institutionalism," 936; Inazu, "Freedom of the Church," 365n151.

91. Schragger and Schwartzman, "Against Religious Institutionalism," 945–946.

92. Schragger and Schwartzman, 966–967.

93. Floyd Abrams, *The Soul of the First Amendment* (New Haven: Yale University Press, 2017), 57.

94. We will return to the relation of this thesis to religious liberty in chapter 4.

95. Horwitz, *Institutions*, 5.

96. Quoted in Horwitz, 12. Original quotation from Paul Horwitz, "Grutter's *First Amendment*," 46 *B.C. L. Rev.* 461, 589 (2005).

97. Horwitz, *Institutions*, 9.

98. Horwitz, 12.

99. Horwitz, 13.

100. "In looking at [current values, theories, and judicial doctrines of the First Amendment] we will see a common thread: they routinely emphasize the individual and deemphasize the institutional." Horwitz, 27.

101. Inazu criticizes Horwitz on similar grounds. See John D. Inazu, "Institutions in Context," *Tulsa Law Review* 50 (2015): 491, 495.

102. Horwitz, *Institutions*, 14. Emphasis in original.

103. Horwitz, 242–243.

104. We will use the example of a Shaker community in chapter 4 to demonstrate this point.

105. Horwitz deftly explains the importance of the First Amendment institutions that he defends. However, even while acknowledging that such institutions have nondiscursive roles (i.e., churches are for saving souls [chap. 8], associations are where people and ideas meet [chap. 9]) he frames their defense as necessarily attached to their role in public discourse. In chapters 3 and 4 we will explain the important role of associations aside from their value for democratic dialogue.

106. Horwitz, *Institutions*, 277–278.

107. Horwitz, 35–37.

108. Horwitz, 17.

109. See Kelly Sarabyn, "Free Speech at Private Universities," *Journal of Law & Education* 39, no. 2 (2010): 145–182.

110. Horwitz, *Institutions*, 44.

111. Horwitz, 47.

112. Horwitz, 56.

113. Inazu, "Institutions in Context," 501. "The First Amendment implications of those entities are better understood within the public and private ordering of our society. In other words, they are better understood in context."

114. Jacob Levy uses this phrase to point to deeper reservoirs within liberal thought for recognition of a plurality of groups. He writes, "The rise of the language of liberal universalism, of abstract doctrines of rights applicable everywhere, sometimes flattens our sense of what the liberal tradition has consisted of and of what liberal ideas can consist of now. It leads us to overemphasize the dyadic relationship of individual and state, both of which seem abstract and universally necessary, rather than the triadic relations of individual, state, and a plurality of social groups that seem unavoidably locally specific." Jacob Levy, *Rationalism, Pluralism, and Freedom* (Oxford: Oxford University Press, 2015), 12.

115. See Stephen V. Monsma and Stanley W. Carlson-Thies, *Free to Serve: Protecting the Religious Freedom of Faith-Based Organizations* (Grand Rapids, MI: Brazos Press, 2015) and Marci A. Hamilton, *God vs. the Gavel: Religion and the Rule of Law* (Cambridge, UK: Cambridge University Press, 2005) for two sides to this debate.

116. We will discuss state funding in more detail in chapters 3 and 4.

117. Horwitz, *Institutions*, 24.

118. While not strictly a First Amendment case (as we have said, the First Amendment is not mentioned in the opinion), the tendency to attach association to speech is present and affects later jurisprudential developments.

CHAPTER 2. PLURALISM AND THE "SOCIAL" NATURE OF THE SOCIAL GROUP

1. The notion that a group has qualities that are not reducible to its individual members need not implicate "metaphysics or spiritual essences" but simply "legal ideas and real social facts." See Levy, *Rationalism*, 247. Levy is discussing F. W. Maitland's pluralism, and the English pluralists more generally, but the principle that the social reality of groups goes beyond the individuals who compose them is important to a broader understanding of the complex reality of associational dynamics.

2. This process was discussed briefly in chapter 1.

3. Robert Nisbet, *The Quest for Community* (Wilmington, DE: ISI Books, 2010), 62–63.

4. Nisbet, 63.

5. While Nisbet's broad claims about the impersonality of modern associations may be true in the aggregate as indicated by overwhelming evidence for increased alienation and anomie (see generally Putnam, *Bowling Alone*), some associations, such as labor unions, seem to have an integrating effect on their members that Nisbet did not fully appreciate. See Crain and Inazu, "Re-Assembling Labor," 1791.

6. Nisbet, *Quest*, 50.

7. Nisbet is writing during the social turmoil of the 1970s, but his argument is increasingly relevant today in the wake of riots in response to incidents of police violence in Ferguson, Missouri, and Baltimore, Maryland, among other places.

8. For the case that the voluntary association is Nisbet's antidote to alienation by being able to effectively reintegrate the individual into meaningful community in the context of liberal democracy, see Sheahan, "Antidote."

9. Nisbet, *Twilight*, 247. Emphasis in original.

10. Nisbet, 246.

11. Nisbet, 251–252.

12. Nisbet, 215.

13. Nisbet, 217.

14. Nisbet, 217.

15. Nisbet, 218.

16. Nisbet, *Quest*, 256, 257; *Twilight*, 252–259.

17. Nisbet, *Twilight*, 252–259; *Quest*, 256.

18. Nisbet, *Twilight*, 255–256.

19. Nisbet, 257.

20. Nisbet, 256–257.

21. Nisbet, 257. In *The Social Bond*, Nisbet praises the reforms of Cleisthenes and the rise of the political state in Athens. He writes, "To the historian, to the social scientist, to any humane mind, the changes effected by Cleisthenes must rank among the greatest to be found anywhere in history. No one will question the moral values that lay behind his works, or the personal courage and insight." Nisbet, *The Social Bond*, 397–398.

22. Nisbet, *Quest*, 226.

23. Nisbet, 256.

24. Nisbet, 227.

25. Nisbet, 209.

26. Nisbet, *Social Bond*, 45.

27. Nisbet, 45.

28. Nisbet, 45.

29. As noted in the introduction, Jacob Levy writes, "The rise of the language of liberal universalism . . . leads us to overemphasize the dyadic relationship of individual and state, both of which seem abstract and universally necessary, rather than the triadic relations of individual, state, and a plurality of social groups that seem unavoidably locally specific." Levy, *Rationalism, Pluralism, and Freedom*, 12. This insight explains some of the difficulty encountered by discussions of the social group in political philosophy that focuses too much on abstract concepts to the detriment of the concrete and the contextual.

30. Nisbet, *Social Bond*, 83.

31. Nisbet, 80.

32. Nisbet, 81.

33. Nisbet, 81. Emphasis added.

34. Nisbet, 82.

35. Robert Nisbet, *The Degradation of the Academic Dogma: The University in America, 1945–1970* (New York: Basic Books, 1971), 43.

36. Nisbet, 43.

37. Nisbet, 44.

38. Nisbet, 44.

39. Nisbet, 45.

40. "Conceptual distinctions, yes; separations, no." Nisbet, *Social Bond*, 232.

41. Nisbet, 85. This type of aggregate will be described in chapter 3 as an "intimate association."

42. Nisbet, 88.

43. Nisbet, 88.

44. Nisbet, 88–89.

45. Nisbet, 89.

46. *Roberts v. United States Jaycees*, 468 U.S. 609, 610 (1984)

47. Nisbet, *Social Bond*, 91.

48. Nisbet, 92.

49. Nisbet, 92.

50. Nisbet, 94.

51. Nisbet, 97–98.

52. Nisbet, 98.

53. Nisbet, 98.

54. Nisbet, 99–100.

55. Nisbet, 101.

56. Nisbet, 101.

57. *Minersville School District v. Gobitis*, 310 U.S. 586 (1940) and *West Virginia State Board of Education v. Barnette*, 319 U.S. 624 (1943); Nisbet, *Social Bond*, 104.

58. *Zubik v. Burwell*, 578 U.S. 1 (2016).

59. The riots in 2014–2015 in Ferguson, Missouri, are a prime example of this conflict. See Samantha Storey, "Scenes of Chaos Unfold after a Peaceful Vigil in Ferguson," *New York Times*, August 13, 2014.

60. Nisbet, *Social Bond*, 104.

61. Nisbet, 105.

62. Nisbet, 105. Nisbet's examples.

63. Nisbet, 106.

64. Nisbet, 106.

65. Nisbet, 107.

66. Nisbet, 108.

67. Nisbet, 109.

68. Nisbet, 110.

69. Nisbet, 111.

70. Nisbet, 148.

71. Nisbet, 149.

72. Nisbet, 149–150.

73. Nisbet, 152.

74. Nisbet, 157.

75. Nisbet, 181.

76. Nisbet, 182.

77. Nisbet, 182–184.

78. Nisbet, 187.

79. Nisbet, 209.

80. Nisbet, 201–202.

81. Nisbet, 200.

82. Nisbet, 222.

83. Nisbet, 223.

84. Nisbet, 223.

85. Nisbet, 226–227.

86. Nisbet, 233.

87. Nisbet, 233.

88. Nisbet, 233.

89. Nisbet, *Sociological Tradition*, 150.

90. Nisbet, 150–151.

91. Nisbet, 151.

92. Nisbet, 153.

93. Nisbet, 153.

94. Nisbet, 163.

95. Nisbet, *Social Bond*, 117.

96. Nisbet, *Sociological Tradition*, 166. Emphasis in original.

97. Nisbet quoting Simmel, in Nisbet, *Sociological Tradition*, 167.

98. Nisbet, *Social Bond*, 117.

99. Nisbet, 121.

100. Nisbet, 122.

101. Nisbet, 122.

102. Nisbet, 129–130.

103. Nisbet, 130.

104. Nisbet, 130–131.

105. Nisbet, 131.

106. Nisbet, 132.

107. Nisbet, 133. Nisbet writes, "The totalitarian state is but an intensification of tendencies present in the modern limited state, an extension of political powers possessed under the doctrine of sovereignty even by the democratic state. There is still a profound difference between a political order in which power stemming from government is limited and significant areas of intellectual, cultural, and economic autonomy are left intact, and a political order whose aim is systematic extermination of these areas of autonomy."

108. Nisbet, 140.

109. Nisbet, 141.

110. Nisbet, 142.

111. For a brief discussion of the sociological character of the voluntary association, see Sheahan, "Antidote," 296–297.

112. Nisbet, 89. Nisbet makes the same point in *Twilight*, 247.

113. See chapter 3.

114. Alexis de Tocqueville, *Democracy in America* (Indianapolis: Liberty Fund, 2012), 896.

115. Nisbet, *Social Bond*, 108.

116. Nisbet, 149.

117. CLS's statement of faith at issue in the *Martinez* case will be discussed in detail in the next chapter.

118. Nisbet, *Sociological Tradition*, 163.

CHAPTER 3. THE FIRST AMENDMENT DICHOTOMY AND FREEDOM OF ASSOCIATION

1. Inazu, *Liberty's Refuge*.

2. Inazu, 97.

3. Inazu, 105.

4. Quoted in Inazu, 99.

5. Inazu, 99–100.

6. Quoted in Inazu, 101.

7. Quoted in Inazu, 101.

8. Inazu, 106–107.

9. James Madison, Alexander Hamilton, and John Jay, *The Federalist Papers* (New York: Penguin Group, 2003), 72.

10. Inazu, *Liberty's Refuge*, 104.

11. Inazu, 131.

12. Inazu, 129.

13. Inazu, 131.

14. Ronald Dworkin, *Freedom's Law: The Moral Reading of the American Constitution*, excerpted in *Constitutional Theory: Arguments and Perspectives*, 3rd ed., ed. Michael Gerhardt, Stephen M. Griffin, and Thomas D. Rowe Jr. (Newark: Matthew Bender, 2007), 360.

15. Dworkin, 360.

16. Dworkin, 354–355.

17. Nisbet, *Twilight of Authority*, 248–249.

18. Robert J. Bresler, *Freedom of Association: Rights and Liberties under the Law* (Santa Barbara, CA: ABC-CLIO, 2004), 4.

19. Bresler, 39–40.

20. *NAACP v. Alabama*, 357 U.S. 449 (1958).

21. *NAACP*, 357 U.S. 449, 460.

22. *NAACP*, 357 U.S. 460.

23. Inazu, *Liberty's Refuge*, 82. Inazu's research indicates that the Court was split as to the origins of the right, with Frankfurter insisting that Harlan cite only the Fourteenth Amendment and Douglas and Black pressing him to cite the First Amendment.

24. *DeJonge v. Oregon*, 299 U.S. 353, 364.

25. *DeJonge*, 357 U.S. 461.

26. See Inazu, *Liberty's Refuge*, 82n44. Most of the scholars he cites understand the case as a First Amendment case.

27. Inazu, 82. See Thomas Emerson, "Freedom of Association and Freedom of Expression," *Yale Law Journal* 74, no. 1 (November 1964): 1–35.

28. *Bates v. City of Little Rock*, 361 U.S. 516 (1960).

29. "It is now beyond dispute that freedom of association for the purpose of advancing ideas and airing grievances is protected by the Due Process Clause of the Fourteenth Amendment from invasion by the States." *Bates*, 361 U.S. 516, 523.

30. *Bates*, 361 U.S. 516, 528.

31. *Shelton v. Tucker*, 364 U.S. 479, 485–486 (1960).

32. *Bates*, 364 U.S. 479, 497.

33. Inazu, *Liberty's Refuge*, 74–75.

34. *Louisiana v. NAACP*, 366 U.S. 293, 296 (1961).

35. *NAACP v. Button*, 371 U.S. 415, 428–429 (1963).

36. *Uphaus v. Wyman*, 360 U.S. 72 (1959), *Barenblatt v. United States*, 360 U.S. 109 (1959), *Communist Party v. Subversive Activities Control Board* (SACB) 367 U.S. 1 (1961), *Scales v. United States*, 367 U.S. 203 (1961).

37. *Gibson v. Florida Legislative Investigation Comm.*, 372 U.S. 539 (1963).

38. *Gibson*, 372 U.S. 539, 540.

39. *Gibson*, 372 U.S. 539, 544.

40. *Runyon v. McCrary*, 427 U.S. 163 (1976).

41. Inazu, *Liberty's Refuge*, 123–124. Italics in original.

42. The importance of conduct as an aspect of belief was discussed in chapter 2, and we will return to it in chapter 4. The term used there for conduct is "prescribed practices," which are associated with the "central tenets" that form the core of a group's beliefs.

43. Inazu, *Liberty's Refuge*, 125–126.

44. *Roberts v. United States Jaycees*, 468 U.S. 609 (1984).

45. Inazu, *Liberty's Refuge*, 133.

46. *Roberts*, 468 U.S. 620 (1984).

47. Kenneth L. Karst, "The Freedom of Intimate Association," *Yale Law Journal* 89, no. 4 (March 1980): 629. Quoted in Inazu, *Liberty's Refuge*, 136.

48. *Roberts*, 468 U.S. 619. Subsequent privacy cases such as *Planned Parenthood v. Casey*, 505 U.S. 833 (1992) have reinforced this notion.

49. Tracey, "In Hindsight," 71.

50. *Roberts*, 468 U.S. 624.

51. Andrew Koppelman and Tobias Barrington Wolff, *A Right to Discriminate? How the Case of* Boy Scouts of America v. James Dale *Warped the Law of Free Association* (New Haven: Yale University Press, 2009), 19.

52. Inazu, *Liberty's Refuge*, 136. This fourth type of association is just as important as the rest. We explained the importance of associations, regardless of whether they are expressive, in chapter 2, and we will return to the point in chapter 4.

53. *Lawrence v. Texas*, 539 U.S. 558 (2003) relied on the Due Process Clause and ignored the category of intimate associations. See Inazu, *Liberty's Refuge*, 138–139.

54. Tracey, "In Hindsight," 53.

55. *Rotary International v. Rotary Club of Duarte*, 481 U.S. 537 (1987).

56. *New York Club Ass'n v. City of New York*, 487 U.S. 1 (1988).

57. *Hurley v. Irish-American Gay, Lesbian, and Bisexual Group of Boston*, 515 U.S. 557 (1995).

58. *Boy Scouts of America v. Dale*, 530 U.S. 640, 648 (2000).

59. *United States v. O'Brien*, 391 U.S. 367 (1968) (upholding the conviction of a protester who burned his draft card). The O'Brien test holds that "a government regulation is sufficiently justified if it is within the constitutional power of the Government; if it furthers an important or substantial governmental interest; if the governmental interest is unrelated to the suppression of free expression, and if the incidental restriction on alleged First Amendment freedoms is no greater than is essential to the furtherance of that interest." 391 U.S. 377.

60. *Dale*, 530 U.S. 659.

61. Bresler, "Freedom of Association," 96.

62. Tracey, "In Hindsight," 54.

63. This implicates the discussion of "dogma" at the core of associations, including expressive associations, discussed in chapter 2.

64. Charles J. Russo and William E. Thro, "Another Nail in the Coffin of Religious Freedom? *Christian Legal Society v. Martinez*," *Education Law Journal* 12 (2011): 20.

65. The policy states, "[Hastings] shall not discriminate unlawfully on the basis of race, color, religion, national origin, ancestry, disability, age, sex, or sexual orientation." Quoted in *Martinez*, 561 U.S. 661, 670 (2010).

66. "Trusting in Jesus Christ as my Savior, I believe in: One God, eternally existent in three persons, Father, Son and Holy Spirit. God, the Father Almighty, Maker of heaven and earth. The Deity of our Lord, Jesus Christ, God's only Son, conceived of the Holy Spirit, born of the virgin Mary; His vicarious death for our sins through which we receive eternal life; His bodily resurrection and personal return. The presence and power of the Holy Spirit in the work of regeneration. The Bible as the inspired Word of God." Brief for Petitioner at 6, *Martinez*, 561 U.S. 661 (No. 08–1371).

67. Brief for Petitioner at 7, *Martinez*, 561 U.S. 661 (No. 08–1371).

68. The policy was relatively uncontroversial for students on campuses with CLS chapters. "Nationwide, CLS has only once had to expel a member for beliefs inconsistent with the Statement of Faith, and it is unaware of any homosexual person being expelled from any chapter." Brief for petitioner at 7, *Martinez*, 561 U.S. 661 (No. 08–1371).

69. *Martinez*, 561 U.S. 661, 668. The Court wrote, "Hastings interprets the Non-discrimination Policy, as it relates to the RSO program, to mandate acceptance of all comers." This interpretation arose during deposition of the former law school dean Mary Kane, who stated, "In order to be a registered student organization you have to allow all of our students to be members and full participants if they want to." See Brief for Respondent, Addendum at 7, *Martinez*, 561 U.S. 661 (No. 08–1371).

70. *Martinez*, 561 U.S. 661, 672–673.

71. *Martinez*, 561 U.S. 661, 669–670.

72. Brief for Petitioner at 12, *Martinez*, 561 U.S. 661 (No. 08–1371).

73. *Martinez*, 561 U.S. 661, 673.

74. *Martinez*, 561 U.S. 661, 675.

75. Tracey, "In Hindsight," 73. Tracey served on CLS's legal team.

76. The nondiscrimination policy was not ruled constitutional by the Court and, according to some legal scholars, remains presumptively unconstitutional until the Supreme Court rules otherwise. See Tracey, 72n3.

77. *Martinez*, 561 U.S. 661, 678.

78. *Martinez*, 561 U.S. 661, 669.

79. *Martinez*, 561 U.S. 661, 685. Internal citations omitted.

80. *Martinez*, 561 U.S. 661, 685, 689.

81. The Court dismissed the free exercise claim in a footnote and did not address it at all in the main text of the opinion. See *Martinez*, 561 U.S. 661, 697n27. "CLS briefly argues that Hastings's all-comers condition violates the Free Exercise Clause. Our decision in *Smith*, 494 U.S. 872, forecloses that argument." Internal citations omitted.

82. *Martinez*, 561 U.S. 661, 680.

83. Erica Goldberg, "Amending *Christian Legal Society v. Martinez*: Protecting Expressive Association as an Independent Right in a Limited Public Forum," *Texas Journal on Civil Liberties & Civil Rights* 16, no. 2 (2011): 148.

84. *Dale*, 530 U.S. 640, 648 (2000).

85. Jonathan Winters, "Thou Shall Not Exclude: How *Christian Legal Society v. Martinez* Affects Expressive Associations, Limited Public Forums, and Student's Associational Rights," *University of Toledo Law Review* 43 (Spring 2012): 752.

86. *Martinez*, 561 U.S. 661, 680.

87. We will discuss problems with this description of limited public forums in detail later in the chapter.

88. *Martinez*, 561 U.S. 661, 681. The Court wrote, "Implicit in the concept of a limited public forum is the State's right to make distinction in access on the basis of . . . speaker identity." Internal citations omitted.

89. *Martinez*, 561 U.S. 661, 682.

90. *Martinez*, 561 U.S. 661, 683.

91. In the next section we will tie the Court's use of forum analysis in *Martinez* to the concept of the state.

92. *Martinez*, 561 U.S. 661, 679. Internal citations omitted.

93. *Martinez*, 561 U.S. 661, 686.

94. *Martinez*, 561 U.S. 661, 687.

95. *Martinez*, 561 U.S. 661, 695.

96. *Martinez*, 561 U.S. 661, 696.

97. *Martinez*, 561 U.S. 661, 692.

98. *Martinez*, 561 U.S. 661, 692. "This catchphrase confuses CLS's preferred policy with constitutional limitation—the *advisability* of Hastings's policy does not control its *permissibility*. . . . A State's restriction on access to a limited public forum need not be the most reasonable or the only reasonable limitation." Italics in original. Internal citations omitted.

99. *Martinez*, 561 U.S. 661, 692. The Court was incorrect in stating that a hostile takeover is a hypothetical fear. Actual cases have been documented where hostile students took over student groups for reasons of ideological disagreement. See Brief for the Foundation for Individual Rights in Education and Students for Liberty as *Amicus Curiae* at 8–12, *Martinez*, 561 U.S. 661.

100. *Martinez*, 561 U.S. 661, 693–694.

101. Tracey, "In Hindsight," 95.

102. Tracey, 86.

103. *Widmar v. Vincent*, 454 U.S. 263 (1981), 268–269. Also see *Shelton v. Tucker*, 364 U.S. 479, 364 U.S. 487 (1960); *Tinker v. Des Moines Independent Community School District*, 393 U.S. 503 (1969); *Healy v. James*, 408 U.S. 169, 180 (1972).

104. We will discuss the student organization forum as a limited public forum in detail below.

105. Tracey provides a list of diverse commentators who agree that the decision applies narrowly to the "all-comers" policy at Hastings. See Tracey, "In Hindsight," 72n3, 74n20. Also see William N. Eskridge Jr., "Noah's Curse: How Religion Often Conflates Status, Belief, and Conduct to Resist Antidiscrimination Norms," *Georgia Law Review*, 45:657, 720 (2011). Eskridge argues that *Martinez* is an example of a "narrow" constitutional ruling.

106. This is Tracey's opinion. See Tracey, "In Hindsight," 116–123.

107. B. Jessie Hill, "Property and the Public Forum: An Essay on *Christian Legal Society v. Martinez*," *Duke Journal of Constitutional Law and Public Policy*, special issue 6, no. 51 (2010).

108. David Brown, "Hey! Universities! Leave Them Kids Alone! *Christian Legal Society v. Martinez* and Conditioning Equal Access to a University's Student-Organization Forum," *Penn State Law Review* 116 (2011): 165–167.

109. Goldberg, "Amending *CLS*," 160–162 and Hill, "Property," both see this as an important jurisprudential innovation in the decision. But the dissent dismissed the subsidy aspect as "play[ing] a very small role" in the majority decision. 561 U.S. 718 (Alito, S., dissenting). See analysis below in the section "Government Property and Subsidy."

110. Compare Goldberg, "Amending *CLS*" and Julie A. Nice, "How Equality Constitutes Liberty: The Alignment of *CLS v. Martinez* (The Constitution on Campus: The Case of *CLS v. Martinez*)," *Hastings Constitutional Law Quarterly* 38, no. 3 (2011):

631–672. Goldberg and Nice come to opposite conclusions in terms of the soundness of the holding, but both agree on the potential effect of the decision on freedom of association. See also Ashutosh Bhagwat, "Associations and Forums: Situating *CLS v. Martinez*," *Hastings Constitutional Law Quarterly* 38, no. 3 (2011): 549.

111. Edward J. Schoen and Joseph S. Falchek, "*Christian Legal Society v. Martinez*: Rock, Paper, Scissors," *Southern Law Journal* 21 (Fall 2010): 222–223. "The manner in which these three competing interests are resolved in *Christian Legal Society* strikes the authors as being rather like the ancient game of 'Rock—Paper—Scissors' in which participants use hand gestures symbolizing the rock, paper, and scissors to defeat an opponent. . . . In *Christian Legal Society*, First Amendment principles are like the competing hand gestures."

112. See Nice, "Equality" and Max Kanin, "*Christian Legal Society v. Martinez*: How an Obscure First Amendment Case Inadvertently and Unexpectedly Created a Significant Fourteenth Amendment Advance for LGBT Rights Advocates," *Journal of Gender, Social Policy & the Law*, 1324–1326 (2011). Both Nice and Kanin see the case as a significant achievement of constitutional rights for gays and lesbians on par with *Lawrence*, 539 U.S. 558 (2003) and *Romer v. Evans*, 517 U.S. 620 (1996).

113. "In my view . . . Hastings probably should have won. . . . The university's right to sponsor groups like the CLS, or to exclude them altogether, trumps the nested rights of the associations in question." Paul Horwitz, *First Amendment Institutions* (Cambridge, MA: Harvard University Press, 2013), 237.

114. Horwitz, 236.

115. "A true victory for diversity and pluralism in CLS would have involved neither demanding that student groups include all comers nor insisting that universities cannot tell them to do so. It would have involved adopting a robust institutional framework that would help us see that there is room for universities to reach different decisions on this question." Horwitz, 238.

116. Horwitz, 236.

117. While concurrences are noncontrolling, they can provide insight into the votes of particular justices, in this case, Justices Anthony Kennedy and John Paul Stevens.

118. Justice Samuel Alito authored the dissent and was joined by Chief Justice John Roberts, Justice Antonin Scalia, and Justice Clarence Thomas.

119. For example, see Inazu, *Liberty's Refuge*, especially ch. 3, Bhagwat, "Associations and Forums," and Ashutosh Bhagwat, "Associational Speech," 120 *Yale Law Journal* 978 (2011).

120. Below we will relate speech to the concept of the state. See "Speech and the Democratic State."

121. Inazu writes, "The assembly right necessarily invokes a relational context: one can speak alone; one cannot assemble alone." John D. Inazu, "The First Amendment's Public Forum," *William & Mary Law Review* 56:1159 (2015): 1169.

122. See *Roberts*, 468 U.S. 609, 618 (1984); *NAACP v. Alabama*, 357 U.S. 449 (1958). Also see Bhagwat, "Associations and Forums," 566. "The modern Court . . . has treated association as a right derivative of and subsidiary to free speech."

123. *Martinez*, 561 U.S. 661, 680.

124. The majority cited one case to justify this "unprecedented maneuver." *Citizens against Rent Control Coalition for Fair Housing v. Berkeley* 454 U.S. 290 (1981). See *Martinez*, 561 U.S. 661, 680. The Court ruled in that case that the actions of the California ordinance in question violated both the right to free speech and the right to expressive association. That did not imply that they were not separate rights with separate streams of jurisprudence. An analysis under the freedom of association line of jurisprudence would have required stricter scrutiny, but would still have failed to free the Court's analysis from the First Amendment Dichotomy.

125. *Martinez*, 561 U.S. 661, 681.

126. Brown, "Leave Them Kids Alone!" 180.

127. *Martinez*, 561 U.S. 661, 704 (Kennedy, A., concurring).

128. *Martinez*, 561 U.S. 661, 706 (Alito, S., dissenting).

129. *Healy*, 408 U.S. 169 (1972). See *Martinez*, 561 U.S. 661, 718–722 (Alito, S., dissenting).

130. *Martinez*, 561 U.S. 661, 721 (Alito, S., dissenting). Internal citation omitted. Emphasis added. The Court is so enmeshed in its dichotomous theory of association that even a victory for CLS would not have secured the right of association, as the alternative majority opinion would have still justified association on the basis of the individual right to speech.

131. See generally Inazu, *Liberty's Refuge*; John D. Inazu, "The Four Freedoms and the Future of Religious Liberty," *North Carolina Law Review* 92 (2014): 787, 814; John D. Inazu, "The Forgotten Freedom of Assembly," *Tulane Law Review* 84 (2010): 565, 601–603.

132. See the discussion of Inazu in chapter 1.

133. For example, see *Roberts*, 468 U.S. 609 (1984) (distinguishing between the status of sex and the belief in advancing young men in business), *Dale*, 530 U.S. 640 (2000) (distinguishing between the status of homosexuality and belief in the morality of homosexual acts), and *Runyon vs. McCrary*, 427 U.S. 163 (1976) (distinguishing between the status of race and racist beliefs). Also see Eugene Volokh, "Freedom of Expressive Association and Government Subsidies," *57 Stan. L. Rev.* 1919, 1938 (2006). "A religious group . . . that condemns homosexuality might demand that its members share those views. Such a demand would be neither religious discrimination nor sexual orientation discrimination, but only discrimination based on holding a certain viewpoint that secular people could hold as well as religious ones. But such a group rule wouldn't just exclude practicing homosexuals, or at least those practicing homosexuals who believe that homosexuality is proper—it would also exclude heterosexual Catholics who disagree with church teachings on this issue. And if the group tolerates these dissenting heterosexual Catholics but excludes dissenting homosexual Catholics, then it would be engaging in prohibited sexual orientation discrimination, not permitted religious discrimination."

134. Goldberg, "Amending *CLS*," 153.

135. As we discussed above, the Court had developed a concept of a status/belief distinction in *Runyon*.

136. *Roberts*, 468 U.S. 609, 624–626. Also see Nice, "Equality," 655–656, for analysis.

137. See *Robinson v. California*, 370 U.S. 660, 665 (distinguishing between the status of drug addiction and the conduct of illegal drug use).

138. *Lawrence*, 539 U.S. 558, 575 (2003). Inazu links this to Ginsberg's "inattention to religious liberty." John D. Inazu, "Justice Ginsberg and Religious Liberty," *Hastings Law Journal* 63 (2012):1213–1241.

139. *Martinez*, 561 U.S. 661, 689 (quoting *Lawrence*, 589 U.S. 661, 575). Emphasis inserted by *Martinez* Court.

140. Nice, "Equality," 670.

141. Kanin, "Obscure," 1324–1326.

142. *Martinez*, 561 U.S. 661, 688. See also *Christian Legal Society v. Walker*, 453 F.3d 853 (7th Cir. 2006). The 7th Circuit ruled in favor of the CLS chapter in question on a nearly identical case because the group discriminated in membership on the basis of same-sex conduct, but not the immutable characteristic of sexual orientation.

143. See the discussion of *Roberts* above. *Roberts*, 468 U.S. 609, 623–624, 628–629 (1984).

144. Goldberg, "Amending *CLS*," 153.

145. For example, in *Dale*, 530 U.S. 640, 655 (2000), "An association must merely engage in expressive activity that could be impaired in order to be entitled to protection."

146. Nice, "Equality," 672.

147. See *Romer*, 517 U.S. 620 (1996) and *Lawrence*, 539 U.S. 558 (2003). Nice, "Equality," 645–648.

148. *Romer*, 517 U.S. 624.

149. *Lawrence*, 539 U.S. 575.

150. Constitutional scholar Bruce Frohnen explains the individual right to act corporately: "A multitude of authorities, aiming at differing ends . . . allowed space for each person to carve out his or her own sphere of autonomous action while also pursuing substantive goods in common with his or her fellows." Bruce P. Frohnen, "The One and the Many: Individual Rights, Corporate Rights, and the Diversity of Groups," *West Virginia Law Review* 107 (2005): 789–845, 845.

151. *Rosenberger v. Rector & Visitors for the University of Virginia*, 515 U.S. 819 (1995). See Brief for Gays and Lesbians for Individual Liberty as *Amicus Curiae* at 9n2, *Martinez*, 561 U.S. 661. "The expressive freedom claims of religious and gay student groups have long been mutually reinforcing. The plaintiffs in *Rosenberger* relied heavily on *Gay & Lesbian Students Assn. v. Gohn*. . . . And many high school gay rights groups have found refuge in the Equal Access Act, which was enacted in part at the behest of religious-liberty advocates." Internal citations omitted.

152. Brief for Petitioner at 12–13, *Martinez*, 561 U.S. 661 (No. 08–1371). The dissent pointed out that plenty of student groups at Hastings were allowed to have membership requirements in their bylaws. The university only objected to the membership requirements of those groups after CLS's litigation was underway. See 561 U.S. 712–13 (Alito, J., dissenting).

153. The women's rights movement and the civil rights movement are two prominent examples. See Inazu, *Liberty's Refuge*, 44–48.

154. And now *Obergefell v. Hodges*, 576 US __ (2015) can be added to the list of gay rights victories coming out of the Supreme Court.

155. See Dale Carpenter, "Expressive Association and Anti-Discrimination Law after *Dale*: A Tripartite Approach," *Minnesota Law Review* 85, 1515 at 1528–1531 (2001).

156. "[The First Amendment's] chief value may be the role it plays in protecting people who want to combine with others to promote common causes. This lesson holds for gay people, who have benefited politically and personally when they organize and who have suffered terribly when the state impeded their ability to do so." Carpenter, 1519.

157. Many went even further. The first gay rights organization, the Chicago Society for Human Rights, required that members be both homosexual and male. Even bisexual males were excluded. Carpenter, 1529.

158. Carpenter, 1588. Internal citations omitted.

159. *Martinez*, 561 U.S. 661, 694. Emphasis in original.

160. Hastings regulations for student groups require that groups submit "a statement of *its purpose*." See *Martinez*, 561 U.S. 661, 729 (Alito, J., dissenting), quoting Hastings Regulations 34.10.A.1.

161. Goldberg, "Amending *CLS*," 154.

162. *Martinez*, 561 U.S. 661, 694.

163. Goldberg, "Amending *CLS*," 156.

164. Brown, "Leave Them Kids Alone!"187.

165. *Martinez*, 561 U.S. 661, 669.

166. Inazu is the most perceptive scholar on this point. He traces the relationship between free speech and the democratic state in Supreme Court doctrine. See the sections above "The Legal Theory Background" and "A Brief History of Freedom of Association," which draw heavily from Inazu's scholarship.

167. *Martinez*, 561 U.S. 661, 689.

168. *Martinez*, 561 U.S. 661, 689. "Hastings can rationally rank among RSO-program goals development of conflict-resolution skills, toleration, and readiness to find common ground."

169. *Martinez*, 561 U.S. 661, 705 (Kennedy, A., concurring).

170. "An association is a coming together of individuals for a common cause or based on common values or goals." Bhagwat, "Associational Speech," 998. Those values or goals need not have anything to do with state objectives.

171. *Martinez*, 561 U.S. 661, 706 (Kennedy, A., concurring).

172. *Martinez*, 561 U.S. 661, 734 (Alito, S., dissenting). Internal citation omitted.

173. *Widmar*, 454 U.S. 263 (1981).

174. *Widmar*, 454 U.S. 263, 274.

175. *Martinez*, 561 U.S. 661, 680.

176. Robert Post argues that the limited public forum is virtually useless as a category and that there are really only two categories, public and non-public. Robert C. Post, "Between Governance and Management: The History of the Public Forum," *UCLA Law Review* 34 (1987): 1713, 1757. Also see Winters, "Exclude," 752.

177. Traditional public forums are places "which had traditionally been open to the public for purposes of assembling and exercising free-speech rights." Winters, "Exclude," 751. Public parks and public sidewalks are the paradigmatic examples. See *Hague v. CIO*, 307 U.S. 496, 515–516 (1939).

178. "The second category of public property is the designated public forum, whether of a limited or unlimited character—property that the state has opened for expressive activity by part or all of the public." *International Society for Krishna Consciousness, Inc. v. Lee*, 505 U.S. 672, 678 (1992), citing *Perry v. Perry Local Educators' Association*, 460 U.S. 37, 45 (1983). Also see *Perry*, 460 U.S. 37, 48 and *Heffron*, 452 U.S. 640, 655.

179. A limited public forum happens when the government designates a forum public and further restricts the forum to a certain class of speakers or for a certain purpose. *Cornelius v. NAACP Legal Defense & Education Fund*, 473 U.S. 788, 802–803 (1985), *Heffron*, 452 U.S. 640, 655. For example, public universities restricting student groups to students. See *Widmar*, 454 U.S. 263, 267–268 (1981). There is ambiguity as to the distinction between designated and limited public forums. One interpretation the Court has given is that the limited public forum is a type of designated public forum. See *Perry*, 460 U.S. 37, 45.

180. A nonpublic forum is a government-sponsored forum that is *not* public. The only restriction on the government in a nonpublic forum is that the government cannot restrict speech on the basis of mere opposition to the speaker's views. Winters, "Exclude," 752. Also see Bhagwat, "Associations and Forums," 559.

181. "The forum concept has been criticized for, among other things, its rigidity, its lack of a coherent theoretical foundation, and its myopic focus on property characteristics to the exclusion of expressive rights." Timothy Zick, "Space, Place, and Speech: The Expressive Topography," *George Washington Law Review* 74 (2006): 439, 440.

182. "[Limited public forums] can be limited to a particular class of people (like students on public university campuses) or to a particular topic (like a public hearing on a proposed policy)." John D. Inazu, *Confident Pluralism: Surviving and Thriving through Deep Difference* (Chicago: University of Chicago Press, 2016), 50–51.

183. Winters, "Exclude," 752. See *Perry*, 460 U.S. 37, 48. "A limited public forum [was] generally open for use by employee organizations, and that once this occurred, exclusions of employee organizations thereafter must be judged by the constitutional standard applicable to public forums."

184. *Widmar*, 454 U.S. 263, 267n5. The "Court has recognized that the campus of a public university, at least for its students, possesses many of the characteristics of a public forum." Also see *Rosenberger*, 515 U.S. 819, 828–830 (1995).

185. *Rosenberger*, 515 U.S. 819, 828–829. *Perry*, 460 U.S. 37, 45.

186. *Widmar*, 454 U.S. 263, 267n5. See Winters, "Exclude," 756–757; *Rosenberger*, 515 U.S. 819, 829; *University of Wisconsin v. Southworth*, 529 U.S. 217, 234.

187. *Healy*, 408 U.S. 169 (1972). While the Court doesn't use the "limited public forum" language in *Healy*, it applied the same principles there.

188. *Pleasant Grove City v. Summum*, 555 U.S. 460 (2009).

189. *Summum*, 555 U.S. 460, 469–470. Emphasis added.

190. Winters, "Exclude," 753.

191. *Martinez*, 561 U.S. 661, 679n11. In *Martinez*, the Court uses the term "limited public forum" to describe the third category, which it did not do in *Summum*.

192. Discussing the context of the public forum doctrines, Inazu writes, "The reasonableness requirement is an inherently squishy standard that can almost always be met." Inazu, *Confident Pluralism*, 54.

193. *Widmar*, 454 U.S. 263, 267n5.

194. The dissent cites *Rosenberger*, 515 U.S. 819 (1995), *Healy*, 408 U.S. 169 (1972), and *Southworth*, 529 US 217 (2000), among other cases that deal with the presence of religious groups on public school property. *Martinez*, 561 U.S. 661, 722. However, it neither cites nor references *Summum*.

195. *Martinez*, 561 U.S. 661, 726–727 (Alito, S., dissenting).

196. *Martinez*, 561 U.S. 661, 728 (Alito, S., dissenting).

197. *Martinez*, 561 U.S. 661, 683. Emphasis added.

198. Hill, "Property," 52.

199. Hill, 53.

200. Hill, 53.

201. *Martinez*, 561 U.S. 661, 682.

202. *Dale*, 530 U.S. 640, 648 (2000).

203. *Martinez*, 561 U.S. 683.

204. *Martinez*, 561 U.S. 661, 689–690. This is in reference to Cal. Educ. Code Ann. § 66270 (West Supp. 2010) (prohibiting discrimination on various bases including, but not limited to, disability, gender, gender identity, gender expression, nationality, race or ethnicity, religion, and sexual orientation).

205. Winters, "Exclude," 767.

206. Goldberg, "Amending *CLS*," 160. See *Rosenberger*, 515 U.S. 819 (1995) and *Southworth*, 529 U.S. 217 (2000).

207. Goldberg, "Amending *CLS*," 160.

208. *Healy*, 408 U.S. 169, 181.

209. *Widmar*, 454 U.S. 263, 267 (1981). Emphasis added. Internal citations omitted.

210. *Widmar*, 454 U.S. 263, 267–268.

211. *Widmar*, 454 U.S. 263, 274. Internal citations omitted.

212. *Widmar*, 454 U.S. 263, 274–275.

213. *Rosenberger*, 515 U.S. 819, 834.

214. *Southworth*, 529 US 217 (2000).

215. Tracey, "In Hindsight," 120. Internal citations omitted.

216. Tracey, 116.

217. *Healy*, 408 U.S. 169, 180. See *Shelton v. Tucker*, 364 U.S. 479, 487 (1960): "The vigilant protection of constitutional freedoms is nowhere more vital than in the community of American schools."

218. *Rosenberger*, 515 U.S. 819, 832.

219. *Southworth*, 529 U.S. 217.

220. *Gay and Lesbian Students Ass'n v. Gohn*, 850 F.2d 361 (1988).

221. *Healy*, 408 U.S. 169.

222. *Widmar*, 454 U.S. 263.

223. *Rosenberger*, 515 U.S. 819.

224. See *Gay Student Services v. Texas A&M University*, 737 F.2d 1317 (5th Cir. 1984); *University of S. Mississippi Chapter of the Mississippi Civil Liberties Union v. University of Southern Mississippi*, 452 F. 2d 564 (5th Cir. 1971); *Gay Alliance of Students v. Matthews*, 544 F. 2d 162, 168 (4th Cir. 1976); and *Gay Lesbian Bisexual Alliance v. Pryor*, 110 F.3d 1543 (11th Cir. 1997).

225. Bhagwat, "Associations and Forums," 651.

226. Julie Nice is one scholar who sees the subsidy issue as important to the case, since it implicates state recognition and involvement. Nice," Equality," at 648.

227. *Martinez*, 561 U.S. 661, 682.

228. *Martinez*, 561 U.S. 661, 669.

229. *Martinez*, 561 U.S. 661, 682.

230. *Forsyth County v. Nationalist Movement*, 505 U.S. 123, 134–135 (1992). "Listeners' reaction to speech is not a content-neutral basis for regulation. . . . Speech cannot be financially burdened, any more than it can be punished or banned, simply because it might offend a hostile mob."

231. Inazu, *Confident Pluralism*, 67.

232. Inazu, 67.

233. Inazu, 67. Italics in original.

234. Inazu, 70–71.

235. *Rosenberger*, 515 U.S. 819, is Inazu's example of proper use of generally available funds.

236. Inazu, *Confident Pluralism*, 80.

237. Goldberg, "Amending *CLS*," 153.

238. See *Martinez*, 561 U.S. 661, 688.

239. *Martinez*, 561 U.S. 661, 689. Referring to the relationship between being homosexual and engaging in homosexual conduct, the *Martinez* Court noted that its "decisions have declined to distinguish between status and conduct in this context."

240. *Lawrence*, 539 U.S. 558, 575 (2003). "When homosexual conduct is made criminal *by the law of the State*, that declaration in and of itself is an invitation to subject homosexual persons to discrimination." Emphasis added.

241. *Martinez*, 561 U.S. 661, 700 (Stevens, J., concurring).

242. *Martinez*, 561 U.S. 661, 700 (Stevens, J., concurring).

243. *Martinez*, 561 U.S. 661, 706 (Kennedy, J., concurring).

244. See Article VI of the U.S. Constitution, "no religious Test shall ever be required as a Qualification to any Office or public Trust under the United States." But the Court will recognize religious tests for groups where they are relevant. See *Hosanna-Tabor Evangelical Lutheran Church and School v. EEOC*, 565 U.S. 171, 181 (2012). "Both Religion Clauses bar the government from interfering with the decision of a religious group to fire one of its ministers."

245. *Martinez*, 561 U.S. 661, 687. This is one possible interpretation of the Court's ruling, although it is belied by the Court's use of limited public forum analysis, which infers government involvement.

246. See note 113.

247. Horwitz, *Institutions*, 185. "Disputes within hierarchical religious organizations, such as the Roman Catholic Church, would be resolved by accepting as final the decision of the highest church adjudicator to address the question."

248. Horwitz, 237. "Whichever path it chooses, the university, as the primary institution involved, should be able to make that choice for itself."

249. These are associations that "are themselves internally pluralistic." Jacob Levy, *Rationalism, Pluralism, and Freedom* (Oxford: Oxford University Press, 2015), 266.

250. Levy, *Rationalism*, 268–269.

251. Horwitz, *Institutions*, 137, and Levy, *Rationalism*, 271n5.

252. It is beyond the scope of this chapter (and indeed this book) to comment on the application of the public/private distinction to libraries or other institutions. For a counterargument to Horwitz on the public/private distinction, see John D. Inazu, "Institutions in Context," *Tulsa Law Review* 50 (Spring 2015): 491–501.

253. See "Dismantling the Status/Belief Distinction" above.

254. *Martinez*, 561 U.S. 661, 696.

255. "Although registered student groups must conform their conduct to the Law School's regulation by dropping access barriers, they may express any viewpoint they wish—including a discriminatory one." *Martinez*, 561 U.S. 661, 696n26. In other words, a group may not express its views via exclusion, but the individual members may continue to express their individual views, possibly in the presence of disagreeing members. Speech, not association, is what matters.

256. *Martinez*, 561 U.S. 661, 725 (Alito, S., dissenting).

CHAPTER 4. FIRST AMENDMENT PLURALISM

1. Robert Nisbet, *The Degradation of the Academic Dogma* (New Brunswick: Transaction, 1997), 43.

2. The purpose of expression was the Court's justification for association prior to *Martinez*. See discussion of *Roberts v. United States Jaycees*, 468 U.S. 609 (1984) in chapter 3.

3. This discussion draws from Alasdair MacIntyre's meditation on intrinsic and extrinsic goods in *After Virtue*, 3rd ed. (Notre Dame, IN: University of Notre Dame Press, 2007), 187–189.

4. MacIntyre, 189.

5. "Trusting in Jesus Christ as my Savior, I believe in: One God, eternally existent in three persons, Father, Son and Holy Spirit. God, the Father Almighty, Maker of heaven and earth. The Deity of our Lord, Jesus Christ, God's only Son, conceived of the Holy Spirit, born of the virgin Mary; His vicarious death for our sins through which we

receive eternal life; His bodily resurrection and personal return. The presence and power of the Holy Spirit in the work of regeneration. The Bible as the inspired Word of God." Brief for Petitioner at 6, *Christian Legal Society v. Martinez*, 561 U.S. 661 (No. 08-1371).

6. Nisbet, *Quest*, 256.

7. Nisbet, 257.

8. Nisbet, xxxii.

9. Nisbet, xxxii.

10. *DeJonge v. Oregon*, 299 U.S. 353, 364 (1937) referring to the right of assembly.

11. Robert Nisbet, "The Coming Problem of Assimilation," *American Journal of Sociology* 50, no. 4 (January 1945): 270.

12. See *Sherbert v. Verner*, 374 U.S. 398 (1963) and *Wisconsin v. Yoder*, 406 U.S. 205 (1972).

13. I use the term "authority" instead of "hierarchy" because it emphasizes precisely what is at issue with associations: the authority of the association to act as a unit. Of course, authority is exercised by a hierarchy. But use of the term "hierarchy" may confuse more than illuminate the issue.

14. Below I will argue that race may be a compelling interest in a limited public forum.

15. Robert F. Nagel, "States and Localities: A Comment on Robert Nisbet's Communitarianism," *Publius: The Journal of Federalism* 34, no. 4 (Fall 2004): 134.

16. *Employment Division v. Smith*, 494 U.S. 872 (1990).

17. *City of Boerne v. Flores, Archbishop of San Antonio*, 521 U.S. 507 (1997).

18. *DeJonge*, 299 U.S. 353, 364 (1937) referring to the right of assembly.

19. Inazu, *Liberty's Refuge*, 185–186.

20. Inazu, 186.

21. Erica Goldberg, "Amending *Christian Legal Society v. Martinez*: Protecting Expressive Association as an Independent Right in a Limited Public Forum," *Texas Journal on Civil Liberties & Civil Rights* 16, no. 2 (2011): 158.

22. Goldberg, 159.

23. Jack Willems, "The Loss of Freedom of Association in *Christian Legal Society v. Martinez*, 130 S. Ct. 2971 (2010)," *Harvard Journal of Law & Public Policy* 34, no. 2 (Spring 2011): 818.

24. David Brown, "Leave Them Kids Alone!" 195.

25. Brown, 196.

26. Brown, 197.

27. Kyle R. Cummins, "The Intersection of *CLS* and *Hosanna-Tabor*: The Ministerial Exception Applied to Religious Student Organizations," *University of Memphis Law Review* 44 (2013): 177.

28. Rene Reyes, "The Fading Free Exercise Clause," *William & Mary Bill of Rights Journal* 19, no. 3 (March 2011): 725–750.

29. There is tension on this point between what I argue and what Nelson Tebbe argues regarding "values organizations." See Nelson Tebbe, *Religious Freedom in an Egalitarian Age* (Cambridge: Harvard University Press, 2017), 85–87.

30. See a discussion of Levy's views on *Martinez* in chapter 3.

31. See Kelly Sarabyn, "Free Speech at Private Universities," *Journal of Law & Education* 39, no. 2 (2010): 145–182. Sarabyn argues that private universities are not bound by the First Amendment, but they are bound by whatever promises they make to their students and faculty members.

32. *Widmar v. Vincent*, 454 U.S. 263, 267n5. The "Court has recognized that the campus of a public university, at least for its students, possesses many of the characteristics of a public forum." Also see *Rosenberger v. Rectors of the University of Virginia*, 515 U.S. 819, 828–830 (1995).

33. *Perry Educ. Ass'n v. Perry Educators' Ass'n*, 460 U.S. 37, 48. "A limited public forum [was] generally open for use by employee organizations, and that once this occurred, exclusions of employee organizations thereafter must be judged by the constitutional standard applicable to public forums."

34. Inazu, *Liberty's Refuge*, 145.

35. Inazu, 166–168. Inazu makes noncommercial groups the focus of his theory of assembly, finding that there is little constitutional, economic, social, or popular support for revamping employment laws to allow commercial groups to discriminate in employees and customers. He also bars from the full protection of assembly groups that operate "under monopolistic or near-monopolistic conditions" in a manner similar to the state.

36. *Runyon v. McCrary*, 427 U.S. 160 (1976). Discussed in chapter 3.

37. *Bob Jones University v. United States*, 461 U.S. 574 (1983). Discussed in more detail below.

38. So it would not overturn *Shelley v. Kraemer*, 334 U.S. 1 (1948) (striking down a racially discriminatory housing covenant). In chapter 2, I noted that territorial authority was a characteristic constitutive of the political state. When a private association takes on a sort of quasi-state function, such as exerting authority over a particular geographical territory, it may be required to abide by the same limitations as the state, which includes a bar on racial discrimination. No locality, state, or federal initiative would be able to discriminate on the basis of race, and neither can these groups.

39. I take these categories from Inazu's discussion. See John Inazu, "The Four Freedoms and the Future of Religious Liberty," *North Carolina Law Review* 92 (2014): 787, 828–852.

40. Inazu, 835.

41. Inazu, 837.

42. *Christian Legal Society v. Martinez*, 561 U.S. 661, 689 (2010).

43. See Dale Carpenter, "Expressive Association and Anti-Discrimination Law after *Dale*: A Tripartite Approach," *Minnesota Law Review* 85 (2001): 1515, 1529, and *Gay Students Organization of the University of New Hampshire v. Bonner*, 509 F.2d 652, Note 1 (1st Cir. 1974).

44. Inazu, "Four Freedoms," 837.

45. Inazu, 842; Inazu, *Confident Pluralism*.

46. *National Socialist Party of America v. Village of Skokie*, 432 U.S. 43 (1977). The Supreme Court denied a stay of the trial court's injunction against the National Socialist

Party of America that forbade it from marching or protesting in the village of Skokie, Illinois, where many Holocaust survivors lived. While this was essentially a procedural ruling, the implication is that the rights of free speech and free assembly of even a neo-Nazi group are protected in a traditional public forum, such as a street through a small town.

47. *Martinez*, 561 U.S. 661, 683.

48. Inazu, *Confident Pluralism*, 69.

49. See *Regan v. Taxation with Representation of Washington*, 461 U.S. 540, 544 (1983). "Both tax exemptions and tax deductibility are a form of subsidy that is administered through the tax system."

50. See *Texas Monthly, Inc. v. Bullock*, 489 U.S. 1, 14 (1989) "Every tax exemption constitutes a subsidy that affects nonqualifying taxpayers. . . . *Insofar as that subsidy is conferred upon a wide array of nonsectarian groups as well as religious organizations in pursuit of some legitimate secular end, the fact that religious groups benefit incidentally does not deprive the subsidy of the secular purpose and primary effect mandated by the Establishment Clause*" (emphasis in original; internal citations omitted).

51. See "Tax Guide for Churches & Religious Organizations," Publication 1828 (Rev. 8–2015), Catalog Number 21096G, Department of the Treasury, Internal Revenue Service. https://www.irs.gov/pub/irs-pdf/p1828.pdf.

52. See Internal Revenue Code, 26.I.A.1 § 1.501(c)(3)–1.

53. Inazu, *Confident Pluralism*, 67.54. For example, see *National Endowment for the Arts v. Finley*, 524 U.S. 569 (1998) and *Harris v. McRae*, 448 U.S. 297 (1980).

55. Inazu, *Confident Pluralism*, 67.

56. *Widmar*, 454 U.S. 263, 267–268.

57. *Rosenberger*, 515 U.S. 819, 839.

58. *Rosenberger*, 515 U.S. 819, 833–34. Internal citations omitted.

59. *Rosenberger*, 515 U.S. 819, 834. Internal citations omitted.

60. *Gay and Lesbian Students Ass'n v. Gohn*, 850 F.2d 361 (1988).

61. Tax exemption as a form of generally available funding is the reason Inazu describes *Bob Jones* as "normatively attractive to almost everyone, [but] conceptually wrong." Inazu, *Confident Pluralism*, 75.

62. *Bob Jones*, 461 U.S. 574 (1983).

63. Revenue Ruling 71-447, 1971-2 C.B. 230.

64. *Bob Jones*, 461 U.S. 574, 582.

65. *Bob Jones*, 461 U.S. 574, 604. Internal citations omitted.

66. *Bob Jones*, 461 U.S. 574, 604, note 29. Emphasis in original.

67. Eugene Volokh, "Freedom of Expressive Association and Government Subsidies," *Stanford Law Review* 58 (2006): 1919, 1963.

68. Volokh notes that while there may be a *rational basis* for excluding discriminatory groups from tax exemptions, there is not a *compelling interest*. Volokh, 1965.

69. Inazu, *Confident Pluralism*, 76.

70. *Roberts v. United States Jaycees*, 468 U.S. 609 (1984).

71. *Doe v. Kamehameha Schools/Bernice Pauahi Bishop Estate*, 470 F.3d 827 (9th Cir.).

72. 347 U.S. 483 (1954).

73. See Douglas Laycock, "Tax Exemptions for Racially Discriminatory Religious Schools," *Texas Law Review* 60 (1982): 259, 265. "Many private schools were established for the express purpose of creating a segregated alternative to forcibly integrated public schools."

74. *Runyun*, 427 U.S. 160 (1976).

75. *Grutter v. Bollinger*, 539 U.S. 306, 343 (2003). (Emphasis added. Internal citations omitted.) In *Grutter*, the Court ruled that using race as one factor in an admissions policy at a public educational institution does not violate the Equal Protection Clause as long as the policy was narrowly tailored and in the compelling interest of promoting diversity in the student body. As such, it seems like the Court expects that at some point diversity would be achieved without considering the race of applicants and when that happens a policy considering race as one factor in admissions would no longer enjoy exemption from the Equal Protection Clause.

76. "Ethnic minorities will be at a record level in the House—at least 118." Susan Milligan, "Destiny in the Demographics: Midterm Voting Trends among Subsections of the Population Say a Lot about Where the Major Political Parties Are Headed," *U.S. News & World Report*, November 16, 2018. https://www.usnews.com/news/the-report /articles/2018-11-16/women-and-minorities-deliver-for-democrats-in-midterm -election. Accessed March 21, 2019.

77. National Center for Education Statistics, "Undergraduate Enrollment," https:// nces.ed.gov/programs/coe/indicator_cha.asp, and "Bachelor's, master's, and doctor's degrees conferred by postsecondary institutions, by sex of student and discipline division: 2015–16," https://nces.ed.gov/programs/digest/d17/tables/dt17_318.30.asp. Accessed March 21, 2019.

78. See Leigh E. Fine, "Penalized or Privileged? Sexual Identity, Gender, and Postsecondary Educational Attainment," *American Journal of Education* 121, no. 2 (February 2015): 271–297.

79. For example, Wheaton College, a prominent evangelical Christian college in Illinois, requires its students to adhere to the "Community Covenant," which requires among other things that students "uphold chastity among the unmarried (1 Cor. 6:18) and the sanctity of marriage between a man and woman (Heb. 13:4)." "Community Covenant: Living the Christian Life." https://www.wheaton.edu/about-wheaton /community-covenant/. Accessed March 25, 2019.

80. Robert Cover, "The Supreme Court, 1982 Term—Foreword: *Nomos* and Narrative," *Harvard Law Review* 97, no. 4 (1983): 66.

81. This is Inazu's formulation. See Inazu, *Confident Pluralism*, 75.

82. See Mayer G. Freed and Daniel D. Polsby, "Race, Religion, and Public Policy: *Bob Jones University v. United States*," *Supreme Court Review* no. 1 (1983).

83. Inazu, *Confident Pluralism*, 79.

84. Nancy Rosenblum, *Membership and Morals: The Personal Uses of Pluralism in America* (Princeton, NJ: Princeton University Press, 1998), 274–276.

85. Rosenblum, 8.

86. Rosenblum, 349.

87. Rosenblum, 5.

88. Referring to a race-based exception, Inazu writes, "Neither the Court nor the American public is always careful about recognizing the boundaries of these kinds of arguments." Inazu, "Four Freedoms," 839.

89. The question came up in oral argument for *Obergefell v. Hodges*, 135 S.Ct. 2071 (2015). Solicitor General Donald Verrilli noted that the government would have to consider the application of *Bob Jones* to colleges and universities that had policies opposed to same-sex marriage. *Obergefell v. Hodges* No. 14-556 (April 25, 2015), Oral Argument, 38.

CONCLUSION: FIRST AMENDMENT PLURALISM AND THE FREEDOM OF ASSOCIATION

1. Robert Nisbet, *Twilight of Authority* (Indianapolis: Liberty Fund, 1975), 247.

2. *Martinez*, 561 U.S. 28.

Bibliography

Abrams, Floyd. *The Soul of the First Amendment*. New Haven: Yale University Press, 2017.

Aristotle. *The Politics*. Translated by Ernest Barker. London: Oxford University Press, 1946.

Bhagwat, Ashutosh. "Associational Speech." *Yale Law Journal* 120 (2011): 978–1030.

———. "Associations and Forums: Situating *CLS v. Martinez*." *Hastings Constitutional Law Quarterly* 38, no. 3 (2011): 543–568.

Birzer, Bradley J. "Leviathan, Inc.: Robert Nisbet and the Modern Nation-State." *Political Science Reviewer* 42, no. 2 (2018).

Bresler, Robert J. *Freedom of Association: Rights and Liberties under the Law*. Santa Barbara, CA: ABC-CLIO, 2004.

Brown, David. "Hey! Universities! Leave Them Kids Alone!" *Christian Legal Society v. Martinez* and Conditioning Equal Access to a University's Student-Organization Forum." *Penn State Law Review* 116 (2011): 163–198.

Carpenter, Dale. "Expressive Association and Anti-Discrimination Law after *Dale*: A Tripartite Approach." *Minnesota Law Review* 85 (2001): 1515–1590.

Cover, Robert. "The Supreme Court, 1982 Term—Foreword: *Nomos* and Narrative." *Harvard Law Review* 97 (1983): 4–68.

Crain, Marion, and John Inazu. "Re-Assembling Labor." *University of Illinois Law Review* (2015): 1791–1846.

Cummins, Kyle R. "The Intersection of *CLS* and *Hosanna-Tabor*: The Ministerial Exception Applied to Religious Student Organizations." *University of Memphis Law Review* 44 (2013): 142–182.

Durkheim, Emile. *Suicide: A Study in Sociology*. Translated by John A. Spaulding and George Simpson. New York: Free Press, 1979.

Dworkin, Ronald. *Freedom's Law: The Moral Reading of the American Constitution*. Excerpt in *Constitutional Theory: Arguments and Perspectives*. 3rd ed. Edited by Michael J. Gerhardt, Stephen M. Griffin, and Thomas D. Rowe Jr. Newark, NJ: LexisNexis Matthew Bender, 2007.

Emerson, Thomas. "Freedom of Association and Freedom of Expression." *Yale Law Journal* 74, no. 1 (November 1964): 1–35.

Eskridge, William N., Jr. "Noah's Curse: How Religion Often Conflates Status, Belief, and Conduct to Resist Antidiscrimination Norms." *Georgia Law Review* 45 (2011): 657–720.

Field, Constance N. "My Father, Robert Nisbet." *Society* 52 (2015): 344–350.

Fine, Leigh E. "Penalized or Privileged? Sexual Identity, Gender, and Postsecondary Educational Attainment." *American Journal of Education* 121, no. 2 (February 2015): 271–297.

Foundation for Individual Rights in Education and Students for Liberty as *Amicus Curiae* in Support of Petitioner, *Martinez*, 561 U.S. 661.

Freed, Mayer G., and Daniel D. Polsby. "Race, Religion, and Public Policy: *Bob Jones University v. United States.*" *Supreme Court Review* 1983, no. 1 (1983): 1–31.

Frohnen, Bruce P. "The One and the Many: Individual Rights, Corporate Rights, and the Diversity of Groups." *West Virginia Law Review* 107 (2005): 789–845.

Galston, William A. *Liberal Pluralism: The Implications of Value Pluralism for Political Theory.* Cambridge: Cambridge University Press, 2002.

———. *The Practice of Liberal Pluralism.* Cambridge: Cambridge University Press, 2005.

Gays and Lesbians for Individual Liberty as *Amicus Curiae* in Support of Petitioner, *Christian Legal Society v. Martinez*, 561 U.S. 661.

Goldberg, Erica. "Amending *Christian Legal Society v. Martinez*: Protecting Expressive Association as an Independent Right in a Limited Public Forum." *Texas Journal on Civil Liberties & Civil Rights* 16, no. 2 (2011): 129–169.

Hamilton, Marci A. *God vs. the Gavel: Religion and the Rule of Law.* Cambridge: Cambridge University Press, 2005.

Hill, B. Jessie. "Property and the Public Forum: An Essay on *Christian Legal Society v. Martinez.*" *Duke Journal of Constitutional Law and Public Policy*, Special Issue, 6 (2010): 49–57.

Horwitz, Paul. *First Amendment Institutions.* Cambridge: Harvard University Press, 2013.

———. "Grutter's *First Amendment.*" *Boston College Law Review* 46, no. 3 (2005): 461–590.

Inazu, John D. *Confident Pluralism: Surviving and Thriving through Deep Difference.* Chicago: University of Chicago Press, 2016.

———. "The First Amendment's Public Forum." *William & Mary Law Review* 56, no. 4 (2015): 1159–1197.

———. "The Forgotten Freedom of Assembly." *Tulane Law Review* 84 (2010): 565–612.

———. "The Four Freedoms and the Future of Religious Liberty." *North Carolina Law Review* 92 (2014): 787–853.

———. "The Freedom of the Church (New Revised Standard Version)." *Journal of Contemporary Legal Issues* 21 (2013): 335–367.

———. "Institutions in Context." *Tulsa Law Review* 50 (Spring 2015): 491–501.

———. "Justice Ginsberg and Religious Liberty." *Hastings Law Journal* 63 (2012): 1213–1241.

———. *Liberty's Refuge: The Forgotten Freedom of Assembly.* New Haven: Yale University Press, 2012.

Kanin, Max. "*Christian Legal Society v. Martinez*: How an Obscure First Amendment Case Inadvertently and Unexpectedly Created a Significant Fourteenth Amendment Advance for LGBT Rights Advocates." *Journal of Gender, Social Policy & the Law* (2011): 1324–1326.

Karst, Kenneth L. "The Freedom of Intimate Association." *Yale Law Journal* 89, no. 4 (March 1980): 624–692.

Koppelman, Andrew, and Tobias Barrington Wolff. *A Right to Discriminate? How the Case of* Boy Scouts of America v. James Dale *Warped the Law of Free Association*. New Haven: Yale University Press, 2009.

Laycock, Douglas. "Tax Exemptions for Racially Discriminatory Religious Schools." *Texas Law Review* 60 (1982): 259–277.

Levy, Jacob. *Rationalism, Pluralism, and Freedom*. Oxford: Oxford University Press, 2015.

MacIntyre, Alasdair. *After Virtue*. 3rd ed. Notre Dame, IN: University of Notre Dame Press, 2007.

Madison, James, Alexander Hamilton, and John Jay. *The Federalist Papers*. New York: Penguin, 2003.

Meiklejohn, Alexander. *Free Speech and Its Relation to Self-Government*. New York: Harper, 1948.

Monsma, Stephen V. *Pluralism and Freedom: Faith-Based Organizations in a Democratic Society*. Lanham, MD: Rowman & Littlefield, 2012.

Monsma, Stephen V., and Stanley W. Carlson-Thies. *Free to Serve: Protecting the Religious Freedom of Faith-Based Organizations*. Grand Rapids, MI: Brazos Press, 2015.

Nagel, Robert F. "States and Localities: A Comment on Robert Nisbet's Communitarianism." *Publius: The Journal of Federalism* 34 (Fall 2004): 125–138.

Nice, Julie A. "How Equality Constitutes Liberty: The Alignment of *CLS v. Martinez* (The Constitution on Campus: The Case of *CLS v. Martinez*)." *Hastings Constitutional Law Quarterly* 38, no. 3 (2011): 631–672.

Nisbet, Robert A. "The Coming Problem of Assimilation." *American Journal of Sociology* 50, no. 4 (January 1945): 261–270.

———. *The Degradation of the Academic Dogma: The University in America, 1945–1970*. New York: Basic Books, 1971. Reprinted with a new introduction by Gertrude Himmelfarb. New Brunswick NJ: Transaction, 1997.

———. *The Making of Modern Society*. Brighton, Sussex: Wheatsheaf Books, 1986. Published concurrently by New York University Press.

———. *The Quest for Community: A Study in the Ethics of Order and Freedom*. New York: Oxford University Press, 1953. Republished as *Community and Power*. New York: Galaxy Book, 1962. Reissued in 1969 as *The Quest for Community*. Reprinted with a new preface. San Francisco: Institute for Contemporary Studies, 1990. Reprinted with a new introduction. Wilmington: ISI Books, 2010.

———. *The Social Bond: An Introduction to the Study of Society*. New York: Knopf, 1970. Reissued in a new edition coauthored with Robert G. Perrin. New York: McGraw-Hill, 1977.

———. *The Social Group in French Thought*. PhD diss., University of California, Berkeley, 1939. Reprint. New York: Arno, 1980.

———. *The Social Philosophers: Community and Conflict in Western Thought*. London: Heinemann, 1973.

———. *The Sociological Tradition*. New York: Basic Books, 1966. Reissued with a new introduction by the author. New Brunswick, NJ: Transaction, 1993

———. *Tradition and Revolt: Historical and Sociological Essays*. New York: Random House, 1968. Reissued with a new introduction by Robert G. Perrin. New Brunswick, NJ: Transaction, 1990.

———. *Twilight of Authority*. New York: Oxford University Press, 1975. Reprinted with a new preface by Robert G. Perrin. Indianapolis: Liberty Fund, 2000.

Post, Robert C. "Between Governance and Management: The History of the Public Forum." *UCLA Law Review* 34 (1987): 1713–1835.

Putnam, Robert D. *Bowling Alone: The Collapse and Revival of American Community*. New York: Simon & Schuster, 2001.

Reyes, Rene. "The Fading Free Exercise Clause." *William & Mary Bill of Rights Journal* 19 (March 2011): 725–750.

Rosenblum, Nancy. *Membership and Morals: The Personal Uses of Pluralism in America*. Princeton, NJ: Princeton University Press, 1998.

Rowling, J. K. *Harry Potter and the Order of the Phoenix*. New York: Scholastic, 2004.

Russo, Charles J., and William E. Thro. "'Another Nail in the Coffin of Religious Freedom?' *Christian Legal Society v. Martinez*." *Education Law Journal* 12 (2011): 20–30.

Sarabyn, Kelly. "Free Speech at Private Universities." *Journal of Law & Education* 39, no. 2 (2010): 145–182.

Schoen, Edward J., and Joseph S. Falchek. "*Christian Legal Society v. Martinez*: Rock, Paper, Scissors." *Southern Law Journal* 21 (Fall 2010): 201–223.

Schragger, Richard, and Micah Schwartzman. "Against Religious Institutionalism." *Virginia Law Review* 99 (September 2013): 917–985.

Sheahan, Luke C. "Antidote to Alienation: The Voluntary Association in the Work of Robert Nisbet." *Perspectives on Political Science* 48, no. 4 (2019).

———. "Conservative, Pluralist, Sociologist: Robert Nisbet's Burke." *Studies in Burke and His Time* 28 (2019).

———. "Robert Nisbet: Reappraisal of a Political Sociologist," Introduction to Symposium on Robert Nisbet. *Political Science Reviewer* 42, no. 2 (2018).

———. "The State as Historical Necessity: Robert Nisbet's Critique of Developmentalism," *The Political Science Reviewer* 42, no. 2 (2018).

Smith, Steven D. *The Rise and Decline of American Religious Freedom*. Cambridge: Harvard University Press, 2014.

Tebbe, Nelson. *Religious Freedom in an Egalitarian Age*. Cambridge: Harvard University Press, 2017.

Tocqueville, Alexis de. *Democracy in America*. Indianapolis: Liberty Fund, 2012.

Tracey, Timothy J. "*Christian Legal Society v. Martinez*: In Hindsight." *University of Hawaii Law Review* 34 (Fall 2012): 71–123.

Volokh, Eugene. "Freedom of Expressive Association and Government Subsidies." *Stanford Law Review* 57 (2006): 1919–1968.

Willems, Jack. "The Loss of Freedom of Association in *Christian Legal Society v. Martinez*, 130 S. Ct. 2971 (2010)." *Harvard Journal of Law & Public Policy* 34, no. 2 (2011): 805–818.

Winters, Jonathan. "Thou Shall Not Exclude: How *Christian Legal Society v. Martinez* Affects Expressive Associations, Limited Public Forums, and Student's Associational Rights." *University of Toledo Law Review* 43 (Spring 2012): 747–776.

Zick, Timothy. "Space, Place, and Speech: The Expressive Topography." *George Washington Law Review* 74 (2006): 439–505.

CASES

Barenblatt v. United States, 360 U.S. 109 (1959).

Bates v. City of Little Rock, 361 U.S. 516 (1960).

Bob Jones University v. United States, 461 U.S. 574 (1983).

Boy Scouts of America v. Dale, 530 U.S. 640 (2000).

Chi Iota Colony of Alpha Epsilon Pi Fraternity v. City Univ. Of N.Y., 502 F.3d 136 (2007).

Christian Legal Society v. Martinez, 561 U.S. 661 (2010).

Christian Legal Society v. Walker, 453 F.3d 853 (7th Cir. 2006).

Citizens against Rent Control Coalition for Fair Housing v. Berkeley, 454 U.S. 290 (1981).

Citizens United v. Federal Election Comm'n, 558 U.S. 310 (2010).

City of Boerne v. Flores, Archbishop of San Antonio, 521 U.S. 507 (1997).

Communist Party v. Subversive Activities Control Board (SACB), 367 U.S. 1 (1961).

Cornelius v. NAACP Legal Defense & Education Fund, 473 U.S. 788 (1985).

DeJonge v. Oregon, 299 U.S. 353 (1937).

Doe v. Kamehameha Schools/Bernice Pauahi Bishop Estate, 470 F.3d 827 (9th Cir. 2006).

Employment Division, Department of Human Resources of Oregon v. Smith, 494 U.S. 872 (1990).

Forsyth County v. Nationalist Movement, 505 U.S. 123 (1992).

Gay Alliance of Students v. Matthews, 544 F. 2d 162 (4th Cir. 1976).

Gay and Lesbian Students Ass'n v. Gohn, 850 F.2d 361 (1988).

Gay Lesbian Bisexual Alliance v. Pryor, 110 F.3d 1543 (11th Cir. 1997).

Gay Student Services v. Texas A&M University, 737 F.2d 1317 (5th Cir. 1984).

Gay Students Organization of the University of New Hampshire v. Bonner, 509 F.2d 652 (1st Cir. 1974).

Gibson v. Florida Legislative Investigation Comm., 372 U.S. 539 (1963).

Grutter v. Bollinger, 539 U.S. 306 (2003).

Hague v. CIO, 307 U.S. 496 (1939).

Harris v. McRae, 448 U.S. 297 (1980).

Healy v. James, 408 U.S. 169 (1972).

Heffron v. Soc'y for Krishna Consciousness, 452 U.S. 640 (1981).

Holder v. Humanitarian Law Project, 561 U.S. 1 (2010).

Hosanna-Tabor Evangelical Lutheran Church and School v. EEOC, 565 U.S. 171 (2012).

Hurley v. Irish American Gay, Lesbian, and Bisexual Group of Boston, 515 U.S. 557 (1995).

Lawrence v. Texas, 539 U.S. 558 (2003).

Louisiana v. NAACP, 366 U.S. 293 (1961).

Minersville School District v. Gobitis, 310 U.S. 586 (1940).

NAACP v. Alabama, 357 U.S. 449 (1958).

NAACP v. Button, 371 U.S. 415 (1963).

NAACP v. Claiborne, 458 U.S. 886 (1982).

National Endowment for the Arts v. Finley, 524 U.S. 569 (1998).

National Socialist Party of America v. Village of Skokie, 432 U.S. 43 (1977).

New York Club Ass'n v. City of New York, 487 U.S. 1 (1988).

Obergefell v. Hodges, 135 S.Ct. 2071 (2015).

Perry v. Perry Local Educators' Association, 460 U.S. 37 (1983).

Planned Parenthood v. Casey, 505 U.S. 833 (1992).

Pleasant Grove City v. Summum, 555 U.S. 460 (2009).

Regan v. Taxation with Representation of Washington, 461 U.S. 540 (1983).

Roberts v. United States Jaycees, 468 U.S. 609 (1984).

Robinson v. California, 370 U.S. 660 (1962).

Rosenberger v. Rector & Visitors for the University of Virginia, 515 U.S. 819 (1995).

Rotary International v. Rotary Club of Duarte, 481 U.S. 537 (1987).

Runyon v. McCrary, 427 U.S. 163 (1976).

Scales v. United States, 367 U.S. 203 (1961).

Shelley v. Kraemer, 334 U.S. 1 (1948).

Shelton v. Tucker, 364 U.S. 479, 485-6 (1960).

Sherbert v. Verner, 374 U.S. 398 (1963).

Texas Monthly, Inc. v. Bullock, 489 U.S. 1 (1989).

Tinker v. Des Moines Independent Community School District, 393 U.S. 503 (1969).

United States v. O'Brien, 391 U.S. 367 (1968).

University of S. Mississippi Chapter of the Mississippi Civil Liberties Union v. University of Southern Mississippi, 452 F. 2d 564 (5th Cir. 1971).

University of Wisconsin v. Southworth, 529 U.S. 217 (2000).

Uphaus v. Wyman, 360 U.S. 72 (1959).

West Virginia State Board of Education v. Barnette, 319 U.S. 624 (1943).

Widmar v. Vincent, 454 U.S. 263 (1981).

Wisconsin v. Yoder, 406 U.S. 205 (1972).

Zubik v. Burwell, 578 U.S. 1 (2016).

Index